LOVING

INTERRACIAL INTIMACY IN AMERICA

LOVING

AND THE THREAT TO WHITE SUPREMACY

. . .

Sheryll Cashin

BEACON PRESS
BOSTON

BEACON PRESS
Boston, Massachusetts
www.beacon.org

Beacon Press books
are published under the auspices of
the Unitarian Universalist Association of Congregations.

20 19 18 17   8 7 6 5 4 3 2

This book is printed on acid-free paper that meets the uncoated paper
ANSI/NISO specifications for permanence as revised in 1992.

Text design and composition by Kim Arney

Library of Congress Cataloging-in-Publication Data

Names: Cashin, Sheryll, author.
Title: Loving : interracial intimacy in America and the threat
to white supremacy / Sheryll Cashin.
Description: Boston : Beacon Press, [2017] | Includes
bibliographical references and index.
Identifiers: LCCN 2016055091 (print) | LCCN 2016056910 (ebook) | ISBN
9780807058275 (hardcover : acid-free paper) | ISBN 9780807058268 (e-book)
Subjects: LCSH: Interracial marriage—United States—History. |
Miscegenation—United States—History. | Interracial dating—United
States—History. | Racially mixed families—United States—History. |
Interracial friendship—United States—History. | Intimacy
(Psychology)—Social aspects—United States. | Loving, Richard
Perry—Trials, litigation, etc. | Loving, Mildred Jeter—Trials,
litigation, etc. | United States—Race relations. | White supremacy
movements—United States.
Classification: LCC HQ1031 .C383 2017 (print) | LCC HQ1031 (ebook) |
DDC 306.84/50973—dc23
LC record available at https://lccn.loc.gov/2016055091

For Dorothy Reed,
my cousin-angel

CONTENTS

AUTHOR'S NOTE

As a daughter of civil rights activists and a descendant of slaves and slaveholders, I wrote this book from a personal perspective. Because my life experience and voice shape this and all my work, I feel obligated to disclose the source of my admiration for agitators who cross lines. It begins with amazing parents who lived their personal creeds, sometimes at great cost.

Joan and John Cashin were among the happy warriors who planned and participated in the sit-in movement in Huntsville, Alabama, in 1962. Tired of waiting for equality, they and other Huntsvillians organized, marched, and demanded to be served. One element of their strategy was to recruit white allies from the local Unitarian church. The Unitarians, too, would march for black freedom. My parents and some of these long-haired people became dear friends. This biracial group of activists laughed a lot and called themselves the Drek Set. They were irreverent and playful in undermining white supremacy.

They infiltrated white citizens' council meetings. They desegregated the Grand Ole Opry in Nashville through a ruse in which a white couple played maid and chauffer to my resplendent parents as they stepped out of an antique Rolls Royce. Another white couple purchased a house with my parents' money and deeded it to them, enabling Cashins to integrate a neighborhood and a public school with a program for hearing-impaired children—a program that my brother needed. My parents were proud graduates of Fisk, a venerable, historically black university. They celebrated the genius of black folk and devoted their lives to helping those who had less than they did. They also opened their home to a steady stream of people of all races and ethnicities. The common thread among our guests was that they had stimulating things to say and were passionate about social justice.

In 1962, as part of their strategy for bringing national attention and allies to Huntsville's sit-in movement, my mother sat down at a lunch counter, with me—a four-month-old infant—in her arms. She was arrested and taken to jail, along with another black doctor's wife, who was eight months pregnant. This was the turning point in their movement. A city concerned with its image and future in the space industry soon relented and desegregated its public accommodations a year before the children of Birmingham ignited the conscience of the nation.

Then my parents turned to politics. My father grew up hearing about his grandfather's exploits as a member of the Alabama legislature during Reconstruction. Herschel V. Cashin, the son of a white slave owner and a mixed-race woman of African descent, was a Radical Republican and my father's hero. Dad had a lifelong dream of reigniting the spirit of Reconstruction in Alabama, of finishing Grandpa Herschel's work. Dad was a dentist by profession but an agitator by disposition. He founded a political party, the National Democratic Party of Alabama (NDPA), to give poor black sharecroppers newly enfranchised by the Voting Rights Act an alternative to the party of George Wallace.

NDPA was born in 1967, the same year that *Loving v. Virginia* was decided. Both were assaults on white supremacy. The traditional Alabama Democratic Party reluctantly had given up its official slogan, "White Supremacy for the Right," the year before. Through NDPA, blacks elected themselves to local office throughout the Black Belt, where the plantation economy had once reigned. And they returned a black man to the Alabama legislature for the first time since Reconstruction. NDPA was also backed by a biracial group of riotously humorous change agents. I inherited their sense of humor, irreverence, and impatience with supremacy. I also learned from my parents that good people come in all colors and that with allies and activism, any situation can be made better.

INTRODUCTION

To love beyond boundaries is the most radical of acts. It also requires optimism. Richard Loving must have followed the light of his surname. In news clips he didn't smile much, perhaps because his teeth were irregular. He didn't look the part of an ardent integrator. His buzz cut, rugged face, and tobacco-scarred Southern accent marked him as a white, working rural man of simple means and tastes.

Like many Southerners, Loving knew people of color. But his relations with them were more intimate than most whites were willing to countenance. His father worked on a farm for a prosperous man of color, and his parents' home was "down in the community where all the Indians lived," according to a resident. Loving and friends would gather at a favorite bend in the road or at the back of a general store they had turned into a juke joint. Someone would bring a guitar or a fiddle, and this motley crew would play music and hang out together. They were black, white, racially ambiguous "high yellow," or "Indian," depending on the perspective of who was observing and who was claiming labels. Their crossing of color lines irritated the county sheriff, who literally was the race police and tried to break up their fun. Loving was perhaps the most culturally dexterous among this group. He could blend in with anybody, people said.[1] He was playful and lived the life he wanted, loved the red-brown girl he wanted, drag-raced cars with his high-yellow friends. In the 1950s, in Central Point, Virginia—a hamlet with a penchant for race mixing—he and others willfully defied the old Jim Crow.

Mildred Jeter Loving accorded with central casting. In a documentary about the couple and the Supreme Court case that she and her husband brought fifty years ago, she played herself better than any actress could.[2] She was dignified, slender, and pretty, with a quiet voice that made people lean in to hear her. Richard called her "Bean," short for "String Bean." She dressed like the housewife that she was; her short, bobbed hair was fuzzy at the roots but ended in shiny curls that betrayed either her complicated lineage or the pressing comb. She appeared to be a Negro or colored, words then used to describe African Americans, although as this book later describes, she identified herself as a descendant of an indigenous nation rather than slaves.

In 1958, Mildred and Richard were arrested and jailed for the felony crime of marrying. Virginia was among sixteen states in that era still sufficiently obsessed with the purity of its white citizens' bloodlines to ban whites from marrying nonwhites, with varying definitions for who could claim whiteness. From 1661 until the Supreme Court ruled against such measures in the *Loving* case, forty-one states had enacted statutes that penalized interracial marriages.[3] Every state with such laws discouraged or prohibited whites from marrying blacks, but many statutes also named other groups that could not intermarry with whites: Chinese, Japanese, Filipinos, American Indians, native Hawaiians, and South Asians, among others.[4]

There were legal bans, and there were social ones. Marrying, loving, and having sex across lines of phenotype were not considered normal or acceptable among most people in pre-civil-rights America. In 1958, only 4 percent of Americans approved of marriages between blacks and whites.[5]

On June 12, 1967, the Supreme Court sided with the Lovings. The civil rights revolution had roiled from a Woolworth's lunch counter in Greensboro, North Carolina, to a thousand similar nonviolent protests in over one hundred Southern cities, resulting in over twenty thousand arrests.[6] When Police Commissioner Bull Connor turned water hoses and attack dogs on child protesters in Birmingham, Alabama, people of goodwill supported the protesters, as did moderate Republicans in Congress, who added their votes to overcome the staunch opposition of segregation-forever Southern Democrats. The Civil Rights Act of 1964 barred discrimination in education and employment and allowed people of color to dine, shop, and travel where they wanted. The Voting Rights Act of 1965 began to desegregate politics. In *Loving v. Virginia*, the Supreme Court added to the movement's momentum.

Chief Justice Earl Warren, writing for his unanimous brethren, plainly stated that Virginia's ban on interracial marriage was "designed to maintain White Supremacy," an objective no longer permitted by the Constitution. It was the first time the court used those potent words to name what the Civil War and the resulting Fourteenth Amendment should have defeated. Twice Warren mentioned "the doctrine of White Supremacy" animating these laws, implicitly acknowledging that the case was not only about intermarriage but also the ideology itself. This idea, created and propagated by patriarchs, had required separation in all forms of social relations. The ideology told whites in particular that they could not marry, sleep with, live near, play checkers with, much less ally politically with a black person. It built a wall that supremacists believed was necessary to elevate whiteness above all else. A dominant whiteness, constructed by law, was embedded in people's habits. Perhaps Warren thought being transparent about this pervasive racial dogma would help cure the nation of its mental illness.

The onset of the long hot summer of 1967 may also have hastened the court's desire to help dismantle the architecture of division. A race riot had erupted in the Roxbury neighborhood of Boston on June 2 and raged for three days. The day before the court announced its *Loving* opinion, Tampa, Florida, had ignited. By the end of the year, 159 race riots had roiled the United States, most lethally in Detroit, where a police raid on an after-hours bar set off a revolt that ended five days later with forty-three deaths and two thousand injuries.[7]

There was an "impasse in race relations," as Dr. Martin Luther King Jr. delicately phrased it—a wide gap in perception between blacks and most whites about the aims of the civil rights movement and the riots.[8] Black people were outraged by the inequality they suffered. They wanted opportunity and freedom from police harassment, squalor, and isolation. According to Dr. King, whites wanted improvement for the Negro, but not necessarily economic equality.

When black folks moved beyond sitting down to order a hamburger to trying to integrate the neighborhoods, workplaces, and schools that whites dominated, a firm, even violent resistance ensued. Black people trapped in high-poverty ghettoes expressed rage at their limited possibilities, and white people considered riots evidence that blacks were unconstructive and undeserving. This was the impasse Dr. King described, alas, solely in terms of Negro and white.[9] In 1967, the many-hued people of the United States were more focused on the Vietnam War and ameliorating or fleeing the aftermath of the riots than on the Lovings' victory for quiet acts of interracial love.

Mildred Loving was motivated more by her desperation to end her family's years of exile from Virginia than by the civil rights movement. In lieu of prison, a Virginia judge had banished them from the state for twenty-five years. They had settled, unhappily, in Washington, DC, a world away from tight-knit Central Point. For Mildred, the last straw came when one of her children was hit by a car. At her cousin's urging, she wrote a letter to Attorney General Robert Kennedy, asking for help.[10] This infant step toward her personal liberation ultimately led to a transformation in national consciousness about the freedom to love.

Loving v. Virginia was one of a series of antiracist decisions by the Warren Court. Neither it, nor its famous predecessor, *Brown v. Board of Education*, would dismantle segregation, the enduring structures of white supremacy. While *Loving* removed legal barriers to interracial intimacy, the true import of the case is only beginning to emerge, as social barriers to interracial love have fallen and will continue to play out in coming decades.

In the long arc of history, the meaning of the case becomes clearer. It is impossible to understand America's persistent race business without examining its origins, and antimiscegenation was an enduring protagonist. Enacting laws to ban or penalize interracial sex and marriage and stoking loathing about race mixing were key legal and rhetorical tools for constructing and propagating white supremacy. This ideology, in turn, was the organizing plank for regimes of oppression that were essential to American capitalism and expansion—from slavery, to indigenous and Mexican conquest, to exclusion of Asian and other immigrants, and, later, to Jim Crow.

This book does not purport to offer a comprehensive social or legal history of attempts to thwart race mixing.[11] Instead it simply tries to tell a coherent story about what transpired with interracial intimacy before *Loving* and what has and has not changed since the case was decided. For married couples, anniversaries mark time and the miracle that a marriage, whether rocky and redemptive, prosaic or blissful, has endured another year. The fiftieth anniversary of *Loving v. Virginia* is an apt time for reflection on the marriage of differences that is America and how we might improve, if not perfect, the Union.

Before *Loving*, lawgivers constructed whiteness as the preferred identity for citizen and country and then set about protecting this fictional white purity from mixture. Over three centuries, our nation was caught in a seemingly endless cycle of political and economic elites using law to separate light and dark people who might love one another or revolt together against supremacist regimes the economic elites created. After *Loving*, the game of divide and conquer continues, but rising interracial intimacy could alter tired scripts.

White people who have an intimate relationship with a person of color, particularly a black person, can lose the luxury of racial blindness if they really are in love with their paramour, their adopted child, their "ace" in that nonsexual way that one can adore a friend. They can lose their blindness and gain something tragic, yet real—the ability to see racism clearly and to weep for a loved one and a country that suffers because of it. For the culturally dexterous, race is *more* salient, not less, and difference is a source of wonder, not fear.

This transition from blindness to seeing, from anxiety to familiarity, that comes with intimate cross-racial contact is a process of acquiring *dexterity*. And if one chooses to undertake the effort, the process is never-ending. Some folks are more dexterous than others. Some, like Richard Loving, are more adventurous and get more practice than others at crossing boundaries or immersion in another culture. I do not make the simplistic and silly claim that interracial intimacy in and of itself will destroy white supremacy or eliminate race. Instead, I argue that a growing cohort is acquiring dexterity and race consciousness through intimate interracial contact, especially in dense metropolitan areas. Although I do not claim that every interracial relationship automatically confers such knowledge, many do, leading us on an arc toward less emotional segregation, of many but obviously not all whites choosing to work at adjusting to difference.

With proximity, race mixing has always occurred in America. In every generation, some people defied color lines to love, befriend, or agitate with racial others. From the founding of Jamestown in 1607, throughout much of the seventeenth century in colonial Virginia, indentured and enslaved people were allies and sometimes lovers without much distinction among themselves about color. After 1660, their masters began to introduce a color line to transition to and sustain the American institution of black chattel slavery. Laws prohibiting miscegenation encouraged struggling whites to see black people as inferior and to police black slaves. The investor class, those with the power to own people and write laws, began to assess special penalties for interracial sex and interracial cooperation, such as when servants and slaves ran away together.

Lawgivers enacted Virginia's first comprehensive slave code in 1705, stripping African slaves of rights they had enjoyed along with indentured servants in the previous century and bolstering the white bonded with new privileges. The code also included penalties against interracial marriage and fornication among bonded people. There was no penalty, however, for master-slave sex, which would become the dominant form of interracial sex in the eighteenth and nineteenth centuries. Mixed-race people were common. The one-drop rule that rendered them black or Negro has roots in the Virginia slave code. Under that law, the child of a slave, no matter how fair the baby's skin or elevated the status of the father, was also a slave.

Virginia's slave code became a model for other states. As the state with the most slaves and the most to lose economically from any efforts to undermine slavery, Virginia relentlessly policed interracial intimacy and interracial cooperation among people who were not themselves slaveholders. The miasma of racism that suffused legal code would soon spread to the consciousness of men without political or economic power. The 1705 code helped reconcile rich and working whites, classes that had been economic antagonists. Race pride would emerge as a source of unity for all who could claim whiteness.

The color line and a discourse against race mixing had a political function as well. In *Notes on the State of Virginia*, Thomas Jefferson expounded on his belief in supremacy of whites over Africans and offered his fear of amalgamation of whites with blacks as part of his justification for not championing black freedom. Slavery was an evil, Jefferson admitted. Blame it on King George, he wrote in his first draft of the Declaration of Independence, for introducing this stain and thousands of dark bodies into the colonies. Jefferson couldn't imagine a country where whites would accept blacks as citizens, much less intermix with them, his relationship with Sally Hemings notwithstanding.[12]

Jefferson's arguments with himself in *Notes* and with others in correspondence are consistent with nearly two centuries of subsequent discourse about the perceived problem of race mixing and American identity. These questions arose in the debate about whether and how the US should conquer northern Mexico, which was replete with Spanish-speaking, mixed-race people. The ideology of white supremacy that animated slavery and Manifest Destiny placed politicians on the horns of an American dilemma. What to do with adventurous people who defied this ideology and muddied the lines? Hence, dog-whistling in the nineteenth century was often about interracial sex and, in turn, American identity.

In seven debates with Stephen Douglas in their bid for senator from Illinois, Abraham Lincoln was forced to address the issue. He countered Douglas with humor and played to the electorate's racism. "Now I protest against the counterfeit logic which concludes that, because I do not want a black woman for a slave, I must necessarily want her for a wife," he said, to laughter.

The Party of Lincoln prosecuted the Civil War, ended slavery, and extended citizenship to black males. During Reconstruction, the Radical Republicans offered the world its first glimpse of racially integrated democracy, and several Reconstruction governments repealed miscegenation laws. But in an odd twist of logic, white supremacy Democrats equated black voting power with black male sexuality, and the myth of the black man as sexual predator was born. Supremacist-orchestrated hysteria about black bodies would soon ferment the regular if strange public ritual of lynching. And when Southern Democrats retook control, they reinstated miscegenation laws throughout the states of the former Confederacy. Lawgivers in

Midwestern and Western states also adopted miscegenation laws in an attempt to insulate whites from myriad groups they might mix or compete with economically. White political power translated into separate social worlds.

For a brief moment in the 1890s, the South saw a resurgence of biracial politics. Economically oppressed whites joined with blacks to create a biracial farmers' alliance that challenged unfair financial policies. Seeing such alliances as a threat, economic elites destroyed them with the offer of supremacy to the white working class. Jim Crow became the only political game to play, and Southern politicians competed with one another by proposing ever-more-ingenious forms of racial apartheid. Voting and full citizenship were reserved for whites who could afford poll taxes. Race mixing was banned in politics and life.

By the early twentieth century, interracial violence seemed much more normal than interracial love. Lynching continued, mainly though not exclusively in the South, and race riots broke out in three dozen cities in the Red Summer of 1919. Violent mobs enforced social codes about the lowly place of the Negro in America's racial pecking order. As Gunnar Myrdal explained two decades later in *An American Dilemma*, his classic treatise on American race relations, the regime of Jim Crow proliferated on the fear of black men having sex with white women.[13] It was easy to use this ruse to garner widespread support for segregation, and false accusations against black men would regularly incite public lynching. Families brought picnic baskets to these ritual atrocities, and people fought over body parts after a body was cut down from the noose. In this context, the Virginia legislature niggardly redrew the color line to narrow the class of people who could claim whiteness.

The state's Racial Integrity Act of 1924, which would cause Mildred and Richard Loving's arrest years later, was enacted at the apex of the American eugenics movement. The ideology of supremacy supported not only Jim Crow but also eugenics laws authorizing state-enforced sterilization of undesired populations and constricted immigration. In 1924, a federal law banned or severely restricted immigration for all nationalities except people from northern Europe. For much of the twentieth century, the nation would continue to limit immigration of colored and olive-skinned people and promote forced sterilization and racial segregation—all of it to the benefit of white upper classes.

Much has changed, although segregation, inequality, and race-baiting endure. Today, the *Loving* decision has a fan base, and most people in the United States now approve of interracial marriage.[14] *Loving* has been chronicled in films, and the decision has its own annual worldwide celebration, Loving Day, on June 12. *Loving* was also a progenitor of the Supreme Court's 2015 decision *Obergefell v. Hodges*, which constitutionalized same-sex marriage.

Since *Loving* was decided, race mixing and same-sex marriage have gained acceptance, and social tolerance is rising for people and lifestyles that diverge from white, patriarchal, heterosexual norms. At least that is what removal of legal and social restrictions against mixing is beginning to mean. Racist or insensitive people often capture our attention. Millennials make news for hanging a noose on a campus, chanting a frat-boy song about lynching, wearing gangsta'-blackface to a Halloween party, or murdering nine African Americans at a Wednesday night Bible study.[15] The majority of millennials, however, are more open to our majority-minority future than are their parents and grandparents. Much less attention is paid to the 54 percent of millennials who have friends of a different race or the 67 percent who say that they view increasing diversity as a good thing.[16]

In the 2010s, the American people changed their minds about same-sex marriage with seemingly lightning speed, although the patrons at the Stonewall Inn rose up against homophobia in 1969. Acceptance spread as straight people had conversations with gay people or their allies about their hardships and dreams for equality. Attitudes about race will also undergo exponential change in coming decades in part because countless individuals will have acquired the scar tissue of seeing how race affects a loved one or a friend. Many already recognize that we are all trapped in the architecture of division supremacists and cynics created. The rise of the culturally dexterous offers a possibility for breaking free, for creating something that might have been, had the first Reconstruction, or the second, been allowed to stand.

Most who love interracially take the time to understand and value racial and cultural differences. I believe that rising interracial intimacy, combined with immigration and demographic and generational change, will contribute to the rise of what I call the *culturally dexterous class*. From cross-racial marriage, adoption, and romance to the simple act of entering the home of someone of another race or ethnicity to have a meal, the dexterous cross different cultures daily and are forced to practice pluralism. Though relatively few today, ardent integrators will inevitably create a tipping point, as Malcolm Gladwell defines it.[17] In this case, integrators are spreading the social epidemic or virus of cultural dexterity—an enhanced capacity for intimate connections with people outside one's own tribe, for seeing and accepting difference rather than demanding assimilation to an unspoken norm of whiteness. For whites in particular, intimate contact reduces prejudice and anxiety about dealing with an out-group.[18]

In a fast future, culturally dexterous people will redefine American culture and, hopefully, politics. The descriptor "American" will no longer imply a dominant norm of English-speaking whiteness. Instead, the majority of "We the People of the United States" will accept that the country is and should be a pluralistic mash-up of myriad human strains, a gorgeous multicolored quilt, not a melting pot of assimilation. It is the difference, say, between those who loved and those who hated a Super Bowl commercial featuring "America the Beautiful" sung in seven languages. The nondexterous recoiled at this montage. No matter. As older generations die, as racial demographics change, and as cultural dexterity proliferates, math will overtake haters. The haters will continue to fight and fear the future, but when a third or more of whites have acquired cultural dexterity, it will be much easier to create a functional, multiracial politics for the common good.

Prediction, of course, is a fool's errand, so this book does not come with a money-back guarantee. There are more dystopian possibilities. The 2016 presidential election demonstrated the enduring power of dog-whistling. Much depends on how individuals and institutions choose to respond to vertigo-inducing diversity. People of all colors have grown used to certain habits that are hard to give up. Race loyalty, benign or otherwise, is the result, whether it is among black women whose fealty to black men in the dating game is not exactly reciprocated or angry racial conservatives who deny racial bias but register pointed antiblack sentiments in opinion polls.[19]

Those who cannot adjust psychically to our nation's browning may already feel overwhelmed by demographic change. In the 2016 presidential election, almost all the counties that candidate Donald Trump won had very low percentages of immigrants. In these counties, whites were the least exposed to nonwhites and therefore lacked cultural dexterity and were likely more receptive to Trump's nativist and race-coded vitriol. In other words, whites exhibiting the most fear about immigrants were the least likely to meet any immigrants.[20]

Dexterous people are more willing to learn about and accommodate cultural differences. They accept that diversity requires negotiation and compromise. Nondexterous people perceive out-groups as risks to be avoided, for example, by crossing the street, or controlled, say, through local zoning that bans apartments, textbook battles for the minds of brown youth, or gerrymandering that distorts and reifies white voting power.

The battle between the dexterous and the nondexterous continues to play out in elections. Fifty years after *Loving*, a biracial president who self-identifies as African American has left the White House. Barack Obama's personal experience with being loved and raised by white people probably helped him understand his potential as a candidate. He knew better than most black folks what was in the minds and hearts of white voters. Like many biracial people, Obama had to learn how to straddle worlds, to code-switch, to observe and ingratiate himself with both the people of his mother and those of his wife. As he began his first presidential campaign, he believed that the white people of Iowa would support him, whereas most African Americans were quite dubious. To the surprise of many, he won a plurality of white working-class voters in 2008. The election results then and in 2016 underscore that people can carry both antidiscrimination values and bias in their heads and that either impulse can be primed by an effective politician.[21]

As Obama departed office in 2017, a multiracial coalition of millions that voted for him, twice, mourned his exit. Many of his supporters learned to see and name racism simply by watching how reactionary forces obstructed and undermined their president for eight years. Obama, the Jackie Robinson of American presidents and their player on the field of politics, inherited multiple crises and batted persistently, hitting some serious fouls, singles, and doubles and an occasional soaring home run. And always, he and Michelle responded to relentless indignities with grace. Meanwhile, reactionaries who wish they could make America white again appreciate a President Trump who winked on the campaign trail at supporters who expressly supported white supremacy. An ancient idea was dressed up in new terms like *nationalism* and *alt-right* to normalize ideologies that never should have existed in America. These ideas were not popular with the 54 percent that voted for someone other than Trump. And those who cannot abide the brawling meanness he unleashed have woken up to the timeworn observation that dog-whistling in American politics gravely harms the Union.

Racial polarization persists, and elites who stoke it for ratings and votes or who simply benefit from the plutocracy it enables can't be depended on to change course or mitigate the damage. African Americans feel besieged by a police state and by other people who do not value them as three-dimensional human beings. Even in the early light of a new millennium, structures of Jim Crow endure like ruins, from mass incarceration to neighborhood and school segregation to racial distinctions that traverse the subconscious of most Americans. Latinos also suffer these burdens of segregation, as well as labor exploitation, the stigma of attributed foreignness, and sometimes the pain of deportation. Indigenous people, too, suffer disproportionately from mass incarceration and police killings and their nations' struggles to maintain a sovereignty that gives adequate protection to Native American interests. Muslim Americans are often stamped as terrorists or deemed incompatible with America. Asian Americans are stereotyped as foreign and as model citizens, while poor, struggling, or trafficked people of Asian heritage are rendered invisible. Struggling whites dislocated by globalization and plutocracy experience rising white mortality, economic upheaval, and newly impoverished white suburban and rural ghettoes.

The difference between 1967 and 2017, however, is that the ranks of tolerant, culturally dexterous people are exploding even as nondexterous reactionaries rage. Activists for #BlackLives, for example, have more allies than they might imagine. About 60 percent of whites under age thirty support this movement and agree with its critique of law enforcement.[22] That the other 40 percent are more circumspect should not diminish the potential power of people not wedded to old ways of thinking. Culturally dexterous whites are quite similar to people of color in their vision for this country. Those who live integrated lives are less racist and more likely to support policies designed to promote diversity and reduce inequality.

Of course, there are potent reasons to be skeptical about the political and cultural influence of racial intimacy. As Brazil and other examples throughout Latin America demonstrate, intense racial mixing does not lead necessarily to racial or economic equality. If America is to be exceptional, a critical mass of whites must act with allies of color to dismantle supremacy. And so I offer suppositions that are both radical and modest.

In his 1967 lecture on race relations, Dr. King spoke of the "millions who have morally risen above prevailing prejudices," people who were "willing to share power and to accept structural alterations of society even at the cost of traditional privilege."[23] Such culturally dexterous, other-regarding souls were not a majority in 1967 and still are not in 2017. I suggest that in the future, there will be a tipping point at which a critical mass, though not a majority, of white people accepts that structural change and sharing power is what rejecting supremacy, with its embedded notions of white cultural and political dominance, actually means and requires.

When a third of whites, or more, no longer fear the loss of centrality of whiteness, when they can accept being one voice among many in a robust democracy, politics in America could return to functionality. Not perfect, not without fierce debate on ideas, but functional. This transformation occurred in California as it evolved from majority-white, to gridlocked, to majority-minority, to functional over a twenty-year period. As went California, so could the nation.

We should aspire to more than just functionality in politics. To harness cultural dexterity in ways that reduce racial and economic inequality and dismantle the structures of our supremacist past, we need intentional effort and mobilization. Those with fixed ideas about

America will put up a fight, and backlash could grow like kudzu. You, dear reader, must enter this fray. And you will necessarily need motley allies if you want to force governments to adopt saner policies.

The ultimate question is whether more loving and more pluralism will lead to the dismantling of stubborn structures born of supremacist thinking. I dare to imagine what the culturally dexterous class could deliberately dismantle and create, that is, what the third Reconstruction might look like. Many a cynic will believe that we cannot overcome supremacy constructed and reified for centuries or the plutocracy that results. Some people are too disappointed by the America they live in to hope for or imagine anything different, too grief stricken by too many killings of innocents, too beaten down by racial or economic oppression. Those who still have hope for a beautiful America owe it both to themselves and to those who have lost faith to keep fighting. This is an agitator's burden. You never get to stop fighting for your vision for this country. And when you tire, you pass the baton to the next generation, which is hopefully more creative at agitation and more open-minded than yours. The story of our trajectory toward a more perfect Union begins, as it must, in colonial Virginia, where supremacy was introduced and propagated.

. . .

PART ONE

Before *Loving,*
1607–1939

CHAPTER ONE

Going Native

Virginia's First Lovers and Haters

In early colonial Virginia, the indentured and enslaved toiled for the same masters. Oppressed souls—red, black, and white—worked alongside each other and sometimes were allies, although black and white everymen learned to hate indigenous people. America was built on violence against red bodies, and black ones. The truth is mean. There were brief interludes of peace and individual examples of friendship, love, and lovemaking between indigenous and non-indigenous, yet these instances were exceptions to the colonizers' greater love for conquest. Slavery, conquest, and the lines of race and territory that these practices produced would reverberate centuries later in Mildred Loving's complicated identity and her family's legal struggle.[1]

In the first written history of the Virginia colony, when Jamestown was an infant, its governor noted that on June 25, 1607,

> an Indian came to us from the great Poughwaton wth the word of peace: that he desired greatly our friendship; that the wyrounnces [chiefs], Pasyaheigh and Tapahanagh, should be our freindes; that wee should sowe and reape in peace, or els he would make wars vpon

them with vs. This message fell out true; for both those wyroaunces
haue ever since remained in peace and trade with vs.[2]

This hospitable attitude was consistent with the original, if ephem-
eral, vision for Jamestown. The founders of the Virginia Company of
London had naïve dreams of extracting gold, silver, and other riches
from the colony. They imagined an integrated community of indigent
Englishmen laboring with willing natives under a mild English government that would not force people to work.[3]

This fanciful vision did not last. When the colonists landed in
what would become Virginia, the so-called New World was hardly
new and it was not a wilderness. Thirty indigenous chiefdoms pressed
into a confederation by paramount chief Powhatan, himself a con-
queror, lived by the thousands in the region now known as the Virginia Tidewater, where four rivers ran into the sea.[4] By the time the
colonists of Jamestown planted their first desperate seeds, some fifteen million indigenous people resided in North America above what
is now Mexico. Most of them lived in villages organized around the
cultivation of agriculture. They had thrived in the fecund, watered,
and agreeable climates of the continent, creating a densely populated
network of First Nations, a paradise for the people of corn.[5]

Indigenous folk had little incentive to leave their own nations,
much less to work for others. In the Chesapeake region, they had
perfected techniques for producing abundant crops of corn, beans,
melon, and squash. Supplementing this harvest with fish and game,
they had full stomachs and some time for leisure.[6] In the new English colony, though, starvation was a challenge. Men who, back
in England, had been idle, unemployed, or landed gentlemen accus-
tomed to living off the labor of others did not take to the demands of
growing crops and feeding themselves in a strange land. Jamestown
quickly grew dependent on the Powhatan Confederation for corn
and other sustenance. Some colonists preferred to run away to live
with natives than endure harsh servitude and starvation.

The rulers of the colony responded nonsensically to their lack
of control over indigenous people and traitorous servants, adopting
methods that would become standard in American history: violence
and forced separation. Perhaps out of resentment of their dependence

on non-Christians, the colony rulers attacked native villages, burned their unharvested corn, and murdered women and children. They were equally violent with Englishmen who chose to commune with indigenous people. Under the colony's "Laws Divine, Morall and Martiall," written largely by the stern new colony governor, Sir Thomas Dale, settlers were forbidden even to speak to natives without his permission or, on pain of death, to run away to them.[7] In 1612, Dale personally meted out penalties for a group of recaptured white men, appointing some to be hanged, others to be "broken on wheles, . . . staked [or] shot to death."[8]

It was an early sign that elites would destroy people who refused to be exploited and would separate motley resisters who might ally themselves against the rulers. Any common ground that the indigent English may have found with indigenous people would soon turn to enmity. The benevolent vision of biracial living and cooperation that some colony founders imagined gave way to a policy of extermination and massacre. Hatred of natives was almost inevitable in a system in which the officers of the colony would grow rich and acquire land while the indentured could not. Anglo-indigenous relations would be marked by resentment among those pale-faced people who occupied the lower rungs of Virginia society, the people who would be relegated to play the role of buffer between indigenous people at the colony frontier and the rich plantations in prime coastal areas.[9]

And yet, some Native American and English individuals became intimates. The mythology surrounding Pocahontas fits with the idea of benevolent cooperation, even love, between pale and red people. Again, it is an exceptional tale that reveals how mythmaking masks the truth of genocidal Anglo–Native American relations. The famous tale about her saving Captain John Smith, de facto military leader of Jamestown, from being bludgeoned by placing her body over his and pleading with her father, Chief Powhatan, to spare Smith is almost certainly untrue. Or it originates from a misunderstanding on Smith's part about an indigenous ritual whereby the Powhatans adopted Smith and the English colony into their world.[10]

It is well documented that Smith and Pocahontas were friends.[11] Both exhibited extraordinary cultural dexterity in their ability to traverse disparate worlds. They conversed with each other, exchanging broken English and Algonkian. Smith bothered to write down Algonkian words and phrases that he learned, and Pocahontas acquired enough English to make herself understood.[12] Ultimately, though, Pocahontas showed more respect for Anglo religion and culture than Smith did toward the Algonkian-speaking polities of the Powhatan Confederation.

Pocahontas was a preternaturally curious child of about ten or eleven when Smith first encountered her. Perhaps for this reason, Powhatan selected her to be cultural mediator to the English, a role that indigenous women commonly played in their nations' practice of trying to incorporate outsiders. Pocahontas's first foray to the Jamestown fort was a diplomatic mission. Her father sent her as an envoy, bearing gifts, along with an adult escort—a clear signal that the Powhatan sought peace.[13] Subsequently, she would visit the fort on her own to chat with Smith and to play with the few boys there.[14]

For his part, Smith took excursions deep into indigenous lands and, as a survival strategy, tried to gain a realistic understanding of the natives' customs and thinking. During this time among natives—once as a prisoner—he may have become irritated with his inability to press the quasi-nomadic Algonkian polities into service.[15] Smith advocated the brutal ways of Spanish colonizers. His primary motive was English occupation, and the role he contemplated for indigenous people in these settlements was not as voluntary participants but something akin to serfs or slaves.[16]

While he traded with natives to keep the colony fed, Smith preferred violent intimidation to kindness. After Powhatan changed his mind about the English and directed those under his leadership to stop trading with or giving the colonists food, Smith would enter a village, burn down one of the homes, and then threaten to burn down the entire village and kill women and children unless they gave the colony half or more of its corn. His defenders argue that intimidation was Smith's means of avoiding the outright massacre and atrocities against natives that his successors committed after he returned to England.[17]

There is an alternative explanation. Powhatan had engineered a political association of Algonkian chiefdoms that paid taxes or tributes to him by creating kinship ties with those nations he conquered or coaxed into alliance. He was perhaps the most powerful man in North America at the time. He would take young women from other chiefdoms as brides and send sons or daughters of his to be married into such polities, a strategy not unlike alliances among European noble families.[18] Exogamy, cohabitation, and incorporation of people from different nations were part of the cultural traditions of many indigenous nations, and this openness to intermarriage and mixing was initially extended to Europeans and Africans. Powhatan also created kinship ties by adoption. For example, the event that Smith interpreted as an act of rescue by Pocahontas may have been an adoption ritual. Powhatan certainly treated Smith as something of a son and an ally for a period and offered a trade alliance with the colony.[19]

According to Smith's written account, Powhatan entreated: "Let this therefore assure you of our loves and everie yeare our friendly trade shall furnish you with corne, and now also if you would come in friendly manner to see us, and not thus with your gunnes and swords, as [if] to invade your foes." "What can you get by war, when we can hide our provision and flie into the woodes, whereby you must famish?" he asked.[20]

The colony response to this predicament defies logic. It burned crops when its people were starving. A people told for a millennium that they are better than others become enraged and disoriented when their eminence is threatened. European supremacy was bound up in the ideology of conquest, the idea of the superiority of the Christian to the infidel. Christian soldiers and conquistadors had wielded this ideology at least since the Crusades of the Middle Ages.[21] It was beyond Smith's imagination and, later, that of others to supplicate to a First Nation. Supremacy and power sharing could not coexist. The ideology of white supremacy became, and still is, the chief impediment to successful human relations in America. Each generation struggles to throw off its yoke.

As a teenager, Pocahontas demonstrated brave cultural agility that seems unparalleled in her time. Although her marriage to John Rolfe, an English tobacco planter, depicts intercultural love, warfare birthed their romance. Their courtship probably would not have occurred had she not been captured and held for ransom in the colonists' first war with the Powhatan Confederation.[22]

While in captivity for over a year, Pocahontas, then fifteen or sixteen, decided to try the ways of the English and accept Rolfe's offer of marriage. She became the first native of record in the colony to convert to Christianity, although this was likely a syncretic melding with her prior spiritual understandings rather than a complete abandonment of indigenous beliefs. Again, she played the role of intercultural mediator. Her conversion was announced only after a truce was negotiated between her father and the colonists. She took the Christian name Rebecca. The Reverend Alexander Whitaker, who had served as her religious tutor, probably chose the name. In the Bible, the beautiful Rebecca journeyed from one homeland to marry Isaac in another and would hold "two nations" and "two manner of people" in her womb.[23]

Pocahontas's choices seem those of a survivor—the best means of bridging dissonant cultures and protecting herself and her people. She must have seen advantages to becoming the wife of a man with property and connections among a people who treated her like a Powhatan princess, when in her matrilineal culture she, the daughter of a commoner, was no princess at all. For Pocahontas, love may or may not have had something to do with it.[24]

Rolfe left written evidence of his feelings. Clearly, he was besotted. In a four-page letter, he sought approval of the marriage from the colony governor, Sir Thomas Dale, and struggled aloud to reconcile his ardor for Pocahontas with his Anglo-Christian identity. Some of his references to Pocahontas or her people reflect the thinking of colonizers: a native not yet brought to Jesus was a savage, a heathen. Yet because he loved her, he wrestled: "[What] should provoke me to be in love with one, whose education hath byn rude, her manners barbarous, her generation Cursed, and so discrepant in all nutriture from my selfe?"[25]

In the letter, Rolfe describes his anguished attempts to free himself of this love. He tried leaving the thriving settlement of Henrico, where Pocahontas, as a prisoner of war, had been sent to be cultivated. By 1614, when Rolfe wrote the letter, English forts and settlements had sprung up and down the James River. During his self-imposed exile from love and its lure, Rolfe may have traveled downriver to the Jamestown fort. By then it was populated mainly by

Englishmen and, invisible in most histories of the fort, native women who lived with them.[26] Reverend Whitaker had been a vocal critic of "whoring" in the colony and of these Anglo–Native American couples.[27] That he later welcomed Pocahontas's marriage to Rolfe suggests that Whitaker had viewed Jamestown's intercultural liaisons as dangerous because of unmarried sex. Other leaders in the colony strenuously objected to the English marrying people they considered degraded heathens. By the end of the century, when the idea of white racial purity was being formalized in law, the Virginia Assembly would ban marriage between whites and people of color, including Native Americans.[28]

Absence from Pocahontas did not cure Rolfe. As the adage suggests, it may have made his heart ache more. He thought of Pocahontas "daylie, howerly, yea in my sleepe" and seemed perplexed by her hold on him. His first wife, a young English woman, had died four years before, and he seemed to feel guilt and surprise that a Native American girl could replace her in his heart. "These many passions and sufferings," he wrote of Pocahontas, "have happened to my great wonder, even when she hath byn farthest separated from me, which in Common reason (were it not undoubted the worke of god) might breede a forgettfullnes of a farre more worthy creature."[29] No doubt, Rolfe viewed his deceased, Anglo-Christian wife as superior to any indigenous woman. Yet he declared his love for Pocahontas and married her. As Richard Loving would do nearly 350 years later in another small corner of Virginia, John Rolfe broke ranks with other white men who were known to cohabit with women of color, and he chose to solemnize his affection.

In his letter to Dale, Rolfe ultimately rationalized the marriage as a patriotic, even sacrificial act for the good of the colony—a union that would accelerate Pocahontas's conversion to Christianity. After rehearsing these rationalizations, however, he concluded with language that suggests that above all, he desperately needed to be with her. He confessed that his "hearty and best thoughts" of Pocahontas had "a long time been so entangled and enthralled in so intricate a labyrinth, that I was even a-wearied to unwind myself thereout."[30]

Dale approved, apparently as heartened as Powhatan was by the opportunity the marriage presented to negotiate an end to war.

Perhaps because of the scarcity of women in the colony, Dale, the executioner of his laws more martial than divine, himself became enamored of the idea of having a native bride and bedmate. He sent a deputy to ask Powhatan if he would be willing to part with a second, younger daughter to be the governor's wife, although Dale already had a wife back in England. Powhatan refused.[31]

The Rolfes' marriage did bring about a momentary peace between the English and the Powhatan Confederation. And it was powerful propaganda for the Virginia Company's theory that "savages" could be Christianized and could live happily among transported Englishmen. Rebecca Rolfe, née Pocahontas or Matoaka, does appear to have been content living as the lady of an English-style house on a plantation on Hog Island, directly across the river from Jamestown. She had native companions or servants to help her manage, and her husband, John, lived happily among them. He became a rare defender of indigenous interests, one of the only colonists to state that First Nations had legitimate title to the lands they occupied and that their land should only be procured by negotiated purchase, not bloodshed.[32]

In taking this position, John Rolfe contradicted the international law of discovery and its embedded notions of supremacy, the rules European nations had adopted for how they would carve up the non-Christian world. Acquisition of new lands by conquest, meaning war, was the legal right of the Christian European "discoverer."[33] It is hard to imagine that Rolfe would have come to the exceptional view that the colonists should nevertheless honor the claims of indigenous nations to their land, and resist taking it by force, had he not himself loved a Native American. In this sense he, too, was a cultural mediator.

The Rolfe plantation was among the leaders in the early tobacco trade. Rolfe had pioneered the trade through years of experimentation with strains of tobacco cultivated by the Spanish in the West Indies. Pocahontas may have helped refine Rolfe's techniques for curing tobacco by incorporating native methods. The finicky plant was emerging as the golden resource to fulfill the colony founders' dreams. The Rolfes bore not just a strain of successful tobacco plant but also a son they named Thomas. As the Rolfes prospered, so did the colony.

In this peaceful interlude, Anglo-indigenous friendship was such that the English even began to trade weapons with Algonkian chiefdoms and teach natives how to use them. For a time, the colonists honored native territorial boundaries and tried not to traverse them or demand too much. The colonists finally began to thrive and grow their own food. Above all, the tobacco trade took off. In 1617, the Virginia Company exported twenty thousand pounds of what Rolfe called "the esteemed weed." By 1618, it had doubled that amount and had broken the Spanish monopoly on tobacco. The labor-intensive plant would be the source of the colony's growth and fortune.[34]

In a bid to raise more investment for the colony, the Virginia Company sent the Rolfe family to England as ambassadors. Although Rebecca Rolfe died in England, her legend would live not just in our national imagination but also as the only acceptable cross-racial bloodline for white Jim Crow–era Virginians. Descendants of Pocahontas, the line in Virginia created by her son Thomas, would be exempted from the one-drop rule of the Racial Integrity Act of 1924, the source of Mildred and Richard Loving's problems. Edith Wilson, First Lady to President Woodrow Wilson, proudly claimed to descend from Pocahontas, even though her husband supported Jim Crow segregation.[35] Cultural anthropologist Renato Resaldo wrote that "imperialist nostalgia . . . for the very forms of life [that colonizers] intentionally altered or destroyed" also contributed to the invisibility if not erasure of native people. Virginia aristocrats used the "Pocahontas exception" in the Racial Integrity Act to their advantage. Their claim to native blood legitimated their exalted status and their privilege as heirs to the commonwealth.[36] They would hold the best land in the colony, dominate Virginia politics for generations, and construct and maintain a racial caste that guaranteed their fortunes and prominence.

The interlude of peace between Virginia colonists and the Powhatan Confederation ended when land-hungry settlers refused to be contained and the confederation, led by Powhatan's brother after Powhatan's death, retaliated in 1622 with a surprise attack. The Algonkian had had enough of both physical and cultural invasion. They tried to overcome their technological disadvantages through cunning, choosing the hour of breakfast on Christian Good Friday, as they sat at the tables of white colonists, to attack and kill white men, women, and children.[37] Like Nat Turner and other slaves who revolted two centuries later, a people oppressed by those who take what is not theirs—land and bodies—will sometimes respond with inhumane violence.

Insatiable craving, by waves of settlers and land speculators, fueled American expansion. It took a while. The United States signed treaties with First Nations and abrogated treaties. Ultimately, the English, followed by Americans, conquered or removed indigenous people.

Native Americans landed a notch above black people in the racial hierarchy that Jim Crow–era folk carried in their heads. The Pocahontas exception to the Racial Integrity Act of 1924 suggests this, as did Mildred Loving's claim of indigenous identity a few decades later. Tragically, the dogma of racial purity that denied the Lovings the freedom to marry also infected the thinking of First Nations, which would disavow mixing with black people, despite a long history of such mixing. To keep "colored" people from sneaking into the privileges of whiteness (via the Pocahontas exception), Virginia imposed a definition of Native American that required the absence of blackness. Remarkably, given all the forces set against them, several original indigenous nations of the Tidewater survive as distinct polities or less-well-marked groups, including the Mattaponi, Pamunkey, Chickahominy, and Rappahannock nations. While it was not the only First Nation to engage in such distancing, the Rappahannock adopted a policy of excluding those with "any Negro blood" from membership.[38]

Although Mildred Loving sometimes self-identified as part Negro and Native American, she ultimately pledged allegiance to the Rappahannock people. On her marriage license, she identified herself solely as "Indian." In an interview granted long after the *Loving v. Virginia* case was decided, she said that her mother was "full-blooded Rappahannock" and that her father was Rappahannock and white. This First Nation was pushed and later forcibly removed by the English from its original fourteen towns north of the Rappahannock River to scattered locations across three Virginia counties, including Caroline, where Mildred and Richard lived as children and adults.[39]

In the Lovings' hometown of Central Point, there were many racially ambiguous people born of nighttime integration. When light-skinned people of color in the county claimed a mixed native-white identity, skeptics or the race police would cry foul. One longtime resident had this to say about it:

> The we-only-White-and-Indian thing was what the old folks said and some people still like to believe that, but it's not true. There was a lot of mingling down here between the Blacks, the Whites, and the Indians. Not just in Central Point, but all over Caroline County. As far as the Rappahannocks go, they are mostly light skin, but they got Black relatives right here in this area. I know some of them. Honestly, people are so mixed down here you can't say what you are or what you are not. Sometimes, it is really hard to tell.[40]

Mildred might have been responding to the bitter realities of segregation in distancing herself from the blackness that shows up in census records about her parents and ancestors. "I know my grandmother was from Portugal, but as far as I know, no one in my family was Black," she told a scholar who researched her genealogy and established that both her grandmothers were born in Virginia.[41]

Family lore has a way of weaving together fragments of truth or altering it to accommodate the unknown or the inconvenient. Mildred's identity and her marriage were her business, but her choices were shaped by Virginia's long history of reifying whiteness and denigrating blackness. The Old Dominion insisted on assigning her race as Negro. Where this insistence came from and why it even mattered to the state is bound up in the institution of slavery. Whatever Portuguese antecedents Mildred claimed, others find ties to Portugal in the trans-Atlantic slave trade.

CHAPTER TWO

Sex, Love, and Rebellion in Early Colonial Virginia

Before 1662, Virginia statutes did not penalize people for choosing partners of a different race, although lovers did face the Anglican Church's rules against fornication. Richard Loving's early colonial predecessors, white men who had to work for others, were more likely to be dexterous like Loving than to be segregationists. White workers did not see themselves as superior to darker people, because whiteness as a unifying concept had not yet been invented. The indentured had been paupers in their mother country. The population of seventeenth-century England had ballooned, but the jobs for them had not, creating large ranks of idle unemployed, some of whom turned to thievery in desperation. An English empire on American soil was supposed to create new opportunities for this hardscrabble class of excess people.[1]

In Virginia, masters created something much harsher than what servants had known in England. From the inception of the colony, a small cadre of planter elite acquired large swaths of land through a system known as "headrights." The master was compensated for transporting indentured servants across the Atlantic at the rate of fifty acres per servant, which concentrated land and profit in a relative few patriarchs.[2] Capitalist investors, who could afford to prepay as much as seven years of wages for a servant's contract, set a brutal tone for the New World. Knowing that the servant's term would end and was unlikely to be renewed, the master had incentive to extract as much value as possible from his investment. In England, Virginians soon gained a reputation for "abus[ing] their servants . . . with intollerable oppression and hard usage."[3]

White servitude in Virginia bore other similarities to slavery. As tobacco became king, the demand for labor exceeded its supply. Masters of the colony bought and sold indenture contracts, and hence the bodies attached to them, among one another, with no input from the servant. Masters also controlled their servants' social lives. A servant could not marry or have a family without the master's permission. Because a family might compete with a servant's grueling work schedule, masters had no incentive to consent to such requests. A servant during his or her term of indenture was a draft animal to produce tobacco for the master, nothing more. Elites held the English poor in utter contempt, describing them as "vile and brutish"—a stereotyping nearly indistinguishable from the racism that would be propagated to oppress black bodies.[4]

As the masters pursued a policy of extermination of surrounding indigenous nations, those nations countered with guerrilla warfare. Running away to live with natives quickly evaporated as a viable means of escape for indentured servants.[5] Such was the lowly plight of pale-skinned bonded people in Virginia throughout most of the seventeenth century. Although untold numbers of Native Americans were slaves in Virginia, there were not enough to produce a trade. Most of that work was done by indentured whites, who far outnumbered black and native slaves throughout most of the century.

John Rolfe had returned to the colony, remarried, and resumed his role as colony secretary by the time several Africans arrived, although they may not have been the very first Africans to enter the colony. Rolfe recorded the event: "At the latter end of August 1619 a Dutch man of war of the burden of a [*sic*] 160 tons arrived at Point Comfort . . . brought not anything but 20 and odd Negroes, which the Governor and Cape Merchant bought for victals . . . at the best and easiest rate they could."[6]

The new governor was George Yeardley, and the cape merchant was Abraham Piersey. Both men would become among the wealthiest people in the colony, partly because of this transaction. They had bought highly skilled, pirated slaves for a song.[7]

The *White Lion*, the Dutch man-of-war that Rolfe described, held more than just "20 and odd Negroes." These people had names. Among those likely to have arrived on the *White Lion* or another ship, the *Treasurer*, which docked at Jamestown four days later, were Antonio, Isabell, Maria, Jiro, Francisco, Margarida, John Pedro, and Angelo (or Angola). They all appear in the Virginia census of 1625 or slave inventories of the same period, with hints of their Angolan origin.[8] The "20 and odd" were survivors, a small fraction of the 350 African prisoners who had been bought by Spanish slave traders and put on a frigate called the *San Juan Bautista* in Luanda, Angola, four months before.[9]

This operation marked the beginning of a pattern for the arrival of Africans to the colony. Before 1660, most would come from West Central Africa as prisoners of English and Dutch privateers who waged a war of piracy against Portuguese and Spanish traders. Black slaves were part of the booty the privateers stole in their effort to wrest control of trans-Atlantic commerce and territory in the Americas from Catholic Spain and Portugal.[10]

The *White Lion* flew a Dutch flag because the English privateers at its helm wanted cover in their quest for treasure on the high seas. They had stolen the Africans from the *Bautista* in the Bay of Campeche off the coast of Mexico, although they had been hoping for gold, not slaves. The English privateers continued with their planned scheme of piracy anyway, putting the Africans on the *White Lion* and the *Treasurer* and setting out for English territory, a surprise to the colony when the ship arrived with an offer to sell slaves.

Some of the *Bautista* Africans were probably literate in Portuguese and urban dwellers familiar with the ways of (Portuguese) colonists. Those with Christian names were among the thousands of Africans who had converted to Christianity in Angola during prior decades of Portuguese occupation. All of the transported Africans were from indigenous African polities, including the Ndongo, a powerful kingdom of cattle owners. The Ndongo introduced sophisticated techniques for cattle herding and agriculture to Jamestown. Those who bought most of the Africans on the *White Lion* and the *Treasurer*—white colonists like Yeardley and Piersey—developed the most successful plantations of the colony.[11]

The colony had no legal architecture for slavery in 1619. The House of Burgesses, the first legislative body in the English New World, had only been established a month before the Africans arrived.[12] How Africans were treated depended on whom they were interacting with or who claimed to own them.[13] At the time, there would have been little legal distinction between enslaved Africans and white indentured servants beyond their terms of service. There is some evidence that the Africans were treated as indentured servants, although again, that was a base status. Not all Africans in the colony, however, would be slaves. Some would gain freedom, and some would be indentured. Black skin did not equate to being mere chattel.[14] Investors in black bodies had not yet used law to render white supremacy (and black inferiority) the public policy of the colony.

Aware of the slave trade and its attendant degradations, the planter elite probably considered Africans socially inferior. While the British had not yet begun their own trade in flesh, the Portuguese and Spanish had been hard at it for nearly a century. By 1619, Portuguese and Spanish traders had trafficked a million black people from Africa to South America and the Caribbean.

Extramarital sex of any kind, including between masters and servants, was strictly forbidden and publicly punished. Before the separation of church and state, courts enforced Anglican morals.[15] And some of these court cases attest to intimate relations between dark and light people. The very first reported case from the colony involving a black person was about interracial sex. In 1630, a court called for Hugh Davis to be "soundly whipped . . . before an assembly of Negroes and others for abusing himself to the dishonor of God and the shame of Christians, by defiling his body in lying with a Negro."[16]

Was this case the first salvo in Virginia's centuries-long struggle against race mixing, or was it, to use Reverend Whitaker's phrase, a penalty for "whoring"? One can't be sure, but the context suggests that Davis was a white Englishman who was penalized for the offense of fornication and that this penalty would have applied regardless of the race of his sexual partner. It is also possible that the Negro with whom Davis had lain was a man and that Davis was castigated publicly for "defiling" his body by engaging in sodomy. That Negroes were required to observe the whipping could reflect the adjudicator's desire to hold a public tutorial for a largely unconverted class about acceptable Christian practices.[17]

Whatever this case portends, Davis was not the only white man in colonial Virginia having sex with a person of color. The ugly, pervasive specter of masters raping and defiling unwilling slaves would become the dominant form of interracial sex after the rise of black chattel slavery. But the hoi polloi of early colonial Virginia did not seem to denigrate Africans or otherwise treat them as inferior.[18] Humans ensconced in mutual, withering oppression found one another as friends, lovers, or coconspirators. Proximity brought opportunity to eke out sweaty moments of humanity or to fall in love.

In 1640, Robert Sweat was penalized for impregnating "a negro woman servant." The woman's name was Margaret Cornish, "Margarida," when she was stolen off the *Bautista* two decades before. The court refers to her as a "servant," although she was a slave owned by Robert Sheppard, again suggesting that there was little difference between servants and slaves. Despite her bonded status, Cornish must have had some privileges and spare time as she managed to have both a husband and a lover, apparently neither of whom lived on the premises of her master. She was married to a black man named John Graweere, also an Angolan stolen off the *Bautista*. Graweere was owned by a neighboring master named Evans. Cornish's white lover, Robert Sweat, was the son of a Jamestown assemblyman and came from the upper class.

The affair surfaced when Cornish gave birth to a child that was obviously of mixed heritage. Both Cornish and Sweat were charged with fornication; they were tried and convicted. The court gave Cornish the same penalty prescribed to white men and women who engaged in same-race fornication in that era: thirty lashes. As was also done in medieval England and Puritan New England for immoral acts, she was to be "whipt at the whipping post" in the town square. Meanwhile, Sweat was made to do "public penance for his offense at James city in the time of divine service according to the laws of England."

The disparate penalties imposed on Sweat and the Negro mother of his child suggest a class distinction more than a racial one. Both parties were publicly penalized for fornication, although Sweat seems to have procured for himself a religious alternative to the whipping post—an alternative that literate Christians and first offenders could invoke. Sweat stood in the Jamestown church on a Sunday, wearing a white sheet and wielding a white stick to signal humility and penance.[19] In 1649, another white man, William Watts, and Mary, a Negro servant, were both assessed this ritual penalty for fornication, as were same-race couples. They were made to stand in a church "with the customary white sheet and white wand."[20]

John Graweere, Margaret Cornish's devastated husband, responded to the affair by availing himself of the courts to gain custody of his three-year-old son. The husband's rise from slave to free man with rights attests to the possibilities for black strivers before the construction of a harsh color line. Like other skilled cattle owners of Angola, Graweere took advantage of a common practice in the colony. Some masters allowed their slaves to raise animals and crops on their own and purchase their freedom.

Graweere, apparently still a slave at the time, filed a petition to purchase his son from Sheppard, the master who owned the boy and his mother, and remove the boy from Graweere's cheating wife. The court gave him the relief he sought after he and a godparent assured the court that the child would be made a Christian and "be taught and exercised in the church of England."

The case is astounding in light of the regime of chattel slavery instated by the next century. The court sanctioned a slave's or servant's purchase of another's freedom, condoned his agency in this matter, and approved the boy's being educated (his learning to read and write, presumably) and being raised as a Christian. In other words, the court seemed to contemplate that the child would become a member of the community and was therefore deserving of certain protections. "The court hath therefore ordered that the child shall be free from the said William Evans or his assigns," it concluded, meaning that Graweere's owner could not become the son's owner.

Graweere ultimately purchased his own freedom and moved to Lancaster County, Virginia. He left his wife behind, in slavery. Margaret Cornish continued what would be a long relationship with Robert Sweat. Despite the colony's strong disapproval of extramarital sex, Cornish bore a total of three sons and a daughter by Sweat. The scoundrel in the story, if there is one, is Sweat, as he apparently made no effort to purchase either Cornish or the children she bore him to relieve them from slavery. Cornish was emancipated only when she reached old age and seemingly was of no further use to her master.

As a free man in Lancaster County, Graweere rose to become an officer of the Virginia Court with the duty of punishing lawbreakers at the public whipping post. A black man in the late 1640s oversaw the whipping of white men and women, indentured and free, for infractions of Anglican prohibitions on fornication, adultery, drunkenness, and other sins. One imagines that Graweere found solace in this role for the wounds inflicted on him by his disloyal wife and her lover.[21]

The life of another black *Bautista* Angolan also attests to the complexity of relations in this era. Benjamin Doll began life in Jamestown as a slave, yet he rose to own a three-hundred-acre plantation in Surry County, Virginia, and even had English servants indentured to him. Like Graweere, he earned money by raising animals and crops while still a slave. He invested his savings, purchasing contracts for indenture to acquire land through the system of headrights. Doll was one of the few literate people among bonded workers of any color. He probably arrived literate in Portuguese and learned to read and write in English, perhaps the first African American in Jamestown to do so. In 1659, a white widow in Surry County authorized him to act as her attorney.[22]

Perhaps the most emancipated of the *Bautista* Angolans was Tony Longo. He, too, obtained his freedom and acquired land, 250 acres of it, to farm and raise cattle. He married an Englishwoman named Hannah in 1652. There was no legal prohibition on interracial marriages in Virginia or any other colony at that time—and, apparently, no social prohibitions. The marriage does not seem to have caused any disquiet in the colony.

Longo is famous among legal historians because of a court case in which he demonstrated a sense of entitlement to speak his mind to white people. His uppity ways were tolerated, it seems, until he made the mistake of hitting someone. The penalty he paid for this assault apparently had nothing to do with his status as a black man. Having purchased his freedom, Longo seemed as free as any other man was to do as he pleased, until he traversed the law against assault.

In 1655, Longo was hard at work in his cornfield during harvest time when he was interrupted by John Neene, a white man. Neene tried to serve a warrant on Longo because he needed him to testify in a lawsuit Neene had brought against someone else. Neene and the court system valued Longo's testimony despite his blackness, but Longo could not be bothered. He refused Neene's request to accompany Neene to the home of Judge Peter Walker to testify to what he knew. Neene persisted and soon returned to Longo's farm with Judge Walker demanding that he comply.

In the presence of the judge, Longo unleashed his wrath: "What shall I go to Mr. Walker's for? Go about your business you idle rascal." Neene waved the warrant at Longo, who was unimpressed. "Shitt of your warrant," he said. Longo's wife, Hannah, joined in, berating Neene "with such noise that I could hardly hear my own words," Neene complained. The white plaintiff proceeded to read the warrant in full to Longo, and when he was done, Longo "gave me some blows," Neene testified in a suit he later brought against Longo for assault.

The court gave Longo the heaviest possible penalty for hitting his fellow citizen, thirty lashes on two consecutive days. Although Longo had to pay for being irascible, the episode hints of some egalitarian possibilities for dark people in the first half of the seventeenth century. As a self-emancipated man, Longo felt no need to cower or comply in the face of a warrant. And his testimony was sought in a case on behalf of a white man, possibly against the interests of another white person. A few years later, when the planter elite began to switch from white bodies to black bodies as their main source of labor, the Jamestown assembly would ban Africans from testifying in such cases.[23]

Tony Longo's son, James, was similarly rebellious and independent. He acquired a two-hundred-acre farm and fathered a child with an English, common-law wife named Isabel Hutton. But unlike James's parents, the couple became ensnared in antimiscegenation laws that were introduced in the late seventeenth century. As a "negro or mulatto," Longo was penalized for fathering a child with Hutton. The couple defied the law, stayed together, and had a second child. Like the Lovings centuries later, Longo and Hutton were hauled into local court twice for the crime of creating an interracial family.[24]

Perhaps because he was of mixed heritage and had endured interference from the state in his own mixed family, James Longo once offered to help the child of another interracial couple. George Francis ("Francisco" of the *Bautista*) fathered a child with a young English servant named Dorothy Bestick. Longo and a white neighbor, Jane Fitzgerald, paid Bestick's fine for fornication and agreed to serve as godparents to the child, enabling her to retain custody and saving the child from being bound to servitude as a penalty arising from bastardy.[25] A free white person, Fitzgerald, and a free person of color, Longo, informally adopted a mixed-race child on behalf of an enslaved-indentured, mixed-race couple.

This arrangement attests to friendship, alliances, and caring across what would later become severe social boundaries. Whatever social distinctions infused the ether of the colony, they were not so rigidly established that Longo or Fitzgerald felt inhibited from acting together to help. And the state allowed them to do it, again demonstrating that rigid norms of white supremacy and the need to protect it from infraction by others had not yet been erected, although notions of Christian and English superiority certainly operated in the colony.

In the first half of the seventeenth century, the elites of the colony showed more concern about interracial conspiracies than interracial sex and marriage. In 1640, six white servants and a black man stole a skiff, corn, guns, and ammunition and escaped down the Elizabeth River together. They were captured, tried, and punished. Emmanuel, the black man and probably already a slave for life, was whipped, branded, and required to wear shackles for a year. The leader of the group, Christopher Miller, a Dutchman, was also made to wear shackles for a year. Among the remaining white conspirators, one was also whipped and branded, and three were required to serve the colony for additional years of indenture. That both a white man and a black man could be branded demonstrated their common draft-animal status in the 1640s.[26]

Other bonded people united in acts of resistance. One researcher unearthed fifteen instances in which African Americans and European Americans plotted together to escape—the conspiracies involved a total of seventy-five people. The same researcher found that in fifteen cases, free people tried to assist bonded people in running away.[27]

In the famous case of *In re Negro John Punch*, decided in 1641, an African, a Dutchman, and a Scotsman ran away together to escape life as indentured servants. After they were caught in Maryland, a Virginia court ordered a year of service added to the two white men's terms of indenture. Poor John Punch, from whom President Obama might have descended, was made a slave for "his natural Life here or elsewhere."[28]

Black people were easily distinguishable from the Portuguese, Spanish, French, Turks, Dutch, Scots, Irish, English, and Native Americans who inhabited or traversed the colony. Perhaps this distinctiveness explains why differential treatment emerged. Or perhaps disfavoring Africans was the flip side of a national consciousness favoring the English in the colony. The Dutch ringleaders in the Emmanuel and Punch escapes were also evidently disfavored for being non-English.[29]

By 1649, according to a pamphlet published that year, there were "about fifteene thousand English, and of Negroes brought thither three hundred good servants" in Virginia.[30] One historian claims that there were no more than five hundred blacks in the colony by 1650, out of a total population of about fourteen thousand.[31] Even as late as the 1670s and 1680s, no more than one out of every four or five bonded laborers was African American, while a smaller portion of the bonded was Native American.[32] Indigenous slaves were often prisoners taken as spoils of war.[33] Those struggling to escape the yoke of servitude or to prosper as independent farmers were overwhelmingly white and increasingly rebellious. Even before they were forced or enticed to cross the Atlantic for a term of indenture, indentured whites had lived at the margins of English society, worlds apart from their new masters. These bonded people were Irish slaves, English political prisoners and convicts, beggars snatched off the streets of London, maids targeted to be wives to lonely colonists, and volunteers hoping for better economic circumstances.[34]

For the first part of the seventeenth century, the master-planter class controlled most aspects of bonded people's lives, regardless of the color of their skin, while free people had options. But in 1643, the informal system of requiring permission from masters to marry was replaced with a law forbidding bonded laborers ever to marry. By 1662, any free man who married a bonded woman without her owner's permission was required to pay a fine of fifteen hundred pounds of tobacco or to serve a year of labor to the woman's master.[35] Add to this law the whippings laid on laborers just to make them work harder, the sheer harshness of servitude, and financial hopelessness (economic turbulence during the middle of the seventeenth century made prosperity after indenture unlikely), and bonded people began to revolt.

English servants rebelled in 1659, 1661, 1663, and, most notoriously, in Bacon's Rebellion in 1676, when African and European laborers united initially in a murderous crusade to eliminate indigenous people from Virginia and take their land. Later, these black and white workers sought freedom from the planter elite. This armed, biracial uprising involved six thousand European American and two thousand African American bonded people, in addition to thousands of free men, like the leader Nathaniel Bacon, himself an elite who disagreed with the colony governor's incremental approach to taking native lands. The rebellion lasted nine months and sent shock waves through all the colonies, partly because abolition was one of its goals. Bonded rebels wanted to own their own bodies and be independent farmers rather than wage earners or serfs. In response, the ruling class put down the insurrection and began to fortify and entrench the color line.[36]

The problem for planters was that each year, large numbers of whites would complete terms of indenture and then find that they could not acquire their own farms or otherwise move up the economic ladder. In addition to the growing scarcity of affordable land, the ruling elites were unwilling to kill natives and extend the colony frontier any faster. Restless un-free white labor was becoming dangerous at the same time that Dutch traders were offering a steady supply of African slaves. As one legal historian wrote:

> The institution of white indentured servitude was producing a class of propertyless, mostly unmarried males who proved to be a restless, combustible element of society. . . . Because they had neither wealth nor wives and children to be held hostage by society for their good behavior, these landless ex-servants presented a dilemma to Virginia's rulers. The colony needed cheap, unskilled labor, but it also had to reconcile the interests of ex-servants with the power and expectations of the elite.[37]

In 1660, the planter elite began a multidecade period of transition to black chattel slavery.[38] It was a conscious choice in the sense that black slaves came with life tenures for service and fewer potential headaches. It is less clear whether the rulers of the colony thought through the ramifications of the legal and social architecture they would have to construct to make chattel slavery viable. Nevertheless, those in power began to construct this architecture, and thus began the prohibitions on interracial mixing.

Light and dark bonded people had been working alongside one another in the colony for four decades, and they would continue to do so for at least another century. But interracial alliance among laborers was a serious threat to the planter elite. For this reason, the Virginia Assembly deemed it necessary to counter evident feelings of mutuality among them. In 1660, the assembly penalized "any English servant" who "shall run away in company with any Negroes," rendering the English servant liable to an extension of his or her term of indenture.[39]

In 1662, the Virginia Assembly, which was controlled by the planter class, attached a special penalty to interracial sex, doubling the fine for fornication when it occurred between a "Christian" and a "Negro." The law also mandated that children fathered by an Englishman with a Negro woman would, contrary to English patrilineal tradition, derive their status from the mother. An enslaved or indentured woman would give birth to a slave or a servant, no matter how lofty the father's lineage. In this way, planters could use master-slave sex to expand their slaveholdings.[40]

The assembly's new policy direction apparently was an attempt to shut down the emancipative possibilities of a petition it had granted a few years before. Elizabeth Key was the daughter of an African slave, Thomas Key, an early, respected English settler who had once served in the assembly. Elizabeth Key petitioned for, and won, her freedom. Her legal representative was another Englishman, William Grinstead, who was Key's lover and the father of her two children. In 1655, they brought the case because they wanted to free her and get married. They argued in court that she was a practicing Christian and the daughter of a free Englishman and that the specific terms of her nine-year indenture, negotiated by her father, had expired and been violated.

Thomas Key had returned to England and died, but not before placing Elizabeth with a friend and entering into a written agreement that she would be treated akin to an English servant and be brought to him in England when her period of indenture was complete. The friend betrayed him and presumably sold Key as a slave to another estate. The jury heard testimony from neighbors familiar with Key's birth. Apparently, Key's father owned Key's mother. One witness testified that she saw Key's mother go to bed with Thomas Key many times, and several neighbors let fly the well-spread rumor that Elizabeth, sometimes referred to as Bess, was Key's child. One witness claimed that Thomas Key denied the rumor and claimed that a "Turke" servant or slave to a "Capt. Mathewes" was the culprit. In English usage of the time, a "Turke" was an adherent of Islam.

The hearsay rumors seemed to sway the jury in Elizabeth Key's favor. They believed her claim of free English ancestry. They also may have been sympathetic to the violation of the terms of indenture. During that period, most of the rare servants who had the temerity to sue their masters for violations won their cases. The courts were a source of refuge against extension of indenture.

When an appeals court overturned the jury verdict, Key and her English lover-lawyer pursued an appeal to the Virginia Assembly, which in those days acted as the highest court of the colony as well as supreme legislature. The assembly agreed with the jury and granted Key's petition without explanation, possibly in a nod of respect to a former colleague's arrangements to manumit a daughter-slave. Unlike

Dred Scott two centuries later, Key, a colored slave, was able to petition the courts and be welcomed as a free member of the colony, as
an English subject rather than as a citizen. On attaining her freedom,
Key did marry William Grinstead. While interracial sex was common between white men and Negro or native women in that era, the
Key-Grinstead union was a rare recorded marriage between a white
man and a Negro or mixed-race woman in the colony.[41]

The new 1662 law condemning children of a slave mother to slavery and penalizing interracial sex would prevent others from benefiting from Key's precedent. For the next three hundred years, until
the Lovings brought their successful case before the Supreme Court,
Virginia legislators would maintain some form of penalty or ban on
interracial intimacy. The only class perpetually exempted from these
prohibitions was slave owners who had sex with their property. Virginia's restrictions on love or lust between pale and dark people orig-
inated not from any innate antipathy to interracial sex but from a
capitalist desire to promote black chattel slavery. Consistent with the
Longo men's examples, many free African men in the Chesapeake region took European women as partners or wives in the seventeenth
century. Black women may have been devalued because they were
slaves or because the labor of even free black women was subject to
a tax that did not apply to white women.[42] One researcher examined
fornication cases in Virginia. Among the fifty-four that concerned
male bonded laborers, twenty-two involved black men and white
women. And yet there was no great uproar about black men having
sex with white women in the colony.[43]

There was no lynching, no eyes gouged out, no penises cut off because they threatened Southern womanhood. Wealthy, seventeenth-
century Virginians were rapidly acquiring black labor, but neither
the elites nor the ordinary folk were yet crazed by these dark-skinned
people. Virginia's legislature would not ban marriage between "Christians" and "Negroes" until 1691, nearly thirty years after it first enacted the special penalty for interracial fornication.

Bacon's Rebellion, a biracial revolt with many Native American victims, seems to have accelerated the wealthy's construction
of white racial purity. It is curious, this othering business. The person who is down, his or her back breaking under the foot of an

economic oppressor, fulminates in powerlessness and has few options. The individual can rebel against or even maim the oppressor, and such rebellion happened in colonial Virginia. The downtrodden can also take what they can from other oppressed people. Colonial laborers learned to hate Native Americans because the natives occupied what the masters already had: land. Hatred of the other—racial hatred—would become a standard response to plutocratic oppression among struggling whites in America, although this response had to be inculcated in each new generation. Throughout the ages, plutocrats have honed the skills of divide and conquer, and antimiscegenation laws and rhetoric were primary tools for three centuries. At the close of the seventeenth century, Virginia lawmakers had to contend with many interracial lovers among bonded people and attendant threats to slavery.

CHAPTER THREE

Slavery Begets Antimiscegenation and White Supremacy

One-fifth of the children born out of wedlock at the end of the seventeenth century were mulattoes.[1] In the Chesapeake region of Virginia and Maryland, light and dark bodies had prodigious opportunity to find one another and have sex. Some two thousand slaves and six thousand indentured servants lived in Virginia in 1671, along with even larger numbers of free white persons who had once been indentured. Whether bonded or free, this serving class did the menial work of the colony. Scots, Irish, and English who had been nuisance people in their motherland and Africans and Native Americans who had been captured and sold all labored for masters on the big plantations or on small farms in the interstices not taken by the gentry. Among this colonial underclass, male servants outnumbered females by about three to one. Historians surmise that laboring people simply took lovers where they found them, regardless of color, and created a small cohort of mixed-race people.[2]

Interracial intimacy, then, was a normal part of early colonial life, although alarming to elites. Mating and sometimes marrying produced a steady trickle of mulattoes, half-breeds, quadroons, octo-roons, mustees, or any number of monikers for the mixed people who made up about 2 or 3 percent of the population in the Upper South.[3] Elites who were anxious about this mixing introduced legal penalties and prohibitions.

While Virginia was the first colony to penalize interracial sex, Maryland was the first colony to penalize interracial marriage, albeit indirectly. In 1664, its legislature required that any free woman who married a slave serve the master of that slave during the life of her husband and that any children born of the marriage also be slaves.[4] Maryland may have acted first in penalizing marriage because it had a higher ratio of black slaves to indentured servants in that period than other colonies had.[5] This penalty created the legend of Eleanor "Irish Nell" Butler and "Negro Charles," a true story that appears in most treatises about interracial intimacy and the laws against it.

Nell Butler was an Irish indentured servant to Charles Calvert, the Right Honourable Third Lord Baltimore. His family had established and been proprietor-governors of the Maryland colony from its inception in 1634 through 1676, when he, the third Lord Baltimore stepped down as governor of the colony. Calvert sold Nell's services to Major William Boarman. On the Boarman plantation, Nell did the laundry, cooked, spun, worked in the fields, and served as a midwife. She also fell in love with Charles, one of Boarman's slaves, who likely worked in the fields cultivating tobacco. They may have met in the fields. Court records about them include a witness who recalled that Nell "was a hard laboring body and made good crops."

Nell seems to have been rather willful and outspoken. In 1681, at age sixteen, she informed Calvert that she intended to marry Charles. On the morning of the wedding, Calvert tried to talk her out of it, counseling her to be sensible, lest she become a slave too. Nell cried but would not be deterred and accepted the penalty for her heart's desire. She insisted to Calvert that she would rather marry and go to bed with Charles than with "your lordship." Calvert cursed her but was so disturbed at the prospect of his servant becoming a slave he petitioned the Maryland assembly to change the 1664 law.

The assembly did repeal the provision that forced into slavery any white servant who married a slave even as it prohibited such marriages and imposed punitive fines on slave owners whose slaves entered them. The amendment came too late for Nell, however, and did not apply retroactively. Her marriage, despite being blessed by the Catholic Church, forced her, and the multiple children she bore with Charles, into slavery.

Apparently, after the marriage, "Negro Charles" became Charles Butler, taking the surname of his wife. The couple worked as slaves for the Boarman family for the rest of their lives. He called her his "old woman," and she rejoined with "old man." The main trace of Charles is his name in court records about the struggles of his and Nell's progeny to be free. Their oldest son, Jack, fled to southern Virginia and later purchased his freedom from the Boarmans.[6]

The punitive costs of the Butlers' interracial love would reverberate for at least a century. Their grandchildren and great-grandchildren would also be slaves. In 1770, two of Nell and Charles's great-grandchildren petitioned the court for freedom on the basis that they descended from Irish Nell, a white woman. The court ruled against them, concluding that "many of these people, if turned loose, cannot mix with us and become members of society." By then the color line and the idea of pure whiteness to demarcate who belonged had roots. Another great-grandchild, Mary Butler, would win her suit for freedom in 1787, although the case turned on a technicality: the lack of evidence before the court that Nell and Charles had ever been married. Although the court freed Mary, other enslaved descendants of white women could not benefit from this rare victory.[7]

As Virginia grew, so did the numbers of people engaging in interracial sex. By 1681, some seventy-five thousand people lived in Virginia. The colony governor at the time estimated that fifteen thousand were indentured servants and three thousand were slaves, black and Native American. By 1715, the colony would be home to twenty-three thousand Negro slaves.[8] By design, slavery blackened as the peculiar institution became the most efficient means to create a new "commodity-generating empire" in which "African Americans [would] toil under the hot sun for the profit of the rest of the world."[9]

Virginia had more slaves and more free, formerly indentured, and unmarried white men than any other colony, some fifteen thousand surplus white men. At the turn from the seventeenth century to the eighteenth, the conditions for race mixing were most fertile in Virginia and other Upper South colonies with sizable numbers of slaves, indentured, and formerly indentured people. One scholar of the period describes the circumstances: "The mix of black and white was more intimate in those turn-of-the-century years in the upper South than it was at any other time and any other place in what is now the United States."[10]

Elsewhere, mingling and sex between light and dark depended on the presence and size of an African population. In Northern colonies, social divisions ran primarily between free and bonded rather than between black and white.[11] A community in colonial Pennsylvania with a noticeable presence of mixed-race people garnered the sobriquet Mulatto Hall.[12] In the Lower South, or Deep South, mulatto children, sired primarily by masters who had had sex with their slaves, were the mixed-race fruits of often-violent assault. For nearly two centuries in the Lower South, mulattoes were accorded an elevated status above their aubergine cousins. The Lower South only began to follow the ways of Virginia and the Upper South, adopting a rigid one-drop rule of racial caste in the 1850s, as secessionist sentiments raged.[13]

The planters that ran Virginia began constructing this caste in the late seventeenth century in part because they viewed interracial cooperation as a threat to their interests. They enacted a series of provisions designed to breed white antipathy for blacks, Native Americans, and mixed-race people. By 1670, natives and Negroes, even those like the *Bautista* Angolans who had been baptized as Christians, were forbidden to own Christian servants. The process of aligning laboring whites psychologically with their masters and conscripting all members of colonial society into enforcing black chattel slavery had begun.[14] Black bondage became much harsher than white bondage; with each succeeding decade, the Virginia Assembly reduced the privileges and rights of slaves.[15] In 1682, Virginia eliminated conversion to Christianity as a means by which slaves could gain freedom, as did John Graweere's young son four decades before.[16]

In 1691, the Virginia Assembly explicitly attacked as "abominable" any marriage between a white person and "a Negro, mulatto, or Indian." The offending white person would be permanently banned from the colony, while no penalty would attach to the colored spouse in this marriage, presumably because that person might be owned by a planter. Any free English woman who had a "bastard child by a Negro" had to pay a fine to the church or risk imprisonment for five years. In addition to trying to maintain a clear distinction between black slaves and white nonslaves, these antimiscegenation laws were also motivated by the scarcity of white women in the colony. The lawmakers—free, white, property-owning men—likely wanted free rein in their access both to enslaved Negro women and to free and indentured white women.[17]

Most telling, this ban on interracial marriage was embedded in a larger statute titled "An act for suppressing outlying slaves." Outlying slaves were runaways, and various empathetic actors, from other slaves and servants to friends, lovers, wives, or husbands, could help the runaways evade their masters. The law also made it more difficult for willing masters to free their slaves, requiring the master to pay for any freed slave's transportation out of the country. It authorized the issuance of warrants to capture runaways and permitted killing them if they refused to surrender and return.[18]

By 1705, the Virginia Assembly had adopted the first comprehensive slave code among all the colonies and introduced a crucial demarcation between "white Christian servants" and everyone else in the laboring class. The code conferred new legal rights exclusively on white servants, including a protection against extension of the period of indenture and against becoming a slave. The act's title attested to the assembly's intentions: "An act concerning Servants and Slaves." Race, color, and religion were used to mark the line between the two groups of people. Henceforth, "no negros, mulattos, or Indians, although christians, or Jews, Moors, Mahometans, or other infidels" could purchase "any white christian servant," the code said. The penalty for violation of this new rule was the automatic freeing of the white servant.

White servants were also guaranteed a "wholesome and competent diet, clothing and lodging" and protection against "immoderate correction." White skin was now privileged in a way it had not been before. Masters could no longer whip a white Christian servant on their bare backs without an order from a justice of the peace, and anyone who subjected a white servant to such indignity would pay a fine of forty shillings sterling. And any Negro, mulatto, or Indian, bonded or free, who deigned to "lift his or her hand" against a white Christian would receive "thirty lashes, well laid on" a bare back. Nakedness and public lashing were now reserved for nonwhite bodies. An uppity man like Tony Longo would pay a special price for striking or resisting a white person. And the code gave any aggrieved white servants the protection of the state. They could informally petition the courts with complaints of misusage, for their wages, or for freedom.[19]

The law also clarified that any servants that "were not Christians in their native country, before they were shipped" were now to be accounted as "slaves." Exceptions were made for "Turks and Moors in amity with her majesty" and others who could prove they had been free in a Christian country before being transported to the colony.[20] The new code reaffirmed that baptism and conversion to Christianity would no longer enable a person to gain freedom from slavery.[21]

The code deputized everyone in enforcing the regime of slavery. Landless, free white men could at least become "paddy rollers," as the slaves called them, policing the land and receiving a bounty of one to two hundred pounds of tobacco for capturing an incorrigible runaway. Any person who corrected a resisting slave and happened to kill him or her was immune from liability. For runaways suspected of lying out in the woods, the sheriff was authorized to issue a proclamation to be published and posted at the door of every church and chapel on a Sabbath day and read to all parishioners "after divine worship." The proclamation made it lawful for any person to kill or destroy the named wretch, with impunity. If the proclaimed runaway was captured, the county court was to order a punishment of "dismembering" so as to "terrify . . . others" from escaping.[22]

The code also refined the penalties on interracial intimacy. It required that all mulatto children would be servants at least until they were thirty-one years old. The harshest punishments were reserved for interracial couples that sought to marry. Any white person who married a Negro now faced a fine and imprisonment rather than banishment from the colony, and any master or mistress who married interracially was required to free *all* their Christian white servants.[23] Any minister who wittingly married a white person to a

Negro or mulatto was required to pay a fine of ten thousand pounds of tobacco for each such marriage.[24] There were no such penalties for marriages between whites and Native Americans, or whites and "Jews, Moors, Mahometans or other infidels." Only marriages between whites and Negroes or mulattoes now mattered, likely because these darker people populated the slave class.

Meanwhile, the code rendered black slaves nonpersons, utterly reduced to chattel with no rights or free agency. Their loss of personhood was a horrifyingly inevitable consequence of building a new American capitalism with slavery at its center.[25] Slaves could not leave their masters' plantations without papers. They could not receive coin or engage in exchanges with others without a license from their masters. They could not carry weapons. And if they acquired any horses, cattle, or hogs, the animals were to be seized and sold by the local churchwarden and the proceeds applied by the warden for the use of poor whites. Slaves would no longer be encouraged to better their positions by hiring themselves out and raising their own animals, as the court had commended John Graweere for decades before. And poor whites now had strong incentive to disassociate from and contest such behavior.[26]

The legal rights given white servants greatly improved white master-servant relations and created a sense of racial affinity between these classes. The color line had its intended effect of quieting resistance by white servants. The lawgivers had solved the class tensions of the previous century by creating whiteness. And blackness now meant the opposite in social standing. "Slave" no longer equated with "servant." To be a slave, even a mulatto, light-skinned one, was to be functionally black—disempowered and dehumanized.[27]

Other colonies would soon emulate Virginia's slave code. As bans on interracial intimacy were instrumental in the regulation of slavery, the legal curtain on interracial love or other alliances descended across the colonies. By 1725, seven of the eleven existing colonies had adopted codes banning interracial marriage and four had banned interracial fornication. Virginia and Maryland prohibited both. Four colonies had also defined what constituted "black" or "white" for purposes of delineating which persons could be free or enslaved.[28] While the laws did not formally adopt a one-drop rule that cast persons with *any* African ancestry as black, elites of the Upper South had adopted this rigid social distinction well before the Revolutionary era.[29]

Even in Louisiana, with a history of colonizers mixing with native, African, and Creole women, the civil French Code Noir banned interracial marriage in 1724.[30] Of course, the laws did not stop interracial liaisons like those facilitated by the quadroon balls of New Orleans, elegant affairs in which wealthy European men went looking for a refined mulatto mistress who would become something akin to a common-law wife. Typically, the ingenue's mother would negotiate terms for support and property for her daughter and any children borne of this *mariage de la main gauche,* as mixed-race Creole society called it. This formalized system of interracial coupling known as *plaçage* was common in other places of French or Spanish colonial origin, including Mobile, Alabama; Biloxi and Natchez, Mississippi; and St. Augustine, Florida.[31] In societies with a shortage of white women, a light-skinned mulatto could extract value, whether in the voluntary transactions that plaçage facilitated or involuntarily at slave auctions in which a premium would be paid for mulatto "fancy girls."[32]

Interracial sex continued. In 1757, a Virginian decried that the "country swarms with mulatto bastards" and denounced those "wretches amongst us" who consorted with Negro women and those white women who "prostituted" themselves to Negro men.[33] Even after the creation of a harsh color line, light and dark people interacted with one another daily, and individuals then and for centuries were forced to choose how to respond to the delineation. A line that had initially been a social distinction only among elites eventually came with social and legal penalties for nonelites who defied it. And so the ideology of Christian white supremacy authored by conquering monarchs and aristocrats was imbibed by the white masses. As one historian said of the phenomenon, "southern colonizers were able to forge consensus among upper- and lower-class whites" because race "became the primary badge of status."[34] Racism was the effective answer to preventing a replay of Bacon's Rebellion. In the words of historian Edmund S. Morgan, this new racial caste separated "dangerous free whites from dangerous slave blacks by a screen of racial contempt." Native Americans and mulattoes were lumped in with blacks in a single pariah class to forge a single, white "master class" of small and large planters.[35]

Thus, racism was a mental process that was essential to the creation of remarkable wealth in America. Besides land, slaves were the equity on which fortunes were based, the means by which men of aspiration became respected businessmen and statesmen, especially in the South. Economists estimate that slavery alone accounted for a third of capital assets in the American South during the revolutionary era, the largest source of wealth of Southern patriarchs.[36] Northern fortunes would also be created directly or indirectly through slavery. In the North and South, slave owners sold and leased black bodies to help fund or build esteemed colleges and universities, from Harvard to Princeton, Georgetown to William and Mary and many other institutions, including Yale and the University of Virginia. These would-be citadels of enlightenment also helped propagate supremacist thinking.[37]

After the American Revolution, ironically, race and racism made it easier to reconcile slavery with our founding egalitarian values. Slaveholders in Virginia and elsewhere in the South were among the loudest voices for republican equality among the rich and poor because the color line had disempowered the majority of laborers who might revolt, their slaves.[38] No one seems to embody this irony more than Thomas Jefferson. The color line and the laws against race mixing were central to statecraft in America, delineating who belonged and who did not.[39] Jefferson had much to say on these subjects, and his dissonance about slavery and race mixing—the distance between his republican values and his actions—mirrored that of the nation.

The main transgressors of the color line in the eighteenth century were the masters themselves, including Jefferson. Instead of voluntary couplings between the indentured and the enslaved, in the eighteenth-century master-slave rape and master-slave liaisons would become the dominant form of interracial sex in the Upper South, as it had been in the Lower South. The most significant portion of this sex apparently occurred between the uppermost class of white slaveholding men and the mulatto women slaves who worked for them.[40]

Sally Hemings is the most famous example of the mulatto house-maid who had sexual relations with the master. The Thomas Jefferson Foundation, protector of Monticello and Jefferson's legacy, acknowledges the relationship and has published the evidentiary basis for its conclusion that Jefferson fathered all six of Hemings's children.[41] Beyond DNA evidence linking a Hemings son to a Jefferson male and the fact that Thomas Jefferson was present at Monticello during all the times when Hemings's children would have been conceived, perhaps the most resonant evidence of the relationship is who Hemings was. In her book *The Hemingses of Monticello*, historian Annette Gordon Reed presents circumstances linking Hemings and Jefferson, who may have learned the habit of taking a mulatto slave as a sexual partner from his father-in-law John Wayles. The father of Martha Wayles Jefferson, Wayles had a relationship with a mulatto slave named Elizabeth Hemings, and the relationship produced Sally and five siblings. After Wayles died, the Hemings family—Martha's enslaved half-siblings and their mother—became part of Jefferson's estate. They would live and work for him at Monticello, and a few would accompany him to France, Philadelphia, and Washington, DC. A decade after marrying Jefferson, Martha, weakened by childbirth, extracted a deathbed promise from Jefferson that he would not remarry. Jefferson was thirty-nine at the time.[42]

Honoring this request would have required Jefferson to abstain from sex for the rest of his life, unless he fornicated with someone. He was a man of many interests and appetites, an epicure who arranged to have his slave, James Hemings, brother to Sally, trained to prepare elaborate French cuisine for him. Jefferson had impregnated his wife six times, and he wrote forthrightly in a letter to John Adams that nature had endowed men and women with lustful sexual desire to ensure human procreation.[43] It would have been difficult for Jefferson to quench his thirsts with white women outside marriage. His slave, Sally Hemings, presented an alternative.

While Jefferson was serving as US minister to France, he arranged for Sally Hemings to travel there from Monticello to be a companion and maid to his daughters. By then Hemings was fifteen. The few accounts of her looks suggest she was pretty by white societal norms. Isaac Jefferson, who had been a slave at Monticello, described

Hemings as "mighty nearly white . . . very handsome, [with] long straight hair down her back."[44]

Jefferson seems to have begun a sexual relationship with Hemings while he was in France. Perhaps he loved her, perhaps he didn't. He did not free Hemings during his lifetime or in his will, although he would have been conscious of his legacy and careful not to leave any documentary evidence of the relationship. After he died, his surviving white daughter, Martha, allowed Hemings to leave Monticello to live with one of Jefferson and Hemings's two sons whom Jefferson did free in his will. Jefferson appears to have engineered the freedom of his other Hemings offspring during his life, recording them as having walked off the Monticello plantation, and making no effort to retrieve them. More intriguing evidence of the relationship came from contemporaneous reports that several of Hemings's children resembled Jefferson and the fact that the Hemingses were the only nuclear family at Monticello that ultimately gained emancipation. And the Hemings family's oral tradition, told by Hemings's son Madison, was that Sally had been Jefferson's concubine.[45]

Master-slave liaisons should not be romanticized, because the power relations involved make it impossible to know how much agency the women had. Slavery was illegal on French soil, and while Hemings was in France, she had the right to petition for her freedom. Like Pocahontas, she may have accepted a relationship with a powerful white man because it afforded distinct advantages in a society ruled by such men. In this sense, she, too, was culturally dexterous. Gordon-Reed suggests that Hemings may have used French norms to her advantage in negotiating an understanding with her American master. Born between worlds, Hemings added another world to her competence while in Paris. Ensuring freedom for her children, or a degree of insulation for them and herself from the oppressions of other white people, may have been enough to accept a lifelong role in Jefferson's bed.[46]

It is fair to presume that most master-slave sex was involuntary. In a slave society, no one had authority to constrain a master, not even his wife and certainly not a slave child or woman who did not want to be taken. As slave owners themselves, lawmakers did not impose any penalty on a master who raped a slave, and after the regime of black chattel slavery was established, only masters who had sex with slaves were immune from special penalties for interracial fornication.[47]

Scholars of such relationships depict both violence and complexity. In his book *Interracial Intimacies*, Randall Kennedy describes a forty-year-old master who fancied one of his slaves, a thirteen-year-old girl, and decided to conscript her to sex. This violation produced Amanda America Dickson—a middle name for a daughter and country birthed and nurtured by sometimes-brutal actors. Dickson was fortunate in that her rich white father decided to favor her with support and an education.[48] Other masters were similarly complicated. Kennedy notes that scores of court reports from slave states involve cases in which a white master seeks to confer property, support, and sometimes freedom on his slave paramour and the children they produced. Louisiana contributed the most of such cases, even though its laws prohibited a man from bequeathing more than one-tenth of his assets to a mistress.[49]

This small class of slaveholders who provided for their mixed-race children is not an uncommon story in the oral history of African American families. During Reconstruction, many of the men of color who served in Southern legislatures were sons of slave owners who had provided them with an education.[50] In Virginia, for example, Ralph Quarles, a Revolutionary War hero and wealthy planter, acquired a mulatto slave named Lucy Langston in settlement of a debt, and the two began a relationship that produced four children. Quarles freed Langston and their children and took great care to provide for them. He insisted in his will that he and Langston be buried side by side, last wishes that were honored. The youngest child of this couple was John Mercer Langston, Oberlin graduate, abolitionist, founding dean of Howard Law School, US ambassador to Haiti, and the first man of color elected to Congress from Virginia.[51]

Jefferson may have ensured that his children with Hemings acquired skills to make a living when they were emancipated. He also may have contemplated that they would achieve a citizenship of sorts by escaping into whiteness, although he did not arrange for them to be educated.[52] He was perhaps the first example in a new country of a politician boxed in by racial dogma that his own class created. Throughout his adult life, Jefferson wrote publicly and privately of concerns about, and strategies to avoid, "amalgamation," the term used before *miscegenation* was coined. There was a "Strom-Thurmond-ness," an artificiality, to this cry to maintain racial purity for race and country. Jefferson and all of Southern society objected to what was happening right under their noses or pelvises. As history would prove, no amount of orchestration from on high would stop human urges from muddying lines.

Dog-whistling about race mixing began early. In two screeds published in the heat of 1764–1765 election campaigns for the Pennsylvania Assembly, Benjamin Franklin was accused of keeping Negro paramours. These charges are uncorroborated, probably false allegations.[53] The screeds' authors clearly hoped to tap public sentiment against such mixing. Franklin owned slaves for forty years, bought and sold humans, and allowed others to advertise the sale of slaves in his newspaper, the *Pennsylvania Gazette*. He was also guilty of participating in public discourse about white Anglo-Saxon supremacy and his concern not to diminish the white race and its New World colonies through admixture. Although esteemed for his wide-ranging intellectual and scientific pursuits, Franklin wrote in *Observations Concerning the Increase of Mankind*, published in 1755, of his desire that America be reserved for white Anglo-Saxons and perhaps the "lovely . . . Red." However, Franklin was an equal-opportunity Anglophile, lumping "swarthy" Germans in with Africans among the non-Saxon people he wished to exclude. He even expressed strong misgivings about the harshness of slavery and the fact that it invited whites to become idle and dependent on the work of others.[54] And Franklin evolved. Late in life, he became a leading abolitionist who worked for the integration of free blacks into American society through education and uplift. His slow evolution began when he developed a "higher opinion of the natural capacities of the black race" after observing that African American children in a school were equal in mind to white children.[55]

Like Franklin, Jefferson published thoughts in support of white supremacy and against race mixing. His mistake, perhaps, was that he left a longer paper trail on these issues and actually did take a Negro paramour (if one believes in the one-drop rule).

Writing in 1781 1782 in *Notes on the State of Virginia*, Jefferson answered a series of queries raised by a French official who was then residing in the commonwealth. At the outset, Jefferson approached these queries with a dispassionate empiricism, cataloging Virginia's abundance—its mountains, rivers, quadrupeds, and more. He first mentioned slaves and the other people populating the state in Query VIII, as he analyzed census trends. He observed that Virginia's population of "thythes"—free males and male and female slaves above sixteen years of age—had doubled every 27½ years between 1654 and 1772.[56] He saw progress in this uniform growth and then began to expound his theories on the role of homogeneity in ensuring the republican society he envisioned, one that guaranteed the happiness of all citizens and a peaceable, durable government. Jefferson predicted that too many immigrants from too disparate lands would render America a "heterogeneous, incoherent, distracted mass."[57]

He was prescient in foreseeing an American dilemma, one that would result from "our having such quantities of land to waste as we please," he wrote. In Europe, he surmised, the problem was an excess of labor and limited land, while in America, "here it is to make the most of our labour, land being abundant."[58] Here was the crux of America's exceptional ambiguities and those of Jefferson. He chose to build Monticello atop a mountain, a most inconvenient place, and his plantation sprawled for more than five thousand acres.

The landed American gentry having capitalized on enslaved black bodies to work their vast plantations for free, Jefferson also saw a dilemma in Virginia's census numbers. He noted that in 1782, there were nearly 300,000 free inhabitants and 271,000 slaves. With a ratio of free to slave of "nearly . . . 11 to 10," he worried about the risks slavery presented for whites: "Under the mild treatment our slaves experience, and their wholesome, though coarse, food, this blot in our country increases as fast, or faster, than the whites." In this language, the slaves, not slavery, were the blot on the land. Still, he blamed the British monarchy for having introduced and expanded "this great political and moral evil."[59] Franklin, too, blamed the British for bringing slaves to America for sale: "I do not justify our falling into temptation," he wrote, however, of both his and others' decision to purchase human beings.[60]

Jefferson, the champion of Enlightenment ideals, had to reconcile himself as a slave owner, at least in his own head and heart. Without explicitly saying so, he solved the American embarrassment of appetite for free labor and conflict with professed ideals by articulating an even more shameful justification: black inferiority and white supremacy. A man so smitten with the moral wisdom of Jesus Christ that he spent a decade cutting and pasting the prophet's teachings into his own preferred passages of the four New Testament gospels viewed morality as a matter of reason.[61] And yet, when it came to the question of whether and how Virginia's post-Revolution republican government should revise its legal code to provide for the emancipation of slaves and their incorporation into the polity, the tenor of Jefferson's *Notes on Virginia* turned from clinical reportage to emotional and irrational argument.

In Query XIV on Virginia's laws, he argued that it was not possible to "incorporate the blacks into the state." Racism was now so entrenched in the country that Jefferson seemed to fear that some kind of race war would erupt if black slaves were emancipated and allowed to stay on American soil. "Deep rooted prejudices entertained by the whites; ten thousand recollections, by the blacks, of the injuries they have sustained; [and] the real distinctions which nature has made . . . will divide us into parties, and produce convulsions which will probably never end but in the extermination of the one or the other race."[62]

Then he turned to what he termed "physical and moral" objections to including blacks in Virginian (and hence American) society: "The first difference which strikes us is that of colour." By "us," he must have meant himself and other whites. Black bodies and kinky hair were not beautiful to Jefferson. He wrote:

> Whether the black of the negro resides in the reticular membrane between the skin and scarf-skin, or in the scarf-skin itself; whether it proceeds from the colour of the blood, the colour of the bile, or from that of some other secretion, the difference is fixed in nature, and is as real as if its seat and cause were better known to us. And is this

difference of no importance? Is it not the foundation of a greater or less share of beauty in the two races? Are not the fine mixtures of red and white, the expressions of every passion by greater or less suffusions of colour in the one, preferable to that eternal monotony, which reigns in the countenances, that immoveable veil of black which covers all the emotions of the other race? Add to these, flowing hair, a more elegant symmetry of form, their own judgment in favour of the whites, declared by their preference of them, as uniformly as is the preference of the Oranootan for the black women over those of his own species. The circumstance of superior beauty, is thought worthy attention in the propagation of our horses, dogs, and other domestic animals; why not in that of man?[63]

Jefferson debated the question of the Negro's worthiness for citizenship for seven pages, apparently trying to convince himself and others of the inferiority of black minds and bodies. Perhaps it is unfair to focus on these pages, although they incited controversy even in the era when they were published.[64] Jefferson suffers in the present from being too Jeffersonian in his approach to the subject, engaging in pseudoscientific "reasoning" and bothering to write down detailed musings on color difference.

Notes was first published in France in 1785. Jefferson shared the manuscript with his close friend the Marquis de Chastellux before it was made available to the American public. On reviewing the book, Chastellux challenged Jefferson on the American's speculations on black inferiority. But Jefferson allowed *Notes* to be published largely as he wrote it, acknowledging in a brief prologue that all of the subjects he touches on are "treated imperfectly," then writing elliptically that "to apologize for this . . . would be to open wounds which have already bled enough."[65]

In publishing *Notes* with all its warts, Jefferson left a time capsule that is embarrassing for his present-day admirers. Whatever the current meaning of Jefferson's proffered "evidence" of black inferiority, the pages in *Notes* make transparent the process that the entire country went through in the eighteenth century in establishing white supremacy. When othering a certain group serves a useful purpose, the othering begins.

Jefferson's musings on race in *Notes* also illustrate how even well-educated people can delude themselves into living with, or accepting, unjust arrangements that benefit themselves and harm others. Jefferson did argue against slavery both in *Notes* and during his life. He drafted the Virginia law that banned importation of new slaves to that state in 1778, and as president, he signed the bill that abolished the trans-Atlantic slave trade to America. But on the question of emancipation for slaves already on US soil, Jefferson was more pro-abolition in words than deeds. He lived to be an octogenarian, and when he died, his estate had to sell his slaves to pay his many debts. He and the other gentry so dependent on black bodies were unwilling to reduce their greed, pay a wage for labor, or live a smaller, less grand life. Just as twenty-first-century masters of the universe exploit workers, lobby for tax loopholes, and devise or reap profits from predatory business practices, Jefferson and his peers found it very hard to give up the unearned advantages of systems of exploitation.

And so, in *Notes*, Jefferson rehearsed his thoughts on black inferiority, rationalizing his belief that black people could not be citizens, and, despite his protestations to the contrary, consequently rationalized slavery itself. Among the differences Jefferson alleged between black bodies and white ones were disagreeable body odor (with no account of the differential opportunities slaves had for hygiene), blacks seeming to have less need of sleep, black grief being "transient," black males being more lustful than tender and refined in their relations with women, and other nonsense.

Jefferson did not perceive such differences between white and red bodies. He even marveled at the intelligence and artistry of indigenous people and wrote in a private letter of their "genius" and equality to whites "in body and mind," although he was less charitable in his assessment of Native polities in Virginia.[66] As one historian has pointed out, Jefferson did not depend heavily on indigenous labor, so he did not need to cast their bodies as inferior. Instead, he and all the other presidents in the first decades of the republic proposed a policy of "civilizing" Native Americans and mixing with them to take their land.[67] Instead of avoiding amalgamation between natives and whites, Jefferson championed it. He once proposed to a delegation,

"You will mix with us by marriage." Of course, this policy, far more benevolent than the genocide that would come, was an assimilation not desired by indigenous people, who wanted to be left alone as sovereigns of their own nations. A different objective toward indigenous peoples and their lands meant that most of the states that prohibited marriages between whites and blacks did not constrain whites from marrying Native Americans.[68] Some supporters of the amalgamation of natives and even blacks with whites hoped that through whitening nonwhite people would lose their distinctiveness and create national cohesion; this offensive argument and unwillingness to accept difference would reappear in later centuries.[69]

Jefferson also claimed that blacks were incapable of reason. Even when confronted with Phillis Wheatley, a refined and educated black poet, he denigrated her achievements. Wheatley was a household name in the country. Abolitionists on both sides of the Atlantic repeatedly offered her as an example of black accomplishment.[70] He wrote this of her and all other black people: "Among the blacks is misery enough, God knows, but no poetry. Love is the peculiar oestrum of the poet. Their love is ardent, but it kindles the senses only, not the imagination. Religion indeed has produced a Phyllis Whately [*sic*]; but it could not produce a poet. The compositions published under her name are below the dignity of criticism."[71]

Wheatley addressed scoffers like Jefferson in one of her poems:

Some view our sable race with scornful eye,
"Their colour is a diabolic die."
Remember, Christians, Negro's, black as Cain,
May be refin'd, and join th' angelic train.[72]

Famously, African American naturalist and mathematician Benjamin Banneker wrote Jefferson, sending him a copy of his almanac and chastising Jefferson's failure to extend his Enlightenment egalitarianism to Negroes. French priest and arch abolitionist Henri Gregoire also wrote to Jefferson, sending him a volume on the literature of Negroes and pressing the cause of abolition. These missives, in 1791 and 1808, respectively, were opportunities for Jefferson to recant his views in *Notes*. Yet his replies to both men were mainly polite statements of someday hope for a better future in which Negroes might join the human family on an equal footing.[73]

For Jefferson, whites were "stained" by any mixture with blacks, while blacks were elevated by such mixture. Any future emancipation of slaves that he could contemplate had to be accompanied by the deportation of the freed to some other country or continent populated by dark people, whether in the West Indies or Africa.[74] Jefferson was not unique in his views on supremacy and against amalgamation of blacks and whites. He simply attracts more attention in the present, perhaps, because of the distance between his words in the Declaration of Independence and in *Notes*, and his other, titillating incongruities. He was one of the first politicians to advocate for the colonization of blacks. But with the formation of the American Colonization Society in 1816, this idea became a mainstream movement that attracted evangelical and Quaker abolitionists, slaveholders, and leaders of all political leanings, including the great emancipator, Abraham Lincoln. The colonization movement, however, ultimately led to the migration of a mere trickle of some twenty thousand blacks from America to Africa and the West Indies. Multitudes more Africans in America had the temerity to believe that they deserved to be part of the republic.

Free black people, in particular, were damned inconvenient in a slave society. Their numbers rose dramatically in Virginia in the two decades after the Revolutionary War. In 1782, the Virginia Assembly relaxed restrictions on manumission, and several patriots emancipated their slaves.[75] More slaves were freed in the Upper South, particularly in Virginia, than in any other region. The percentage of free blacks in Virginia rose from 1 to 10 percent of the black population in these decades—about thirty thousand Negroes not under the yoke of a master.[76] This increase in free blacks must have alarmed the lawgivers. By 1806, the Virginia Assembly required freed blacks to leave the state within a year or risk being re-enslaved.[77] One of the most consistent arguments put forth for removal or colonization of free blacks was the supposed licentiousness of black people and the risk of "staining" whites through interracial sex. As the cry of amalgamation and the fear of black sexuality reverberated, the call for colonization gained popular support especially in the North and in the Upper South, the two regions with the largest populations of free blacks.[78]

A second potent fear animating the push for black coloniza tion was the risk of slave rebellion. Free blacks were viewed as a source of agitation and inspiration to their bonded brethren. The idea of the republic, engraved in the Declaration of Independence, gave hope and aspiration to those excluded from it. One of the excluded parties was a literate slave named Gabriel, who was owned by a man named Prosser and therefore referred to incorrectly as Gabriel Prosser. Gabriel was not unlike certain Hemings men of Monticello. They were hired out to others who paid for their skills and could wander beyond the plantation and wonder at their future prospects.[79]

Gabriel may have acquired radical ideas while working as a blacksmith in Richmond foundries among blacks, whites, and mixed-race people. Free people of color had arrived in Richmond as refugees of the Haitian Revolution. In this environment, Gabriel would have learned that Toussaint Louverture had led a slave revolt in Saint-Domingue that ended slavery in Haiti and was on its way to successfully overthrowing the French.[80] It was an era of revolution and choosing. Haitian slaves had been inspired by the radical egalitarian ideas animating the French Revolution and had thrown off their oppressors. France had responded to the pressures of revolt and war by adopting constitutions emancipating slaves in French colonies and rendering free black males citizens, although when Napoléon later reinstated slavery, the struggle for black freedom against French colonialism would continue. Gabriel and the more than one thousand slaves he organized were undoubtedly inspired by these revolts as well as the American Revolution.

Gabriel's rebellion was thwarted before it started, in 1800. He refused to testify at trials after the plot had been exposed by two slave informants. Other rebels did testify and seemed to have been prepared to spare certain whites who were deemed friendly to their cause of liberty, or perhaps innocents in the system of slavery: Quakers, Methodists, French radicals, and "all poor white women who have no slaves." In his fictional account of Gabriel's thwarted revolt, Arna Bontemps depicted a hoped-for mass consciousness by which "the poor, the despised of the earth" of all colors would exert a collective will of the people to be free.[81]

One historian has suggested that the slaves of Gabriel's planned rebellion had white coconspirators, including French radicals, and that then-Governor James Monroe suppressed this evidence to protect Jefferson's chances in the 1800 presidential election. Jefferson himself was influenced by the Haitian Revolution and Gabriel's rebellion in arguing for his plan of black colonization in a letter to Monroe.[82] But because most blacks would not and could not be moved to other shores, mechanisms of social control, including regulation of black-white intimacy, continued.

In the post-Revolutionary era, states in the Upper South generally followed Virginia's lead in refining the color line. In 1785, the Virginia Assembly defined *Negro* as any person with a black parent or grandparent. Anyone with less than one-quarter black ancestry could be white as a matter of law, whereas the line had been drawn earlier at one-eighth white. Anyone who qualified as white could marry a white person. Therefore, the line around whiteness allowed for a sizable portion of blackness and meant that the state officially sanctioned some race mixing, if only among whites and milky mulattoes. This line shaped not just race but also what we have come to call race relations. Those who could do so had great incentive to claim the privileges of whiteness, as whites clearly could be citizens, and hence to distance themselves from those who could not.[83]

Because color lines were drawn at the state level, and states and regions differed by degrees in how tightly, or not, they regulated sexual and other relations, complexity emerged in antimiscegenation law. Like Virginia, most of the original thirteen states regulated interracial intimacy. But New York, New Jersey, New Hampshire, and Connecticut did not.[84]

While regulation of interracial sex was one aspect of the color line, regulation of who could be a citizen was another. Here the laws were even more ambiguous and fragmented. At the founding, the line between white and black, or between citizen and noncitizen, was not airtight. The Founders accommodated slavery as a compromise to ensure a union of Northern and Southern states. The Constitution forbade sympathetic states from protecting fugitive slaves. It rendered slaves three-fifths of a person for purposes of representation in Congress and constrained Congress for a period from abolishing the slave trade.[85] The prerogatives of Southern states won out over those of black lives, and fights about national power interfering with "states' rights," often a dog-whistle, have been imbued with questions of race ever since.

But the Constitution began with "We the People," introducing an ambiguity and a marker for a more capacious republic that might be created by brave future generations. While the Constitution was ambiguous, state laws were more restrictive. Until the Constitution was amended after the Civil War, the main accoutrements of citizenship and who could claim them were defined by individual states. At the time of the founding, free black men, in theory, could vote in a number of the original thirteen states because access to suffrage tended to be based on property ownership, sex, and age, not race. States would begin to introduce racial restrictions only after large numbers of black people began to vote.[86]

In Virginia, Thomas Jefferson authored "A Bill Declaring Who Shall Be Deemed Citizens of this Commonwealth," the first line of which accorded this status to "white persons" who had been born in the state and had resided there for at least two years. Thus, even white indentured servants could be citizens if they met this residency requirement. White migrants from other places could petition the courts to become citizens, and the children of any citizen would also become citizens. After this bill was enacted in 1779, "citizen" in Virginia largely equated with "white."[87]

Pennsylvania chose a different course. In 1780, in the city of brotherly love, the state's legislators enacted a law for the painfully gradual abolition of slavery. As part of this legal reform, they also repealed the state's ban on interracial marriage, the first state in the country to do so.[88] They were motivated by a desire to align their laws and Enlightenment ideals, not to promote interracial intimacy.[89] Still, the repeal was a beginning on the inclusive republic that Benjamin Franklin ultimately decided to agitate for. Other Northern states, including Vermont, Massachusetts, Rhode Island, Connecticut, New York, Ohio, and New Jersey, would sanction immediate or gradual abolition between 1777 and 1804.[90] In 1780, the people of Massachusetts adopted a state constitution declaring that "all men are born free and equal," and a state court enforced this capacious language in 1783, launching an experiment in instant freedom for former slaves. With many free black people in its midst, Massachusetts was less brave than Pennsylvania about the freedom to love. It held on to its antimiscegenation law for six more decades, before becoming the second state to repeal it. Some states, like New York, New Jersey, and Connecticut, would emancipate slaves without ever having restricted interracial intimacy and never choosing to do so.

In 1790, the first Congress of the United States passed a law limiting the right to naturalize to US citizenship to "free white persons." A *Bautista* Angolan like Tony Longo, for example, could not have naturalized, even after purchasing his freedom. Technically, however, federal citizenship was not limited to whites, and some free black sailors received certificates from the US government affirming their citizenship.[91] That said, for the next century and a half, only white people among the huddled masses of immigrants arriving in the United States could naturalize. Here again, law reinforced whiteness as the standard of "American." And this idea endures in current battles about immigration and who belongs. American courts struggled with the question of who could claim whiteness for the purpose of citizenship and sometimes participated in and propagated the ideology of white supremacy in the process. The ultimate determination in these citizenship cases often turned on ocular considerations like whether an aspirant was paler than a walnut or on racism against populations, like the Chinese and Japanese, that resentful whites wished to exclude.[92]

While the first Congress was busy erecting a color line for naturalization, an aged Benjamin Franklin undertook his final public act. In February 1790, he sent a petition to Congress on behalf of the pro-abolition society he led, requesting the gradual abolition of slavery and an end to the slave trade. The petition argued that "mankind are all formed of the same Almighty being" and that Congress had the power under the Constitution to promote the general welfare and secure blessings of liberty for all of the people. It also noted that only one group in "this land of Freedom, are degraded into perpetual Bondage" and entreated Congress to remove "this Inconsistency from the Character of the American People" and "promote mercy and Justice towards this distressed Race."

The Senate refused to take up the petition. The House did take it up, and a heated debate ensued. Members from the Deep South were incensed. James Jackson of Georgia launched a two-hour, proslavery tirade that invoked the Bible, the necessity of slavery to the Southern economy, and even the anti-amalgamation passages of Jefferson's *Notes*. He stoked fears about the risks of a large population of freed slaves and argued that the races could not live together as equals. Franklin died, but not before publishing a parody of Jackson's tirade under the pseudonym Historicus. Ultimately, the House members hid behind the new Constitution, claiming that they were powerless to do anything to restrict slavery before 1808.[93]

Jefferson died in 1826. His last words on slavery and emancipation, written in his penultimate letter, were optimistic about the work of future generations on questions of race and supremacy: "The revolution in public opinion which this cause requires, is not to be expected in a day, or perhaps in an age; but time, which outlives all things, will outlive this evil also."[94] The slow march toward a more perfect Union would continue. Jefferson and other framers of the Constitution left to the future the battle over slavery. By the 1830s, though, white race pride was emerging in public discourse to undergird not only slavery but also westward expansion, and protecting this fictional white purity became a national obsession.

CHAPTER FOUR

Miscegenation, Dog-Whistling, and the Spread of Supremacy

Nat Turner, like the rebel slave Gabriel before him, envisioned something better for Negroes than slavery. He, too, could read and write and plan. He had a relationship with the Lord and said that the revolt he orchestrated was divinely inspired. For forty hours in August 1831, he and other black allies emancipated themselves and killed fifty-five white men, women, and children in Southampton County, Virginia. Turner and his coconspirators were captured, tried, and hanged, but not before Turner gave a composed, detailed confession of their blood-soaked deeds. "Until we had armed and equipped ourselves, and gathered sufficient force, neither age nor sex was to be spared. . . . [']T]was my object to carry terror and devastation wherever we went," Turner said. His inquisitor saw him as a fiend but a smart one: "He possesses an uncommon share of intelligence, with a mind capable of attaining anything [and] the true negro face, every feature of which is strongly marked."[1]

Turner's rebellion struck terror in the hearts of whites. The Virginia Assembly debated how to respond and doubled down on the architecture of supremacy, as did other slave states. Black people, whether slave or free, were prohibited from assembling, owning a gun, or learning to read or write. They could not testify against whites in court and were denied other freedoms accorded citizens.[2] None of the revolutionaries were accused of rape, although they killed several white women. Despite Turner's intelligence, the lawgivers continued to be preoccupied not just with the risks of slave uprisings but also with alleged defects that black slaves might spread to others. A delegate in the Virginia Assembly conjectured that slave "vices must have . . . an injurious influence upon the morals of the free" and suggested that "where so large a mass of the population of the country is corrupt," it would be impossible for "other classes [to] escape the contagion."[3]

This preoccupation with the supposed licentiousness of black people was tied indelibly to debates about slavery. Both the slaver and the abolitionist were threatened by the prospect of amalgamation of blacks and whites, and when an abolitionist excoriated slavery, opponents countered with the risks of free blacks marrying or ravishing a white daughter or son.

This obsession produced a nineteenth-century literature, including cartoons and satire, that dwelled on such fears. For example, Darius Lyman, a translator of aphorisms by ancient Roman author and emancipated slave Publius Syrus, wrote a book titled *Leaven for Doughfaces: Threescore and Ten Parables Touching Slavery*. The year was 1856, and "doughface" was a pejorative term for a Northerner sympathetic to the Southern position on slavery. One of Lyman's parables, "The Besotted Alien," summarizes well the existential threat that nineteenth-century whites perceived. The besotted alien contended that "these blacks have a terrible hankering for amalgamation . . . and we stand in mortal fear that the time is not far distant, when we shall all lose our pure white color, and not know to which race we belong."[4] An author of a serious treatise on slavery wrote of his fears that whites would be debased by mixture with blacks and contended that persons born of all shades and colors would unite against whites and threaten the political and social order of the nation.[5]

In 1839, Edward Williams Clay designed a series of lithograph prints that ran prominently in newspapers and anti-abolitionist literature in the antebellum era, often under the title "Practical Amalgamation."

Clay stoked anxiety with scenes of grotesquely drawn, thick-lipped blacks socializing with and marrying finely rendered whites. In one print, he depicted William Lloyd Garrison, arch abolitionist and founder of the American Anti-Slavery Society, attending a wedding of a lithe white gentlewoman to a black minstrel, while Garrison ushers a rotund black female as his guest.[6] In parallel with this propaganda against race mixing was prodigious literary treatment of the so-called tragic mulatto, beginning with Cora in *The Last of the Mohicans* and continuing with novels, plays, and films well into the twentieth century. Americans were indoctrinated against race mixing but seemed utterly fascinated by the people condemned for being too white or not white enough.[7]

Widely held fears propelled antimiscegenation laws from slave states to new states like Indiana, Illinois, Michigan, and Maine—states that had never allowed slavery. By the onset of the Civil War, twenty-four of thirty-four states had laws barring interracial marriage between whites and Negroes or mulattoes. The prohibition included western jurisdictions like the State of California and Washington Territory, areas with few black people.[8] Free states were relatively better than slaveholding ones in their restrictions on the liberties of blacks, but most free-soil whites did not want Negroes around. Illinois banned entry of both slaves and free Negroes into the state, as did Indiana and Oregon.[9] Settlers in the West were opposed to amalgamation or integration of any kind. Ohio, Illinois, Indiana, Kansas, Nebraska, Wisconsin, and Oregon boasted many members of the American Colonization Society who aspired to pure whiteness for their bloodlines and their territories.[10]

White supremacy was no longer solely about subordinating blacks to enable slavery-based capitalism. Westward expansion and Manifest Destiny were intertwined with the idea that the continent belonged to the Anglo-Saxons, the breed of people exalted above others in the minds of those who could claim such heritage. "Out of all the inhabitants of the world," influential theologian Horace Bushnell said in 1837, ". . . a select stock, the Saxon, and out of this the British family, the noblest of the stock, was chosen to people our country." In the Jacksonian era, many Americans would adopt this view.[11] When poor Irish Catholics began to pour into the country in the 1830s, they were not white yet. Nor were the Italians. Both were cast low on the hierarchy of humans that Anglo-Saxons denigrated.[12]

In the nineteenth century, the ideology of supremacy was useful not only in propagating slavery but also in justifying conquest of lands occupied by indigenous nations and Mexicans and, later, for excluding Asian immigrants. Expansionists cast the Mexican-American War as a glorious conquering of a people who were deemed inferior largely because they were mixed-race. The Spanish colonizers, through intermarriage with and rape of native women, had created a mélange that some found deeply offensive. Senator John C. Calhoun, who espoused a republicanism that included states' rights and structural protections for slavery, spoke against the war and annexing Mexico out of fear that it would taint the Union. "Are we to associate with ourselves as equals, companions and fellow citizens, the Indians and mixed race of Mexico?" Calhoun asked his colleagues on the Senate floor. "Sir, I should consider such a thing fatal to our institutions."[13]

Hunger for the vast lands of northern Mexico, which ultimately became states from Texas to California, won out over antipathy to brown-red people. Annexation created challenges for supremacists. Suddenly, former Mexicans had to be incorporated into the Union— people who had lived in a mixed-race society, without race-based limitations on citizenship. The Treaty of Guadalupe-Hildalgo of 1849 concluded the war and formally extended to Mexicans living within the newly ceded territory the option of either relocating to Mexico's new boundaries or accepting full US citizenship. Most of them were nonwhite and, through the treaty, became Americans.

Marriage between whites and Mexican Americans became common in the West. Such marriages enabled white males to gain access to massive estates that had been held by wealthy Mexican families. Perhaps for this reason, and because of the citizenship terms of the treaty, no US antimiscegenation laws ever barred whites from marrying Chicanos or any other Hispanic group.[14] Similarly, only a small minority of states banned marriages between whites and indigenous people, as a ban would have interfered with white men's ability to marry native women and thereby claim any attendant land.[15] Yet again, miscegenation laws and the racial hierarchy they supported were designed to enable asset accumulation.

With agitation by abolitionists and other radicals, there was some change. Throughout the nineteenth century, there was a dance, then a war, between those who supported slavery and those who did not. There was a huge chasm between the few radical idealists who were open to making people of color equal citizens and the vast majority of whites who were not. Contestation, war, and Reconstruction, followed by a retaking of Southern governments by white supremacists, led some states to repeal and then readopt miscegenation laws. Other states, like Virginia, would keep refining prohibitions on interracial intimacy, uninterrupted. Meanwhile, in the late nineteenth century, Western legislators would develop a lengthy and continually amended list of people, in addition to blacks, that whites could not marry.

Alexis de Tocqueville traveled America in the 1830s and wrote his dispassionate analysis of Jacksonian democracy, in which suffrage became universal among all white men, regardless of property ownership. In *Democracy in America*, he surmised that slavery was "the most formidable evil threatening the future of the United States" and predicted that America would fail to address it successfully and that this would bring the country to disaster. De Tocqueville also wrote that assimilation or integration of Negroes was improbable and undesirable. As he was writing his book, master-slave sex and some voluntary interracial coupling continued, as did dog-whistling about amalgamation.[16]

One of the most prominent nineteenth-century national conversations about race mixing involved Richard Mentor Johnson, the ninth vice president of the United States, who served with Martin Van Buren. Commentary on Johnson's procreating with slaves attests to how common this practice was and to the widely shared, though unstable enterprise of trying to maintain a pure-white nation. But randy patriarchs often refused to abide by their own orthodoxy.

Johnson was a Kentuckian who gained fame as the person who reportedly slayed the Shawnee chieftain Tecumseh in the Battle of the Thames. He rode this national notoriety from the US House to the Senate and then the vice presidency. Johnson also became notorious for fathering two daughters with Julia Chinn, an octoroon slave whom he had inherited. Johnson's father was one of the largest landholders in Kentucky. This patriarch conferred on his sons many slaves and acres as well as a legacy of serving in high office and garnering perhaps more than the family's fair share of government contracts. As a scion of a wealthy, powerful family, Richard Johnson may have felt insulated from the opinions of others when he fell in love with Chinn.[17] Kentucky law may have barred him from marrying Chinn because she did not qualify as white. This proscription did not deter him; he lived with her openly as his common-law wife.

The relationship endured, and Johnson became a political star, though a controversial one. He spent three decades serving in the House and Senate, spanning five presidencies from Jefferson to Jackson. He was devoted to the principles of "Thomas Jefferson, the patriarch of republicanism," as he called him, but as Andrew Jackson ascended to the helm of what would become the Democratic Party, Johnson became a steadfast Jacksonian. By working to abolish the practice of imprisoning debtors and opening his estate in Great Crossings, Kentucky, to constituents of any station and helping them with their problems, Johnson garnered great popularity in his state. He identified deeply with the nonrich farmers of his rural, agrarian district and railed against monopolist creditors.[18]

As his star rose, Johnson was criticized for his relationship with Chinn. He defended his honor and that of Chinn: "Unlike Jefferson, Clay, Poindexter and others I married my wife under the eyes of God, and apparently He found no objections." In pointing his finger at other political leaders suspected of having similar long-term relationships with their slaves, he was identifying the fault line that would contribute to his political problems. Southerners were well aware that masters might take a slave woman as a mistress, and they were used to pretending not to notice the pale-colored babes showing up in the master's yard. But it was virtually unheard-of for a public figure to attempt to make such a relationship official, much less to thrust his mulatto children on polite white society.[19]

Johnson doted on his daughters, Imogene and Adaline, gave them his surname, and educated them. He managed to marry them off to respectable white men, initially quietly, after giving his daughters large dowries, including land. Kentucky's antimiscegenation law may not have been a barrier to his daughters' marriage to white men, because, although they were one-sixteenth black, the law did not define the term *Negro* or *mulatto*.[20]

Social distinctions did stymie the family. When Johnson took Adaline to a Fourth of July barbeque at the home of neighboring whites in 1831, the action sparked controversy. He had been invited to give an Independence Day oration, but his hosts insisted that his lightly colored daughter leave the premises while they celebrated national freedom. The barbeque incident with Adaline and the surfacing of Imogene's recent interracial marriage made the newspapers from Kentucky to Boston. William Lloyd Garrison was kinder than others when he commented on the family in his newspaper, the *Liberator*: "Col. Johnson deserves full condemnation, not for being the father of colored children . . . but for his avowed and shameless libertinism." Garrison also agreed with another commentator that "at the present time mixed marriages would be in bad taste."[21]

When Adaline married the following year, Garrison did not miss an opportunity to attack Southern slavers. In the *Liberator*, he defended Adaline's new spouse as virtuous in taking her as a bride. He compared the marriage with Southern "planters who do not scruple to prostitute their female slaves, and beget as many bastards as possible."[22] Perhaps he was alluding to Johnson. At the time, the Tecumseh slayer, as he was referred to, was one of the most prominent politicians in the United States. His partner, Julia Chinn, was not a tragic mulatto. Johnson empowered her to manage his estate, Blue Spring Farm, while he was away representing Kentucky in Washington. He had created the Choctaw Academy on the farm's grounds—another profitable government contract for a Johnson son. This boarding school was devoted to educating and "civilizing" Choctaws. Johnson appointed a local minister to run it with Chinn's assistance. Problems arose when some Choctaw students were discovered to be having sex with, and otherwise fraternizing with, the slaves. When Chinn succumbed to a cholera epidemic in 1833, Johnson was grief-stricken and spread thin. It was impossible for him or his agent to maintain order and separation among the red, black, and mixed-race people at Blue Spring.

The Choctaw students who copulated with slaves were not following the new racial postulates of the Choctaw Nation (or of the

Cherokees and Creeks), which had cast aside their prior openness to adopting blacks and had taken on the whites' disdain for mixing with them.[23] After Chinn died, Johnson put another slave woman, Parthene, in charge of his household. He apparently also had a sexual relationship with her. When Parthene used her new position to stage an escape to Ohio with a Choctaw student and apparently another slave-Choctaw couple from the farm, Johnson took revenge. He sold Parthene at auction after she was captured and soon took up with another slave, reportedly Parthene's sister. The press ridiculed him for having been "cuckolded" by his slaves and outsmarted by natives. Johnson would father more children with slave women, although he related to these children quite differently than he did to Adaline and Imogene. By 1840, he was excoriated in the antislavery press for producing children with three slave women and selling one mother and the children to another slave owner.[24]

As Van Buren began his run for president in 1836, the entire nation continued to focus on the question of slavery. Southern Democrats supported Johnson as a candidate for vice president because he was a popular Southern slaveholder who assuaged their suspicions about the New Yorker, Van Buren. But Johnson's amalgamating lifestyle was a source of public commentary and discomfort to all sides of the slavery debate. Historian Nicholas Guyatt says of the contretemps: "Defenders of slavery feared a conspiracy in which Johnson would smuggle the radical practices of his private life into the nation's highest councils. . . . Immediate abolitionists [denied] that emancipation would lead to race mixing."[25]

Newspapers on all sides had something to say about him. "He is indeed the most powerful agent of amalgamation," the *Baltimore Chronicle* wrote, "who, by giving fortunes to half-breeds, tempts men greedy of money, but insensible to shame, to mingle the white and African race in a union which merges the fair complexion and the bright intellect of one, in the darkness of color and inferiority of mind which are characteristics of the other." The *Chronicle* argued that the "violent feuds" and instability of Latin American countries were a consequence of race mixing. With Johnson, the "practical amalgamator," on the ticket, "what, we ask, is to prevent . . . a similar result in the United States?"[26] Van Buren won the presidency despite the acrimony, but after he dropped Johnson as a running mate in 1840, Johnson receded from national prominence, except, perhaps, as the butt of jokes.

Abraham Lincoln made light of Johnson in debating Stephen Douglas for a US Senate seat for Illinois. It was one of several ways Lincoln attempted to establish his anti-amalgamation bona fides. "There is a natural disgust in the minds of nearly all white people, to the idea of an indiscriminate amalgamation of the white and black races," Lincoln said in 1857. "Judge Douglas evidently is basing his chief hope, upon the chances of being able to appropriate the benefit of this disgust to himself."[27]

Newspapers attested to this revulsion. "Mormonism is repulsive enough, but abolition-amalgamation makes the soul shudder with a sickening sense of indescribable disgust," the *Richmond Enquirer* wrote with poetic intolerance the same year. The editorial concluded: "The people of this country very well know that there is ten times as much amalgamation under slavery [than] in the free states" and that the "South presented us with a Vice-President who had given us a life-long example of . . . concubinage."[28]

Slavery, abolition, and amalgamation remained prominent issues partly because of the Supreme Court's decision in the *Dred Scott* case in 1857. Dred Scott was a slave who needed to be considered a citizen to bring his case in court. He wished to claim freedom for having lived with his owner for a period in free territory. Infamously, the court concluded that no black person, enslaved or free, could be a citizen. In doing so, Chief Justice Roger B. Taney relied on intentions and habits he imputed not only to the Founders but also to the people who ratified the Constitution.

Taney claimed that there had been a "fixed and universal" opinion "in the civilized portion of the white race" that black people were "altogether unfit to associate with the white race." He cited the many laws prohibiting intermarriage in the colonies as evidence that "a perpetual and impassive barrier was intended to be erected between the white race and the one they had reduced to slavery." Of course, these laws were necessary because some whites were mixing with the "unfortunate race," and, hence, white attitudes could not have been fixed and universal. Taney also ignored evidence of citizenship rights enjoyed by some free blacks at the time of the nation's founding. Taney and a majority of the court had an agenda, a hope of resolving the question of slavery permanently. The court could have declared Scott a noncitizen because he was a slave. It could have left free blacks out of the decision. But it chose to sweep broadly and also reached to essentially nullify the Missouri Compromise, by which Congress had insulated Northern free territories from slavery.

Thus, in 1858, as Lincoln and Douglas debated, the main issue between them was slavery and whether it would be expanded into new states. The two men put on an extraordinary reality show that rode into seven towns across Illinois. The debates, as transcribed by the press, captivated the nation. As slavery was the question at hand, so was amalgamation. Douglas relentlessly exploited the white public's antiblack feelings. He called members of the grand new party "Black Republicans" and painted Lincoln as an abolitionist who supported extending political and social equality to the Negro, including the right to amalgamate with whites. The fight for the soul of America was engaged.

Lincoln was not yet multicultural in his republicanism. He struggled to make sense of the divided house the Founders had created. In the fog of political warfare, which presaged civil warfare, the Declaration of Independence was one weapon Lincoln clung to. Mid-nineteenth-century Americans were not far removed from 1776 and its revolutionary values. Lincoln played to those values as well as to racism in the minds of voters. He was antislavery and procolonization—official planks of his party—and he clearly felt pressure to dispel the notion that he favored amalgamation or black citizenship. He believed that the Declaration of Independence, with its promise of life, liberty, and the pursuit of happiness, extended to Negroes, not as a social equals to whites but to free them and America of slavery. This was a nuanced position compared with Douglas's proslavery popular sovereignty that would allow white men in each new state to decide the slavery question for themselves.

One way Lincoln attempted to gain trust with white crowds was to use the N-word in debate and speeches. For example, at the first debate in Ottawa, Illinois, he said, "When my friend Judge Douglas, came to Chicago . . . he made an harangue there . . . [and] draws out, from my speech this tendency of mine to set the States at war with one another . . . and set the niggers and white people to marrying together [Laughter]."[29] Its cultural meaning clearly had become something different from the term "Negars," which John Smith used in his *Generall Historie* of Virginia to describe the *Bautista* Angolans that landed in 1619.[30] The astute Lincoln used the N-word himself in private, along with "darky," and must have understood its efficiency in signaling that he stood, firmly, on the white side of the color line.[31]

Lincoln was otherwise more eloquent in deflecting Douglas's charge that he favored amalgamation and black citizenship. Lincoln's language and the prominence of the amalgamation issue in the debates attest to how widespread public sentiment was against it and how far white working people had traveled from Virginia's early times, when they had once mixed easily with Africans. Lincoln accused Douglas of attempting to gain public favor by "pandering to the prejudices of the masses" and "pretend[ing] to be horrified by amalgamation," and yet Honest Abe also felt the need to pander.[32] Like generations of politicians before and after him, he had to contend with the monster of white supremacy and the voters' sense of entitlement to subordinate and separate from others.

To parry Douglas, Lincoln also used humor about who was really doing the amalgamating. Nearly fifteen thousand people showed up to watch the fourth debate in Charleston, Illinois. They crowded the fairgrounds just outside of town. Minutes before the debate began Democrats raised a banner depicting a white man, a black woman, and their biracial child under the slogan "Negro equality." Lincoln reasserted that the Declaration of Independence belonged to all people while also denying any intent to make blacks citizens. He explained his compromise position, poking fun at former Vice President Johnson along the way and playing to the crowd's view that it would be absurd for a white man to want a colored woman as a wife. To uproarious laughter, Lincoln declared that he "never had the least apprehension that I or my friends would marry negroes if there was no law to keep them from it." He then suggested that Judge Douglas might wish to return to the Illinois legislature to fight to keep the state's antimiscegenation law and stem any flood of intermarriage.[33]

In another speech, Lincoln drove home the point that slavery was the real source of amalgamation. He cited figures from the census of 1850 to the crowd. It was the first census to count "mulatto" separately from white and Negro, and this new data seemed to fascinate Lincoln. "There were over four hundred thousand mulattoes in the United States," he observed. Then he pointed out how this group was distributed. In "the Republican, slavery-hating State of New Hampshire," he remarked, the census takers found only 184 mulattoes. But in "the Old Dominion—in the Democratic and aristocratic State of Virginia," they found nearly 80,000, he exclaimed, "twenty-three thousand more than were in all the free States!" Throughout the slave states, there were 348,000 mulattoes, "all of home production," Lincoln concluded.[34]

While most of these Southern mulattoes were likely to have been the product of sex between masters and female slaves, this was not the only form of interracial sex in slave states. In her autobiography, *Incidents in the Life of a Slave Girl*, Harriet Jacobs describes how she took a white lover, consensually, as an escape from the persistent assaults of her master. "For years," she writes, "my master had done his utmost to pollute my mind with foul images, and to destroy the pure principles inculcated by my grandmother, and the good mistress of my childhood."[35] Initially Jacobs had fallen in love with a free black man but was beaten by her master when she told him she wanted to marry a free man. Jacobs seems to have avoided rape by her master by taking a lover who impregnated her. Samuel Sawyer, a lawyer who would become a congressman, was attracted to Jacobs and courted her. "There is something akin to freedom in having a lover who has no control over you, except that which he gains by kindness and attachment," Jacobs writes of him.[36] Sawyer bought the two children he fathered with Jacobs from her owner, although the law constrained him from manumitting them, so he deposited them with Jacobs's grandmother. Although Sawyer attempted to buy her, Jacobs's owner would not allow her to marry anyone who wasn't already one of his slaves.

Instead, Jacobs escaped and hid in a crawl space above her grandmother's ceiling for seven years, where she could glimpse but not touch her children. Eventually, she fled north. She also writes of

Southern white women who thrust themselves onto black men in their midst: "I have myself seen the master . . . bowed down in shame; for it was known in the neighborhood that his daughter had selected one of the meanest slaves on his plantation to be the father of his first grandchild."[37]

Plantation lust and rape, and some liaisons off the plantation between willing partners, produced the stark Southern concentration of mixed-race people that Lincoln spoke of. After 1850, the Deep South stopped treating mixed-race people as distinct from Negroes and adopted the rigid one-drop social distinction long established in the Upper South. With antislavery and secessionist sentiment spreading, clear lines were drawn. These in-between people would no longer be allowed to muddy the distinction between enslaved and free, between who was legally black and who was white. As the color line hardened, less mixing would occur in the Deep South outside of slavery.[38]

"The great debates" between Douglas and Lincoln catapulted Lincoln to national prominence and the presidency in 1860. But the issue of race mixing would continue to dog him. The term *miscegenation* was coined during his reelection campaign of 1864. Two reporters at the *New York World*, the leading Democratic newspaper in the North, attempted to drive a wedge between white working-class voters and Lincoln. They published a pamphlet, like *Federalist* papers of old, anonymously. The pamphlet aimed to make readers think a Republican wrote it and to associate its radical ideas with Lincoln.

Miscegenation: The Theory of the Blending of the Races, Applied to the American White Man and Negro, was seventy-two pages long and cost a quarter.[39] It began with an explanation of the new word the authors had created, combining the Latin word *miscere* (to mix) and *genus* (race). The pamphlet advocated the creation of a superior race through mixing. While many readers were suspicious of its origins and motives, others took the bait. In retrospect, its incendiary purposes should have been clear. The authors wrote: "The miscegenitic or mixed races are much superior, mentally, physically, and morally to those pure or unmixed," as the strength of the nation stemmed "not from its Anglo-Saxon progenitors, but from all the different nationalities. . . . All that is needed to make us the finest race on earth . . . is to engraft upon our stock the negro element."

The pamphlet concluded with suggestions that Lincoln should write miscegenation into the Republican platform and adopt race mixing as "the solution to the Negro problem."

The authors generated controversy and free press by sending advanced copies to unsuspecting liberal abolitionists like the Grimké sisters, soliciting approval, which the sisters gave with caveats, and then depositing all of this ammunition with a Democratic pol who was happy to expose it. Sarah and Angelina Grimké, among the most famous of white female abolitionists, had cause to be sympathetic. They had three mixed-race nephews, the offspring of their widowed brother's relationship with a mixed-race slave.[40] The sisters had grown up on their father's South Carolina plantation and had been radicalized by what they observed. They brought two of the nephews north to be educated. One, Francis Grimké, would graduate from Lincoln University and become the minister who married Frederick Douglass to his second wife, Helen Pitts. In 1864, the *Miscegenation* pamphlet helped keep the issue of race mixing before the voters for nearly a year and was not exposed as a hoax until after the election.

The new word *miscegenation* gained traction. Visual anti-Lincoln propaganda began to appear under the new word rather than *amalgamation*. The *New York World* published a political cartoon titled "The Miscegenation Ball," which featured white Republicans dancing or making out with a sable, nappy sweetheart. Another cartoon depicted abolitionist Senator Charles Sumner presenting his plump black arm candy to President Lincoln. Fortunately, Union voters were not swayed. Propagandists misjudged an electorate more concerned with bringing the Civil War to a successful conclusion than with interracial sex. Lincoln won reelection by a landslide, on a platform to introduce an amendment to abolish slavery. But the word *miscegenation* would endure.[41]

Lincoln himself evolved, although he never became a radical racial egalitarian. While he had had very little contact with free blacks before he became president, during the Civil War he met with many prominent black people in the White House, including Frederick Douglass, Sojourner Truth, Martin Delany, Haitian and Liberian diplomats, and a variety of black clergy or leaders pressing black causes. According to historian Eric Foner, these meetings with accomplished black people softened Lincoln's prejudices. He gradually changed his mind about colonization because he, like other Americans, valued the contributions of black soldiers in the Civil War and saw the need for black labor to rebuild the Southern economy after the war.[42]

The Lincolns were the first occupants of the White House to exhibit a measure of cultural dexterity. The president's wife, Mary Todd Lincoln, employed Elizabeth Keckley, an African American dressmaker who was her closest confidante and whom she once described as "my best living friend." In her autobiography, Keckley describes her transformation from slave, who herself endured sexual abuse from her master, to free business owner and intimate of the First Lady. As Mrs. Lincoln's dressmaker, Keckley regularly found herself in the family quarters of the White House not only to fit a dress but also to offer counsel. The dressmaker depicts a warm friendship with Mrs. Lincoln and the president's cordial treatment of her.[43] In an autobiography, Frederick Douglass describes Lincoln welcoming him heartily as the abolitionist entered the White House along with other members of the public on the occasion of the president's second inauguration.[44] These intimate interracial relationships, devoid of the hierarchy of slavery, were something new for an American president.

In his final public speech, President Lincoln hinted at the challenges of reconstructing a war-torn nation and seemed to imagine a society where the differing races would share some measure of equality if not the same schools, neighborhoods, or beds. The speech got him killed. John Wilkes Booth was standing in the audience on the White House lawn and was incensed by what he heard. After assassinating Lincoln three days later, Booth fled to Virginia. He was captured and shot at a farm owned by Confederate sympathizers in Caroline County, where Richard and Mildred Loving would grow up and find each other nearly a century later.

Some Republicans were more radical than others. Like Lincoln, most Republicans contemplated formal equality for the Negro, but not a social equality that included interracial intimacy.[45] Thaddeus Stevens and Frederick Douglass were more insurgent and egalitarian in their politics and their personal lives. Both men had intimate relations with women of another race.

Stevens grew up poor, limped through life with a clubfoot, and gave the planter class hell as a leader of the Radical Republicans in the House of Representatives. For a time, "The Old Commoner," as he was affectionately called, was the most powerful man in Congress. Rumor had it that he also shared his heart and bed with his widowed mixed-race housekeeper, who he insisted be addressed by her name and title, Mrs. Lydia Smith. Smith was the child of an Irish-Catholic father and a free African American mother. As a free, Northern person of color in Pennsylvania, she was used to doing what she wanted and clearly commanded respect as manager of the Stevens household. "Thaddeus Stevens has for years lived in open adultery with a mulatto woman," a Southern newspaper derided. "This mulatto manages his visitors at will, speaks of Mr. Stevens and herself as 'we' and in all other things comports herself as if she enjoyed the rights of a lawful wife."[46] There is much circumstantial evidence to support the rumor.[47] Whether lovers or friends, Smith and Stevens shared a vision of equality that they each helped promote. They used their home as a station on the Underground Railroad, hiding the self-emancipated in a covered cistern that led to a secret tunnel.[48]

Stevens was an irascible voice for the most radical vision of Reconstruction among Republicans. "Free every slave, slay every traitor, burn every rebel mansion if these things be necessary to preserve this temple of freedom," he said of the Union. He wanted to break the back of Southern aristocracy, to confiscate the plantations, and to distribute land to former slaves. He led the effort to adopt the Fourteenth Amendment, which would formally overrule *Dred Scott* and grant citizenship not only to former slaves but also to anyone born on American soil. He advocated for the Fifteenth Amendment to give voting rights to black men, and perhaps to save Republicans in Congress from being overwhelmed by Southern, supremacist Democrats. At his insistence, the words EQUALITY OF MAN BEFORE HIS CREATOR were carved on his headstone, and he was buried in an obscure cemetery that he selected because it was not racially restricted.[49]

The Fourteenth Amendment included the idea of equality for the first time in the US Constitution, and Americans have been arguing ever since about what it means. The Supreme Court would rely on the amendment's guarantee of "equal protection of the laws" to uphold an antimiscegenation law in 1883 and to strike down such laws in *Loving* in 1967.

Frederick Douglass had worked for the ideal of equality his entire life, first for himself in escaping slavery and later for others as an abolitionist, a reformer, and a statesman. He was the child of a slave and a slaveholder—a black woman and a white man—although he never knew who his father was and he was sold away from his mother. His ascent to iconic Negro leader was largely the result of his defiant persistence and the assistance of several women, especially his free African American wife, Anna Murray, who helped arrange his escape and did the prosaic, unacknowledged things required to sustain a great man's child-filled household for four decades.

Douglass did not fight the American origin story that enslaved him. As a child, he taught himself to read and write using *The Columbian Orator*—a seventeenth-century anthology of speeches celebrating republican virtues—and as a free adult, he would claim the country and its founding mythology as his.[50] After the *Dred Scott* decision, he gave a speech decrying its wrongness and used Jefferson's Declaration of Independence to revise the original meaning of the Constitution's we-the-people values. "Your fathers have said that man's right to liberty is self-evident. . . . To decide against this right in the person of Dred Scott, or the humblest and most whip-scarred bondman in the land, is to decide against God," he reasoned.[51]

He was a dexterous bridge builder, a double great-grandfather of rights movements, for African Americans and women. And he was among the tiny class of radicals, like Stevens and John Brown, whose abolitionism and underground subversions bled into intimate friendships across color lines. Douglass identified himself as "a colored man of both Anglo-Saxon and African descent" and, in doing so, apparently resisted the one-drop rule.[52] Critics of his relations with white women considered him too racially dexterous.

Douglass was a magnet for independent-minded women devoted to his causes and wowed by his intellect. Perhaps because of his empathy for anyone who struggled against oppression, he had close friendships with several white feminists, including Elizabeth Cady Stanton, who supported him when he married Pitts. He was especially close to Julia Griffiths, an affluent English woman who crossed the Atlantic to work alongside him at his antislavery newspaper, the *North Star*, for six years. There were rumors of a romance between them, fueled by the fact that Griffiths lived in Douglass's family home for a period. Griffiths and Douglass were undoubtedly true allies in the cause of abolition. Both were station agents on the Underground Railroad in Rochester, New York, and Griffiths raised thousands for Douglass's newspapers. The *North Star* and later iterations of it, *Frederick Douglass' Paper* and *Douglass' Monthly*, were conceived as a community, an outlet for Negro correspondents but also a forum for the connection of abolitionists across the United States and Britain. Griffiths is credited with envisioning and helping to position the papers as the center of an antislavery community.

These newspapers depended on a web of social relationships with Douglass at the center. Color was no barrier to entry, but being antislavery was required.[53] Griffiths also helped Douglass in other ways. She once held the mortgage of his house. To a degree, Douglass emancipated himself not only from slavery but also from the social constrictions of race. He could be seen strolling arm in arm with Griffiths and her sister on the streets of Rochester, provoking some resentment there and a street riot when he once did the same with them in New York City.[54]

Douglass also had a nearly three-decade relationship with Ottilie Assing, a German journalist and intellectual, who spent twenty-two summers at the Douglass home in Rochester and referred to herself in a letter to her sister as Douglass's "natural wife."[55] Assing translated Douglass's second autobiography, *My Bondage and My Freedom*, into German. In a preface, Assing described Douglass to a German readership. Her words are those of a woman in love, although apparently not with the Negroid aspects of his features. She characterized him as a "light mulatto of unusually large, slender, and powerful build [with a] distinctly vaulted forehead," arched nose, "small and nicely formed" lips that revealed "more the influence of the white than . . . black origins." His graying hair was "curly though not woolly," she wrote, and she concluded that "there is the story of past struggle and storm and the expression of great energy" in his whole appearance, "the mark of a rich and original . . . talent . . . both learned and ingenious and highly cultivated."[56]

Douglass's shared knowledge with Assing was more than car-
nal. Together they enjoyed intellectual pursuits, something he could
not do with Anna, who was illiterate. Assing stood with Douglass
on virtually every ideological position he took during their decades
of association.[57] In her correspondence about him to her sister, Assing clearly hoped and expected that Douglass would leave his wife,
Anna, and marry her after slavery was abolished in the United States.
Douglass had other ideas. He stayed with Anna until she died in
1882. He then married Helen Pitts, twenty years his junior, seventeen
months later. Assing committed suicide, leaving an annuity from her
estate to Douglass.[58]

Pitts was a Mayflower descendant, a distant relative of John Adams and John Quincy Adams, and the daughter of lifelong abolitionist Gideon Pitts. She was also a feminist activist and briefly a teacher
at Hampton Institute before becoming Douglass's secretary, a role
in which she assisted Douglass in preparing the final edition of his
third autobiography. The wedding took place in Francis Grimké's
living room in Philadelphia. The marriage was legal in Pennsylvania,
though there were considerable social objections.

At the time, Douglass was America's most influential Negro. Randall Kennedy collected evidence of outrage about the marriage on
both sides of the color line. Douglass was "a lecherous old African
Solomon" and the marriage "a deliberate challenge to the Caucasian
race," wrote one Virginia paper. A black journalist, T. Thomas Fortune, wrote, "The colored ladies take [the marriage] as a slight, if not
an insult, to their race and their beauty," and argued that important
men, whether white or black, "owe some deference to the prejudices
of the people they represent." Another black-owned paper declared
that since "Fred Douglass has married a red-head white girl . . . [w]e
have no further use for him." Booker T. Washington, another child of
an indifferent slave owner and a slave, and the man who would take
Douglass's place as chief spokesman for African Americans, wrote in
his biography that there was "a revulsion of feeling throughout the
entire country" to Douglass's marriage and that Negroes generally
felt "that he had made the most serious mistake of his life."[59]

Neither Pitts's father nor Douglass's grown children were pleased.
Gideon Pitts stopped speaking to his daughter. The Douglass children

were apoplectic, especially his daughter Rosetta, who may have perceived the marriage as a rejection of her dark-skinned mother, if not of her similarly skinned self. "What business has the world with the color of my wife?" Douglass wrote in exasperation to his friend Amy Post, a Quaker abolitionist and women's rights supporter.[60] It was a genre of question that would persist for ardent integrators for another century or more. Stringent social constraints against interracial marriage were now lodged in most black and white minds, and Douglass ignored them all.

Others continued to struggle to reconcile antimiscegenation sentiment with constitutional values. Massachusetts had repealed its antimiscegenation law in 1843. Iowa and Kansas had allowed theirs to lapse in the 1850s. With Reconstruction, and the constitutional and civil rights edicts that came with it, various jurisdictions repealed their laws: New Mexico (1866), Louisiana (1868), South Carolina (1868), Washington (1868), and Mississippi (1870). Three more states, Arkansas, Illinois, and Florida, omitted their antimiscegenation laws from state compilations. And courts in Alabama and Texas set antimiscegenation laws aside.[61]

Black male Reconstruction legislators castigated white men who had had illicit sex with black women, and several states passed bastardy statutes that enabled black or mulatto women to file paternity suits against white men.[62] Reconstruction itself required a mixing of races in politics. Because newly enfranchised black men did not constitute a voting majority in any state of the former Confederacy, except perhaps South Carolina, Reconstruction governments were coalitions of newly freed blacks, white Northern carpetbaggers, and the 2 percent of the white Southern population that had remained loyal to the Union, known unkindly by their confederate brethren as "scalawags."

Though imperfect and a radical change in American history, these multiracial governments tried to make good on the US Constitution's new promise of equality. They tried to create new societies in which sable and pale, formerly enslaved and ordinary yeomen who had never owned slaves, had a chance at liberty and the pursuit of happiness. In *Black Reconstruction*, W. E. B. Du Bois described these governments' achievements. They created new constitutions that extended privileges of citizenship without regard to race, class, or property ownership. Black men could now serve on juries, testify against whites, and buy a gun, among other new privileges. Most importantly to their sense of manhood, they could vote and run for office. The Reconstruction governments also created public education for the first time in the South—integrated education in theory, but segregated education in practice. Public schools in New Orleans actually were integrated. Children of all colors there learned, elbow to elbow with one another and with considerable success, until Reconstruction ended in 1877.[63]

Neither whites nor blacks were cheerleaders for intense integration. Like the revolutionaries of Pennsylvania nearly a century before them, in repealing antimiscegenation laws, Reconstruction legislators were simply trying to align their state laws with the Union's new egalitarian edicts. As in earlier times, interracial couples still hid in plain sight and there is evidence that when such relationships surfaced, they were tolerated or debated at the community level where they occurred, in terms far short of a noose. As antimiscegenation laws were abandoned by some states, others persisted. Virginia held fast to its law, as did Georgia, North Carolina, Tennessee; the upper-border and Midwestern states of Indiana, Kentucky, Ohio, Michigan, and West Virginia; and most western states.[64]

Southern patriarchs lost their minds when they lost control of black bodies. Black male political empowerment quickly came to be equated with black male sexuality.[65] A black body that was owned by someone was valuable, at least in an economic sense, and in a few antebellum cases, when a black man was accused of connecting with a white woman, his master successfully defended him against such charges.[66] Once emancipated, the black men who had done the heavy lifting and skilled-trades work that plantations required became sexual predators in the eyes of their former masters.

One can see this irrational connection in D. W. Griffith's cartoonish depiction of Reconstruction in his infamous film, *The Birth of a Nation*. White actors in blackface play Reconstruction legislators as buffoons who put their feet on their desks in the House chamber in one scene, and then a Southern magnolia is chased down to be devoured by a black-faced rapist in another.

None of this stereotyping made sense, except that Old South patriarchs had constructed racial caste, thrived atop it, and had no intention of giving it up. Slavery had been the system of racial caste before the Civil War. It required a profusion of laws, including antimiscegenation. After emancipation, white supremacists who were used to thinking of blacks solely as workhorses to produce cotton used violence to retake control of government and black bodies.

White civic leaders formed the Ku Klux Klan, initially an underground militia to terrorize black and white Republicans and destroy Reconstruction. As would be the case in subsequent eras, the backlash to multiracial, egalitarian politics was a reassertion of white supremacy for the benefit of elites. Tellingly, the Klan was most active in areas where whites and blacks shared the greatest economic parity. Local Klan cells would round up a posse at the slightest accusation of a black man's glance or touch of a white woman. The fantasy of the black male predator, like the cry of amalgamation-miscegenation before it, had a political function, a way of organizing whites to align with Democrats against the saner vision of interracial cooperation that Reconstruction represented.[67] From the close of the Civil War to the height of the civil rights movement a century later, white supremacy was the central organizing principle of the Democratic Party in the South, and violence was a critical organizing tool.[68]

As with prior generations' cry of amalgamation or miscegenation, there was fakery to this new ritual. The real concern was black men acting like citizens. Black men who gathered political power or had economic success transgressed the racial line that had been drawn during slavery, and these were galling, unforgivable sins in the eyes of supremacists, as galling as the idea of a black man inserting himself between a white woman's legs.[69]

Depraved minds worked terrible deeds. In a case of a Georgia black man who cohabited with a white woman, the mob took him into the woods, drove a nail through his penis into a wooden block, lit a fire around him, and left him with a knife and the decision of whether to slice off his own organ to escape the fire, which he did. Radical Republicans in Congress held hearings and collected this and other cases of domestic terror. It didn't matter whether a black man actually had a relationship with a white woman or not. Either way, he could be maimed or murdered. At the same time, Klansmen routinely raped black women and, sometimes, nonelite white women accused of engaging in illicit sex with black men.[70]

White racism would harden with the ascendance of Democrats.[71] By the late nineteenth century, lynching occurred in staggering numbers and continued well into the twentieth century. A lynching was often a theatrical performance of passion with a fairly standard script. Someone, usually but not always a black man, stood accused of a social crime if not an actual one. The cry of rape of a "respectable" white woman or girl seemed to incite the most delirium. Over decades, even the lowest class of white woman became "respectable" as a critical player in the ritual. Whether of high or low station, whether she had voluntarily taken a black lover or simply happened to know him and was conveniently cast to play the role, she would be forced to tell the crowd that she had been raped or to assent when it was said for her.

The orchestration of the lynching was unusually swift in a tech-free world. Newspapers sometimes published the date and time that the event would take place. Railroads might add extra cars or routes to facilitate crowds from adjoining towns to come watch the spectacle. Children might be let out of school. Men, women, and children would come to watch the ritual. Everyone knew exactly who did the hanging, dismembering, gouging, or burning of the body because much of the town came out to watch and might scramble over body parts. Postcards might be made of the hanging body and the smiling crowd surrounding it. Fingers, teeth, or other souvenirs might be displayed in shop windows, or the body left to swing, until the stench made executioners think better of it. Inevitably, the news accounts afterward would report that "persons unknown" did it.[72] As late as the 1940s, Thurgood Marshall and the National Association for the Advancement of Colored People (NAACP) were flying banners outside the New York office: "A man was lynched yesterday," the banner read, in the group's ongoing effort to save black clients from fabricated rape charges.[73] And a lamb named Emmett Till, a fourteen-year-old Chicagoan innocent of Southern racial codes, would be slaughtered in Money, Mississippi, in 1955 for allegedly whistling at a white female store clerk.

Anyone who criticized or tried to rewrite the sexual-predator script faced grave danger. Ida B. Wells, an African American born a slave and freed by the Emancipation Proclamation, devoted her life to accurately documenting the facts behind lynching and had to flee north to continue doing it. Despite years of reporting and editorializing on lynching, Wells soon realized how little the facts mattered. Congress never succeeded in transcending performance politics about the alleged necessity of protecting white women from black rapists and therefore never passed an antilynching bill.[74]

Not surprisingly, as Democrats retook control of Southern governments, they reenacted or reaffirmed antimiscegenation laws throughout the South. The metaphor of the pure white magnolia could also be applied to the desired, lily-white body politic, and this alleged desire to protect white women was also used in Western states. As whites encountered other groups that they might mix with or that competed with them for resources like land, gold, and silver, Western lawgivers also did their best to insulate the white citizen from competition or "degradation."

By 1869, five Western states had amended their antimiscegenation laws to add new categories like Chinese, Mongolian, and Indians to the club of Negroes and mulattoes that could not marry white people. The same year, the popular *Harper's Weekly* included an illustration of a well-dressed white woman leaving the "Church of St. Confucius" on the arm of her new husband, a realistically rendered, handsome Chinese man sporting the cap, single braid, long mustache, and clothing associated with Chinese railroad workers, under the title "Pacific Railroad Complete."[75] Overt sexualization of Asian men would come later. California, the state with the largest influx of Chinese immigrants, did not get the message about equality embodied in the new Fourteenth Amendment. Its legislators were busy passing laws designed to minimize citizenship rights for Mexican Americans and to squelch economic competition by Asian men. Legislators blamed Chinese workers for undermining the ability of the white man to get a decent wage or support a wife and family. In 1880, California amended its law to ban "Mongolians" from marrying whites.[76]

As interracial marriage was barred everywhere in the South by the 1880s, the Supreme Court effectively sanctioned these laws in a case from Alabama involving a black man, Tony Pace, and white woman, Mary Jane Cox. In an era of lynching, this couple's desires apparently were stronger than their fears. They were accused of fornication in Grove Hill, a tiny hamlet in west Alabama environs that had once been occupied by Creek and Choctaw Indians. White neighbors testified before a grand jury that Pace and Cox lived together, suggesting that folks in Grove Hill were relaxed enough to allow courts rather than vigilantes to handle the matter. Both Pace and Cox were convicted under a statute that assessed a special penalty for interracial fornication or intermarriage. The local court gave them each two years in jail. Pace was fortunate that a sympathetic white lawyer from Mobile took his case on appeal, ultimately to the US Supreme Court, for no fee.[77]

In *Pace v. Alabama*, 1883, the court dispensed with the case in three short paragraphs. It reasoned that blacks and whites were treated equally under the law because both races suffered the same penalty if they engaged in interracial sex.[78] Although the state's penalty on interracial *marriage* was not at issue in this case, the court's formal equality logic would easily apply to that provision, and all antimiscegenation laws escaped scrutiny by the court until the *Loving* case in 1967.

The Supreme Court used similar logic in its 1896 decision in *Plessy v. Ferguson*, sanctioning separate-but-equal railroad cars in New Orleans. Southern states began to use the one-drop rule to police not only whom one could love but also where one could sit in public spaces. Homer Plessy, who was light-skinned and seven-eighths white, was deemed a Negro who therefore had to sit with other Negroes—the pale, caramel, redbone, blue-black, and other gradations of color that the slave trade and amalgamation had produced. The court reasoned that the whites-only and Negro-only cars implied formal equality, not inferiority, of black people. This opinion, too, was fakery, as the court intentionally ignored a violence-backed social meaning of segregation that all Southerners understood well.

In his famous dissent, Justice John Marshall Harlan argued that our Constitution should be "colorblind," a word that judicial conservatives would latch on to a century later. And yet Harlan could not untie the Gordian knot of race and supremacy. He seemed to participate in supremacist thinking when it came to Chinese people, whom he described as "a [race] so different from our own that we do not permit those belonging to it to become citizens of the United States." He argued by way of example that the New Orleans law, in requiring separation only of Negroes from whites on trains, would allow "Chinamen" to "ride in the same passenger coach with white citizens of the United States, while citizens of the black race in Louisiana, many of whom, perhaps, risked their lives for the preservation of the Union . . . are yet declared to be criminals, liable to imprisonment, if they ride in a public coach occupied by citizens of the white race."

After *Plessy*, Southern legislators accelerated the spread of Jim Crow laws.[79] Like antimiscegenation, Jim Crow was rather useful to supremacist politicians. Laws requiring separation of the races in schools, public spaces, restrooms, restaurants, and other areas of life offered status to white working men and security from alleged black rapists for white women. The laws also inculcated a Southern culture of segregation that rendered every black man a "boy" and every white lad "Mister" among a phalanx of other social protocols that denigrated blacks and elevated whites.

Supremacists also moved to rewhiten politics. For a brief period in the 1890s, biracial political coalitions reemerged, fueled by populist, farmer anger at bank and railroad monopolists. But white men of all political stripes grew tired of fighting over who could do a better job of stealing the black vote. Between 1890 and 1910, Southern Democrats in ten of the eleven states of the former Confederacy adopted new state constitutions that introduced poll taxes, literacy tests, and other constraints on voting. The changes disenfranchised not only black men but also many poor, illiterate white men. Black men would largely cease to vote, run for office, or serve on juries.[80]

The nadir continued from the nineteenth century into the twentieth. The reaction to Booker T. Washington's 1901 dinner with Theodore Roosevelt in the White House illuminates Southern society's lack of tolerance for race mixing at the turn of the century. Although Lincoln and other presidents had received black leaders at the White House, not since John Adams dined with a Haitian representative in 1798 had a president invited a Negro to his dinner table. Washington was a close adviser to Roosevelt and an improbable integrator at the White House. He had advised African Americans to stay in and uplift their own communities, yet Southerners in particular reacted with furor to this communion between a former slave and a president.

Hundreds of newspapers across the nation commented on the dinner. Critics made heavy use of the N-word. For Southerners, the dinner suggested social equality for the Negro. An invitation to dine with one's family in the South was an act of intimacy. A guest at a dinner table where a wife and children were present could also ask for the hand of a daughter in marriage. Roosevelt's family had been present at the dinner. Washington, then, could marry Roosevelt's daughter.[81] It was as irrational as equating voting with raping, but there it was, supremacist illogic.

World heavyweight champion boxer Jack Johnson tested the limits of the color line even more, first by winning the title in 1908 and denying it to a series of "Great White Hopes" and then by frolicking with white women and marrying three of them, including a New York society girl. On July 4, 1910, Johnson beat the greatest of white hopes, James Jeffries, in Reno, Nevada, before twenty thousand people. White Southerners were not the only ones affronted; angry whites rioted in more than fifty cities from New York to Colorado. In the history of race riots in America to that date, there had been a conflagration somewhere, every few years since Nat Turner's bloody revolt. But this was the first time the rioting was national in scope. Perhaps the race war that Thomas Jefferson had foreshadowed in *Notes* arrived that Independence Day. Black and white bodies clashed in streets, and at least twenty people died.[82]

Johnson was a supremacist's nightmare. Black as coal, as colorstruck Negroes might say of him, all brawn and bravado and a sharp dresser to boot. He taunted lesser men, white and black, inside the ring and out and bragged publicly about his sexual prowess. He swore off "colored" women, whom he claimed brought him heartache and trouble, and declared he would only associate with white women, at a time when he was the most covered man in the press.[83] And yet he came by his racial dexterity honestly. He grew up in the heavily poor Twelfth Ward of Galveston, Texas, where the laws of survival must have been more important than the codes of supremacy. White families of his childhood chums had invited him to their dinner table, and he even slept overnight in their homes. Used to being treated as Jack rather than black Jack, he behaved as such into adulthood.[84]

Like Richard Mentor Johnson before him, Jack Johnson's amalgamating ways were the subject of intense national scrutiny. Excoriated in the press for his flamboyance and his white women, he gave his critics plenty of fodder. His first wife, New York socialite Etta Duryea, shot herself in the head, the victim of depression and Johnson's physical abuse and philandering. His second wife, Lucille Cameron, a former prostitute, refused to play the role typically assigned to the white woman in the theater of lynching. When prosecutors tried to get her to testify against him for a Mann Act violation of transporting someone across state lines for immoral purposes, Cameron declined repeatedly, professing her love for Johnson and her desire to marry him. As the feds rounded up another white prostitute with whom Johnson had had dealings to play this role, Johnson announced an impromptu wedding and married Cameron before an interracial party in his mother's Chicago home. Johnson's mother, known as Tiny, wore a dark dress that looked more appropriate for a funeral.

The quick wedding produced a national furor. More than a few commentators called for lynching Johnson. The government did succeed in prosecuting him under the Mann Act and eventually imprisoning him. The act was not an antimiscegenation law, but it was prosecuted as such in Johnson's case. His real crime had been traveling with a white woman, and the all-white jury that convicted him in all likelihood saw it that way.[85] He would have been safer with the black women he spurned, but that was not his nonconformist approach to life, sex, and love.

And therein lay the central theme of Johnson's life—how he cunningly beat other boxers, whom he slept with or married, and how he threw his money around was utterly his self-emancipated business. Booker T. Washington and many of the colored people Washington claimed to represent didn't like Johnson's choices any more than did the white men who had difficulty understanding how a white woman could see his swaggering blackness as beautiful. Get over it, America and world, Johnson seemed to say.[86] In this sense, more than Douglass, Johnson was ahead of his time; only the most open-minded souls in America may yet have caught up to him.

W. E. B. Du Bois, eminent scholar, activist, and cofounder of the NAACP, was not enamored of Johnson. Characterizing the boxer as a "bad" person, Du Bois nevertheless defended Johnson's right to marry whomever he wanted and applauded him for solemnizing his relationships rather than just whoring, an activity that Johnson never seemed to give up. The NAACP launched into action and lobbied successfully against multiple new antimiscegenation bills introduced in Northern and Midwestern states because of the Johnson contretemps. With persuasion, this region, Indiana excepted, would try to adhere to principles of liberty and freedom or, like Lincoln, its legislators were content to rely on social rather than legal constraints against intermarriage.[87]

In 1913, a Virginian, Woodrow Wilson, became the first Southern president since before the Civil War. *The Birth of a Nation*, America's first box-office blockbuster, was screened for Wilson at the White House. The NAACP protested the film as whites flocked to see it. Some viewers left movie theaters and attacked blacks in several cities, and the film inspired others to reconstitute the Klan. Wilson's administration birthed segregation in the federal government, which had been integrated since Reconstruction.[88] Race riots erupted again in the Red Summer of 1919 in three dozen cities and a rural outpost in Arkansas. The collective death toll in the hundreds made the 1910 riots look modest. Some of this interracial violence was stoked by claims of black men assaulting white women, but much of it had to do with white World War I veterans disembarking in America alongside black veterans and not being able to accept black veterans' and black people's new assertion of full personhood.[89] Labor strikes raged, and it was easy for captains of industry to pit white and colored workers against each other when a well-entrenched culture of white supremacy decisively shaped the identity of the white working class. Whites saw themselves in racial, superior terms and did not want blacks competing with them for jobs or joining their unions.[90]

Race relations were broken in the United States because patriarchs through the centuries had designed them to be broken.

The problem of the twentieth century was, indeed, the color line, as Du Bois prophesied in *The Souls of Black Folk.* And yet lawmakers kept trying to fortify lines designed to insulate whites of desired stock from everyone else. The year 1924 was a pivotal one nationally and, in particular, in Virginia. Eugenics, immigration, and antimiscegenation law converged in their reliance on pseudoscientific racism. Throughout the nineteenth century, self-appointed experts in fields from ethnology to medicine to anthropology had claimed a scientific basis for classifying people into distinct races, although they fought among each about the constructed racial categories and how to determine who belonged to which ones.[91]

This "science" has been debunked, and while there is no scientific basis for race, Americans necessarily ascribe much cultural and social meaning to racial categories we all live with.[92] In the late nineteenth and early twentieth centuries, eugenicists also had their theories that have since been debunked. They believed that race existed at the cellular level. With care and proper breeding, they thought, the best could be brought out in all the races. Eugenic ideas also reinforced supremacist ones.[93] Anglo-Saxons and pale western and northern Europeans were elevated above other strains of humanity. In a bid to preserve the racial homogeneity and hence the whiteness of the country, Congress passed the Immigration Act of 1924. The law barred the entry of Asians and "Arabians" and severely restricted immigration of darker-complexioned southern and eastern Europeans. It also restricted black migration from the Caribbean and Africa through nationality quotas.[94]

In Virginia, Anglo-Saxon stock was being insulated in other ways. Virginia was a hotbed of eugenic activism in the 1920s. Despite the expansive name of the Anglo-Saxon Clubs of America, this white supremacist organization had outposts only in Virginia. Among other agenda items, the Clubs supported limiting immigration to northern Europeans and tightening antimiscegenation law. Two of its cofounders, John Powell and Walter Plecker (head of the Virginia Bureau of Vital Statistics), were obsessed with white racial purity.

Powell drafted "an act to preserve the integrity of the White Race" and, along with Plecker and the Anglo-Saxon Clubs, successfully lobbied for its passage. Although the legislators changed the name to "an act to preserve Racial Integrity" and watered it down to accommodate Virginia's line of Anglo-Native descendants of Pocahontas, its central feature was a new, narrower definition of whiteness.

Before the 1924 law, a person could be one-quarter nonwhite and still qualify as white for purposes of evading Virginia's ban on whites marrying nonwhites. Plecker in particular was apoplectic about the risk of nearly white Negroes slipping by county clerks to get a license to marry and later procreate with a white person. By applying the one-drop rule to build a wall around whiteness, the act became the most rigid antimiscegenation law in the United States.[95]

The statute did not mince words in its proscription of interracial marriage: "It shall hereafter be unlawful for any white person in this state to marry any save a white person, or a person with no other admixture of blood than white and American Indian." And "white person" was defined as a "person who has no trace whatsoever of any blood other than Caucasian." How one could prove such artifice was an open question. With a narrowly drawn loophole for white people with one-sixteenth Native American blood—the so-called Pocahontas exception—whites could only marry the purest of white people.[96] The other busy work of Virginia eugenicists was the Virginia Sterilization Act of 1924, whereby even poor white women, like Carrie Buck, whom white elites had no use for, could be deemed an imbecile and sterilized.[97]

Plecker would stay in his job as head of Virginia vital statistics until he retired in 1946 and turned over all stones to see the Integrity Act enforced. He kept a county-by-county list of "Mixed Negroid Virginia Families Striving to Pass as 'Indian' or White" to alert clerks to possible violators.

Two family names listed for Caroline County would course through the Lovings' story: Byrd and Fortune.[98] Mildred Loving's mother was a Byrd. Richard Loving raced cars with a light-skinned man of color named Percy Fortune. Mildred and Richard's daughter Peggy would marry a Fortune. Some Byrds and Fortunes identified as Rappahannock and strenuously objected to being cast as Negroes. In 1943, a

Byrd and a Fortune went to trial and risked prison sentences for refusing to be inducted into a black unit in the military.[99]

The subjectivity of racial categories can be seen in Mildred's ancestry. Her parents were Theoliver Jeter and Musiel Byrd. Census records for Caroline County listed people named Jeter and Byrd as early as 1870. One scholar reviewed these records from 1870 to 1930 and found that Jeters were identified as mulatto in the nineteenth century, but by 1930, they were all labeled Negro. The Byrds, overwhelmingly, were listed as black until 1910, when they were identified as colored or mulatto. But by 1930, they, too, were classified solely as Negro.[100] One possible explanation for the blackening of Mildred's people was Plecker's relentlessness after passage of the Racial Integrity Act in policing categories and instructing the small army of people who were accountable to him to use the one-drop rule to designate people as Negro on birth certificates and other government documents. Plecker or state employees would "correct" the race on a child's birth certificate and on any other documents that they considered to have errors in racial reporting.[101]

By 1939, the year Mildred was born, outside of the Northeast and Midwest, most states continued to prohibit whites from marrying nonwhites, with no standard formula for which people were an unacceptable stain on whiteness. All antimiscegenation laws prohibited white-black marriages. Fourteen states banned marriage between whites and Asian Americans, including Chinese, Japanese, Malays, "Corean," and Hindus among the subgroups listed in statutes. Five states, including Virginia, banned marriage between whites and indigenous people.[102] No matter how Mildred identified herself, she could not marry her white lover in Virginia.

PART TWO

. . .

Loving

CHAPTER FIVE

Loving v. Virginia (1967)

Mildred Jeter was eleven years old when she first met Richard Loving, who was then seventeen. "Rich," a buddy of her brothers, played in a band and would stop by the Jeter home to visit. He watched her grow from a skinny girl to a slender but comely teenager whom everyone called "Stringbean." Rich would call her "Bean." At first Mildred did not like Rich. "He was arrogant," she thought, but she came to know him as "a very nice person," she told a documentarian. They started going steady after they noticed each other anew at a dance, a moment when a long family friendship became something more.[1]

Central Point and Caroline County had a history of both mixing and a color line. One practice enabled the couple to meet, and the other rendered the love that would emerge between them forbidden. Mixing began almost immediately after the county was founded in 1728 as white, indigenous, and black people dealt with one another. Yet the color line was just as official in Caroline County as in other parts of the state. The county had strongly supported secession from the Union, and slavery had been a dominant fact of life there. Slavery and the supremacist binary of white and black that supported it rendered the white and "colored" populations nearly equal in Caroline.

They were still nearly fifty-fifty in the 1950s, when Mildred and Richard became lovers.[2]

The small white faction that ran Caroline County aligned with the white-supremacy Democrats who dominated the state. Harry F. Byrd was a US senator and former Virginia governor who descended from Pocahontas and Virginia's colonial planter aristocracy.[3] The Supreme Court's ruling in *Brown v. Board of Education* was an affront to his heritage and supremacist thinking. In 1955, the court ordered states to integrate schools with "all deliberate speed." *Deliberate* meant "with careful and thorough consideration," according to the dictionary, or "slow," as Thurgood Marshall and the attorneys of the NAACP Legal Defense Fund would discover.

Byrd's rural political machine controlled the Virginia General Assembly. He and fellow conspirators invented "Massive Resistance" and passed laws to implement it. They preferred to close public schools and to channel state educational resources to private, segregated academies than give integration a chance. In Norfolk, Charlottesville, Warren, and Prince Edward Counties, schools were actually closed after courts entered desegregation orders there. Other states of the former Confederacy would pick up Virginia's momentum.

Strom Thurmond, the furtive amalgamator who would be exposed after he died as having fathered a daughter with his family's black teenage servant, drafted a "Southern Manifesto" for resistance. Southern politicians signed on and wielded it and the mantra of "states' rights" like a club. A few Southern patriots, Lyndon Baines Johnson and Albert Gore Sr. included, refused to sign it. Otherwise, resistance was the zeitgeist of both supremacists and emerging civil rights revolutionaries. The Caroline County Board of Supervisors took the supremacist approach and voted to withhold funds for all schools rather than integrate them.[4]

Richard and Mildred attended elementary schools that were decidedly separate and unequal. Richard had ridden a school bus five miles west on Sparta Road to a large, modern building at Sparta, Virginia. The school had five or six teachers for each of its seven grades. He continued attending white schools until he dropped out of high school to learn a trade. He was working as a brick mason at the living wage of five dollars an hour in 1967 when the Lovings became famous.

In contrast, Mildred attended one of the nine Rosenwald schools in Caroline County—a two-room wood schoolhouse built shortly after World War I when a group of black parents raised $1,700 to match the Rosenwald Fund's $500 grant. The school had no indoor plumbing, electricity, or central heat and typically employed one teacher for all seven grades of students. As Mildred grew up, Caroline County would put more funds into its Negro schools than other parts of the state, perhaps aiming for "nearly equal." She would attend Caroline County's Union High School for colored students until she dropped out in the eleventh grade, probably because she had given birth to her first child.[5]

Although the schools were segregated, people of different colors in the rural hamlet of Central Point lived near one another. In a documentary about the Lovings, a resident said that Richard's family lived in a section populated by "Indians." Likely these were people who, like Mildred and the Byrds and Fortunes, claimed Rappahannock heritage. According to the laws and social customs of Virginia, they were not white. The Loving family was used to being one of the few white families in their section of Central Point, while the Jeter family lived seven miles "up the road" from the Lovings, as locals would say if giving directions.[6]

Central Point was a tiny, unincorporated community of farmers. Marked on a map as the intersection of Passing and Sparta Roads, the hamlet was about a dozen miles east of Bowling Green, the county seat, and an hour away from Richmond. In the 1950s, when Mildred and Richard met and later married, Passing and Sparta Roads were narrow and unpaved. The intersection had no traffic light and still does not. Today, the roads are known as Routes 625 and 630. The dominant building near the intersection has always been the church Mildred's family belonged to, St. Stephens Baptist, which itself reflected Mildred's complicated ancestry.

In his history of Caroline County, Marshall Wingfield observed in 1924 that St. Stephens was founded by "colored" people during Reconstruction and had "the largest and most costly house of worship in Caroline, white or colored." Wingfield also wrote about the mixed heritage of its members and of the Central Point community. Some "had as much as one-half negro blood" and were "very nearly white." Outside Central Point, he continued, they "could not be recognized or distinguished as people of color. . . . It is said that the predominating blood in them is that of the Indian and white races." According to Wingfield, a man named M. W. Byrd had served as the church clerk for over forty years and was the postmaster of Central Point in 1924.[7] Byrd, whose first name was Mordecai, was a descendant of another Mordecai Byrd, a free man of color who had raised a family in Central Point before the Civil War. In 1943, M. W.'s son Robert would be tried, along with other men of Rappahannock heritage from Caroline County, for refusing to serve in the military with black units.[8]

In 1924, M. W. Byrd must have been the de facto mayor of Central Point. In addition to being a long-serving clerk at St. Stephens, he ran a grocery store across the street from the church and served as postmaster from the same building. When he retired, he passed the job of postmaster to a grandnephew, P. E. Boyd Byrd, and Mordecai F. Byrd inherited the grocery store. The weathered edifice from which Byrds ruled still stands—a boarded ruin with barely legible letters above the front entrance that echo its last emperor, P. E. BOYD BYRD, CENTRAL POINT P.O.

In the ways of Virginia, P. E. Boyd was a "black" Byrd, though a light-skinned one. Both he and Senator Harry F. Byrd claimed William Byrd II, British planter, slaveholder, and founder of Richmond, as a common ancestor. The two men stood on different sides of the color line, the darker Byrd likely created by an amalgamating patriarch more than a century before. An article that appeared in *Ebony Magazine* about the Lovings also covered P. E. Boyd Byrd and his family. It described him as "rotund, amiable" and "possibly the wealthiest Negro farmer in the vicinity." In addition to serving as postmaster, he owned a four-hundred-acre farm on which he employed Richard Loving's father for twenty-three years. In pictures accompanying the article, P. E. Boyd Byrd stands in front of the store-cum-post-office graced with his name, checks on the work of a white and a black employee on his farm, and poses with his similarly light-skinned wife and mother. As *Ebony* would often do for a successful black person, it also published a picture of Byrd's expansive house. Another picture showed Mordecai F. Byrd inside the grocery store, working the cash register, and identifies him as the proprietor.[9]

Simeon Booker, the author of the *Ebony* article, had a long career as a prizewinning journalist, including more than five decades writing for *Ebony* and *Jet*, publications that celebrated black people and their advances. Booker was adept at going into Southern towns, finding the right contacts, and getting people to talk to him to cover a civil rights story. He had managed to cover the trial of Emmett Till's killer with searing truth, without getting himself killed.[10] For his story about the Lovings in 1967, Booker seems to have asked impertinent questions and got answers that explained much about Central Point's habit of mixing.

There is a standard story about Central Point that writers on the Lovings tell. Community lore had it that the name of Passing Road evokes the community's status as the "passing capital of America." Booker mythologized that story by writing about the many light-skinned people of color from Central Point that were doing the passing. Wingfield had described them as "very nearly white." Booker quoted a local who used a phrase well understood by *Ebony* readers to describe brethren that enjoyed skin privileges: "high yaller Negroes." He also labeled them "the creamish-color establishment."

These lighter-skinned residents could leave Central Point for any city in America, pass as white, and reap the benefits of whiteness, and for decades, they did. They went to nearby towns to shop and attend theaters that visibly black people could not frequent in the pre-civil-rights South. They could pass as white to marry white. And when white in-laws came to Central Point to visit, younger siblings would skip school rather than be caught riding the "Negro school bus." Many cream-colored Central Pointers served in white units in the military before it was integrated. A teacher at segregated Union High School told Booker that its light-skinned graduates "always come from Central Point" and said this of them: "We hardly ever hear about them after they finish. They're clannish and proud."[11]

Richard Loving, who spent a lot of time working outside, may have been ruddier than some of these creamy people. His best friends, Raymond Green and Percy Fortune, whom he drag-raced cars with, were light skinned, although they identified themselves solely as black years later.¹² Richard's father worked for the local cream titan, and Richard was surrounded by the light-skinned set as a child. "Everybody looked alike to me," Loving told Booker. "I just never figured out all of this would happen. I just did not know about all of this stuff," he said of the laws that landed him and his wife in jail.

Mildred was "tan-skinned," according to Booker. As an African American who covered African Americans for decades, the journalist would have been aware of the gradations of color that centuries of race mixing had produced and that many Negroes paid attention to.¹³ Mildred would not have been able to pass for white; she looked like a Negro to many people. That was how *Ebony* identified her, as did many reporters and the lawyers who brought the Lovings' case before the Supreme Court. Jim Crow cast her in this role, and her lawyers would need her to play it to help dismantle a system that oppressed visibly dark people. But her race did not matter to Richard. He was so immersed in a world of color that falling in love with a tan girl seemed natural to him.

One of Richard's happy rituals was drag-racing a car with his best friends. Like generations of Byrds, Green and Fortune were also entrepreneurs. Green owned an auto repair shop on Passing Road, Green's Garage and Towing, still open, although in a dilapidated condition. Fortune owned a grocery store in Central Point. Together, Loving, Green, and Fortune could turn a stock Ford sedan into a speed demon.

Richard laid bricks during the week but lived for Saturdays, when the trio would take their car to strip-racing tracks and win. They celebrated over the prize money and trophies as their multicolored entourage of families and friends watched. Fortune usually drove the car, but sometimes Richard made tracks. The trio spent much time together working on their car, replacing an engine they blew out, replacing the rear end nine times. Some claimed that Green and Fortune gained status in their close association with Richard.¹⁴ Jim Crow created a hierarchy. Richard could claim that he didn't know anything about "this stuff," but the large, perching bird's rules shaped habits, and people made distinctions. Richard may not have asked for it, but he, the brick mason, had a higher social status than did his colored entrepreneur teammates when they arrived at the racetrack. Still, they defied the Crow by riding for joy and collecting trophies together.[15]

Central Point farm families had to have known about official segregation, because their children attended segregated schools. They endured color lines that they could not evade, but they seemed to see one another in human terms at home. As Richard told a documentarian, "There's just a few people in this community. There's a few white and a few colored, and as we grew up and they grew up, we all helped one another. It was all mixed together from the start, so it just kept going that way."[16] What many of the white and colored people of Central Point had in common was not having much. Their situation was quite similar to the bonded class of early colonial Virginia—working the land, cooperating with each other, and trying to make a life while political elites tried to divide them. As it had been for bonded colonials, nighttime integration was apparently normal in Central Point and the surrounding environs, even if official law discouraged it.

Simeon Booker got people to talk about the regularity of interracial sex in Caroline County. "There has been plenty of mingling among races for years," said one farmer, "and nobody griped or tried to legalize it. . . . What [Rich] wanted, he wanted on paper and legal." Richard was dangerous both to the creamy class that evaded its Negro-ness and to whites that dated or copulated interracially and surreptitiously. "The power boys in the county despised Rich because he ended the white man's moonlighting in romance," said a county leader. "Now they got to cut out this jive of dating Negro women at night and these high yaller Negroes got to face up to the facts of life. They don't have to pass any more."

The standard story on Central Point also implies that the mixing that went on there was exceptional and would not have been considered normal elsewhere. And yet there were other communities in Virginia with a history of mixing among black, red, and white people. While scholars have debunked this idea of exceptional mixing by unearthing evidence of sex and procreation despite an antimiscegenation regime, most people stuck with their own kind in matters of marriage.[17] Sixteen Southern states still banned whites from marrying nonwhites in 1967. Even in Central Point, centuries of racial regulation made most interracial couples try to stay below the radar of the law.

The Caroline County sheriff gave them good reason to be circumspect. R. Garnett Brooks became sheriff in 1947 and served in that capacity until 1964, when he was voted out of office on the winds of change. He earned his reputation as an oppressor not to be messed with. An imposing man with massive arms and hands, he was known to stop people and ask what they were doing in a particular place. If his victim responded with impertinence, he was not above clubbing them with his nightstick and taking them to jail. The only thing about him that diverged from casting him as the prototypical racist Southern sheriff was his improbably high-pitched voice.[18]

Brooks had tried and failed to separate Richard's motley crew of music buddies. He once entered the grocery store where they were hanging out on a Saturday night, and inspected and tore up their drivers' licenses. He was incensed not only by their mixing but also by the fact that some of the "coloreds" claimed whiteness on their licenses.[19] Because of Brooks's well-earned reputation, Richard had to know that Brooks and others cared about the color line. He surmised that he had to take Mildred to Washington, DC, to marry her. He may not have realized that Virginia law rendered him and Mildred felons for returning to Virginia to live as husband and wife. Perhaps he also did not realize the lengths to which the state would go to prosecute and persecute them. Their fight to live in Virginia and be left alone would take nine years. "I never expected we would have to go through with such a beating. It was right rough," he told Booker.

Mildred was pregnant with her second child when she and Richard married. They did what many 1950s couples did when sex led to pregnancy. They tied the knot and later were coy about the ages of their children. Richard's mother, Lola Jane Loving, was a midwife who delivered most of the children in Central Point. She had delivered Sidney Jeter for Mildred when she was seventeen, and the midwife would eventually deliver her two other children. Sidney would identify Richard as his "stepfather" on a social security form, and the Lovings and their lawyers would take pains to present a family narrative that ignored two out-of-wedlock pregnancies, possibly from different men. Mildred once told a reporter that Richard was the only man she ever loved, but according to one local, she may have had a "black fella'" as a beau before Richard. Sidney was the darkest of her children, with the most Negroid features. One scholar contends that the black-white binary created by Virginia's centuries-long hysteria about protecting and exalting whiteness may have shaped not only Mildred's identity but also her choices about whom to marry, even as the color line also delegitimated her choices.[20]

In 1958, with a baby on the way and Mildred, at eighteen, no longer a child herself, she and Richard must have decided it was time to formalize their love. They drove to Washington, DC, and married on June 2. Lola Jane once said of her son's marriage, "At first I didn't feel too good about it. Then I made up my mind if Richard wanted to, it was fine."[21]

Mr. and Mrs. Loving returned to Central Point and lived with Mildred's parents, enjoying a month of bliss before a cruel interruption. They slept in a bedroom on the first floor of the house and left the front door unlocked. Had they bothered to lock it, they might have had a warning, time to get up to respond to the posse's banging and to retain more of their dignity. Instead, in the middle of a July night, Garnett Brooks and two deputies let themselves into the house and then burst into their bedroom.

All three of Caroline County's law enforcement officers stood over them as Brooks shined a flashlight in their faces and interrogated Richard: "What are you doing in bed with that woman?" or something to that effect. Mildred demurred, "I'm his wife," and Richard pointed to their framed marriage license hanging on the wall. One suspects they had placed it there for protection as much as pride. "That's no good here," Brooks shot back. On the license, Mildred's race was recorded as "Indian," but her identity was irrelevant to Brooks. She was a colored girl to him, and he had no respect for Mildred or Richard as human beings, much less for their marriage.[22]

Nearly thirty-five years later, Brooks was unrepentant and shared thoughts consistent with what Virginia lawgivers had intended to inculcate in its citizens. "I was acting according to the law at the time," he told the *New York Times*, "and I still think it should be on the books. . . . The Lord made sparrows and robins, not to mix with one another." Brooks claimed to have thought little of the Lovings over the years. "If they'd been outstanding people, I would have thought something about it. But with the caliber of those people, it didn't matter. They were both low-class," he opined from his porch in Bowling Green.[23]

In a county known for mixing, it seems that the Lovings were singled out for prosecution because they had bothered to formalize their relationship. One mystery in the Loving story is the identity of the person who tipped off the authorities about their marriage. Richard speculated that it was someone who disliked them; one of his lawyers suggested someone was trying to eliminate competition at the racetrack.[24] Brent Staples, author and editorial writer for the *New York Times*, surmised that the tip could have come from a local white man "who had taken a black lover and used the law as an excuse not to marry."[25]

Mildred was about six months pregnant when Brooks yanked the Lovings from their bed. He carted them to the county jail in Bowling Green, an outmoded facility built in 1902. Richard was released on a thousand dollars bail the next day. When he tried to post similar bail for Mildred, authorities refused and threatened to rejail him if he persisted. They kept her in a five-by-seven-foot, rat-infested cell for five days. One of the jailers threatened to let a white male prisoner share her cell for a night. "It about scared me to death," Mildred recalled.[26]

Donald Loving was born five days before a grand jury agreed with the prosecutor's indictment of his parents. Even if the jurors had been sympathetic, it would have been difficult to avoid indicting them, as they clearly had violated the law. Mildred and Richard each faced prison sentences of one to five years.[27]

Leon Bazile, the judge who presided over their trial, had been a young assistant attorney general when the Racial Integrity Act was passed. He had advised its chief author, John Powell, and its enforcer, Walter Plecker, on how to avoid the one state appellate judge who was hostile to the law. Bazile was a patrician, staunch defender of Jim Crow. Although Brooks did the arresting, Bazile also plays the villain in the Loving story. Black citizens and black lawyers were fighting school segregation in courts across the state. Bazile himself had ruled in a case that the state constitution supported closing public schools if they could not remain segregated, because Virginia's constitution required segregation. For Bazile, the US Constitution and its guarantee of equal protection were irrelevant. States' rights and Virginia's majoritarian prerogatives were his rule of law. The Virginia Supreme Court would disagree with this logic, as would a federal district court.[28]

In the Lovings' case, Bazile wanted to avoid such outside interference. He used a common tactic of courts in other states that were still prosecuting antimiscegenation laws. He persuaded them to change their plea of not guilty to guilty and to go away quietly rather than challenge the law. As a young couple with very young children, the Lovings were anxious to avoid jail time and were easily coaxed into accepting a suspension of a one-year jail sentence if they agreed to leave the state. So began their years of exile in Washington, D.C. They agreed to Bazile's terms that they leave "at once and . . . not return together or at the same time . . . for a period of twenty-five years."[29]

The Lovings moved in with Mildred's cousin Alex Byrd and his wife, Laura, on Neal Street in Northeast Washington. A row house with a narrow porch and patch of grass for a front yard and neighbors sandwiching the family on both sides was a far cry from the open fields of Central Point. The block they lived on was adjacent to Gallaudet University in a neighborhood called Trinidad. Back then, it was a working and middle-class black neighborhood, not yet associated with words like "ghetto" and, later, "gentrification."

The substitution of concrete and sidewalks for unpaved roads and verdant fields was a shock to Mildred. "I missed the open spaces for the children, and just walking down a country lane to pick up my mail," she told a local historian in 1992. Some neighbors were friendly, but it was never enough. In a word, they were miserable in Washington, where they lived for four years. Richard worked when he could get it, Mildred ran the household, and they had a third child, their daughter Peggy. They took frequent clandestine trips back to Central Point, sometimes in separate cars. Twice they were caught and rearrested.[30]

As they struggled for their humanity, so did others. What Mildred knew of the civil rights movement she observed on television. Birmingham was on fire in the spring of 1963. Adults had marched for the big and little things, the right to shop where they wanted and try on the clothes, to get a decent job, to take their kids to public parks and swimming pools, to vote, to be citizens. Martin Luther King Jr. was arrested and wrote his letter from jail. But the movement had faltered until Birmingham children marched, carrying handmade signs: CAN A MAN LOVE GOD AND HATE HIS BROTHER?

Birmingham's public safety commissioner, Bull Connor, was less deft than Judge Bazile. His troops turned fire hoses and dogs on unarmed children but the children kept coming. Arrested, bailed out, and arrested again, some even began to taunt and dance at the men who hosed them. The world watched, horrified, as did President John F. Kennedy. He addressed the country on television and radio on June 11. Invoking the egalitarian words of Jefferson and the emancipating deeds of Lincoln, Kennedy declared, "This Nation, for all its hopes and all its boasts, will not be fully free until all its citizens are free." It was time to end segregation in employment, schooling, and public accommodations, he said, and he sent his draft of the Civil Rights Act to Congress. Although he didn't address the freedom to love, his demand for equal treatment of the Negro must have given Mildred hope.

A mother's love is powerful and the fear that comes with it sometimes excruciating. When Mildred's son Sidney ran into the house to tell her that his brother Donald had been hit by a car while playing in the street, for the endless moments it took to get to him, she did not know whether he was dead or alive. He lived and apparently was not seriously injured. Mildred had had enough of city life, though. Enough of concrete and the dangers of the street for her children. Enough of sneaking around to go to the place she was born and loved. Enough of being arrested and the financial strain of traveling back and forth and perhaps of inconsistent work for Richard. She was done complaining and took her cousin Alex or Laura Byrd's advice. She wrote to Attorney General Robert Kennedy, and the Justice Department put her in touch with lawyers from the American Civil Liberties Union (ACLU).[31]

"Dear sir," she wrote in neat cursive on June 20, 1963, "5 yrs [*sic*] ago my husband and I were married . . . My husband is White, I am part negro and part indian." She capitalized White and did not bother to do so with either strand of her own racial identity. It was probably unconscious on her part. It could mean nothing, or everything, two groups of people reduced to lowercase standing in her mind because she, too, was beaten down. Or perhaps she felt the need to defer to the patriarchal species that ran things, which included her loving husband and the man she was entreating for help, so she used a capital *W* for "White."

Mildred was not a revolutionary. She didn't even expect to win the right to live in Virginia. "We know we can't live there," she wrote, "but we would like to go back once and awhile to visit our families & friends."

"We have 3 children and cannot afford an attorney," she concluded. "Please help us if you can. . . . Yours truly, Mr. & Mrs. Richard Loving."[32]

Bernard Cohen, a young ACLU lawyer in Alexandria, Virginia, took the Lovings' case and was later joined by another young lawyer, Phil Hirschkop. Both attorneys were under age thirty; Hirschkop had only recently graduated from law school. They worked for the Lovings for free and to vindicate their own ideals.[33]

Richard had always hoped that Judge Bazile could be persuaded to reverse course and simply drop the one-year sentence and leave them be. The Lovings quietly moved back to Virginia, renting a house in King and Queen County. Bazile responded to their petition to reconsider with eternal delay. Cohen and Hirschkop filed a class-action lawsuit in federal court to coax him into filing a written opinion that they could appeal. Bazile relented. A few months from retirement, he wrote an opinion that was his last stand for white racial purity. He refused to alter the Lovings' sentence and defended the system that condemned them.[34]

Ironically, Bazile handed the Lovings a gift when he wrote these words in his final order on their case in 1965:

Almighty God created the races white, black, yellow, malay and red, and he placed them on separate continents. And but for the interference with his arrangement there would be no cause for such marriages. The fact that he separated the races shows that he did not intend for the races to mix.

As their lawyers appealed to the Virginia Supreme Court, Mildred and Richard began to speak to the press and find their voices as reluctant agitators. "We loved each other and got married," she told the *Washington Evening Star*. "We are not marrying the state. The law should allow a person to marry anyone he wants." Richard spoke fiercely of his determination and his love: "They said I had to leave the state once, and I left with my wife. If necessary, I will leave Virginia again with my wife, but I am not going to divorce her."[35]

The intensely private pair began to open their lives to reporters, photographers, and a film documentarian, probably because their lawyers told them it might help their case. They even allowed photographers to take pictures of their children, including a shoot for a spread in *Life* magazine. Peggy, Donald, and Sidney usually sported toothy grins, happy kids playing on Virginia soil, oblivious to the stupidity of many adults. In footage, their love shows through, as does the miracle that the family of five could live decently back then on the earnings of a brick mason.

The Virginia Supreme Court voted unanimously to uphold the Racial Integrity Act and its application to the Lovings, although it slapped Bazile on the wrist for banishing them for a quarter century. Again, this law born of eugenic, supremacist obsession with fictional white purity prohibited whites from marrying anyone who had any trace of "non-caucasic blood," with one and only one exception. Whites could marry other whites who had "one sixteenth or less of the blood of the American Indian" and nothing else to taint their whiteness. The act was codified in statutes that declared marriage between whites and blacks unlawful and made it unlawful to leave the state to marry and return to cohabit as husband and wife. In supporting the law, the court cited Virginia's "overriding state interest in the institution of marriage." This outcome was not a surprise.

Three years before the Lovings married, in a case involving a Chinese man and a white woman who had married out of state and returned to Virginia, the court had upheld an annulment of the marriage on grounds that it violated the Racial Integrity Act. In *Naim v. Naim*, the Virginia Supreme Court defended the right of the state to prevent "the corruption of blood," "a mongrel breed of citizens," or "the obliteration of race pride."[36] Despite such overt racism, the

US Supreme Court had declined to review *Naim v. Naim* in all likelihood because the court had already placed its prestige behind *Brown v. Board of Education* and school desegregation and did not want to weigh in on an even more controversial front for race mixing.[37] After a civil rights revolution had blown through the South and bodies were piling up in racial conflagrations from Watts to Boston in 1965 through 1967, the court was less inhibited.

And so the Lovings appealed to the Supreme Court, which agreed to hear their case. Surprised that it had gone this far, Richard was unsure of where it would end. He told Simeon Booker that had they lost, he was prepared to try again in five years. "I'd made up my mind I wouldn't turn back," he said. "I wanted Mildred and was willing to fight for what I wanted." While the Lovings were both motivated to fight for their own liberty and happiness, Mildred had begun to see the importance of their case to others.[38] She told the documentarian that she hoped it would help other people and smiled at the prospect—a reticent warrior queen, surprised to find herself in a position to impact a nation.[39]

As Richard said, the fight continued and was "right rough." While their case was pending and the Lovings were sequestered in King and Queen County, a cross was burned on Mildred's mother's yard in Central Point. Mildred believed it was intended for her and Richard. They would be treated to their own cross burning when they moved back to Caroline County after winning their case.[40]

Their lawyers felt optimistic about their chances with the Supreme Court in part because of what it had done three years before in a case titled *McLaughlin v. Florida*. In Miami Beach, a white woman, Connie Hoffman, lived with her black lover, a Honduran immigrant and hotel porter, Dewey McLaughlin. A few weeks after he had moved in with Hoffman and her five-year-old son, their landlady caught a glimpse of McLaughlin standing stark naked in the apartment as she hung her wash outside. She took umbrage and reported the family to police. Although the case involved criminal penalties against interracial fornication rather than marriage, the court ruled in the couple's favor, rejecting its 1882 precedent in *Pace v. Alabama*. As *Plessy v. Ferguson* had done for segregation laws until it was overturned, the 1882 case had been the precedent that

various states had always relied on when defending their miscegenation laws. In *McLaughlin*, the court jettisoned *Pace*'s logic that
it was constitutional to criminalize interracial sex as long as both
parties received the same penalty. But *McLaughlin* did not reach
laws banning interracial marriage.[41] The court took up that issue in
Loving v. Virginia.

Neither Cohen nor Hirschkop had argued a case before the Supreme Court, although both had received much advice from veteran
litigators at the ACLU and other quarters. In the brief they filed with
the court, they surveyed Virginia's long history of dictating to individuals whom they could love and marry. They emphasized that the
Racial Integrity Act was "a relic of slavery" and "an expression of
modern day racism."[42]

The Lovings did not attend the oral argument, because they did
not want attention. "Tell the Court I love my wife, and it is just unfair that I can't live with her in Virginia," Richard told his lawyers,
who did convey that message to the justices. It helped Cohen drive
home his argument that the state had violated the Lovings' individual rights under the Due Process Clause. Cohen also made arguments
that lawyers for same-sex couples would echo in future cases. He
spoke of the Lovings' right to avail themselves of estate laws and social security benefits and other rights and privileges that redound to
the benefit of children whose parents can marry.

Robert D. McIlawin, an assistant attorney general for Virginia,
argued his state's case. He had lost when arguing before the court
to protect segregation of Virginia's public schools and knew he was
on weak ground. Rather than defend the racist logic animating the
statute, McIlawin tried to paint the state as concerned to protect the
children of mixed marriages. He relied heavily on a 1964 book written by a Harvard social psychologist that included passages about
the "much greater pressures and problems" that arise from interracial unions—a tactic states would try decades later in legal battles
over same-sex marriage. Hirschkop was incensed. He spent his time
during the oral argument on the Equal Protection Clause. Rather
than protecting children, he argued, the Racial Integrity Act violated
the constitution because it was about maintaining a "pure white"
race and controlling and demeaning black Virginians.[43]

Chief Justice Earl Warren assigned the opinion in the case to himself, as he had done for *Brown v. Board of Education*. Warren had been governor of California in 1948 when the California Supreme Court struck down the Golden State's miscegenation law in *Perez v. Sharp*. Andrea Perez, a Mexican American woman, and Sylvester Davis, an African American man, lived in different neighborhoods in Los Angeles and met at work during World War II. The Lockheed Aircraft plant in Burbank hired blacks and women as all hands were needed on the assembly line. Perez and Davis fell in love and, despite the objections of Perez's father, who stopped speaking to her, decided to get married.[44] Perez, an olive-complexioned Chicana, was considered white for purposes of California miscegenation law, first enacted in 1850. The California Supreme Court declared in *Perez* that marriage was "a fundamental right of free men" and could not be restricted by race under the Equal Protection Clause.[45] It was the first state court in the country to make this finding, Warren observed in his opinion in *Loving*. In the same footnote, he hinted at the momentum against miscegenation laws by listing the fourteen states that had jettisoned such laws in the fifteen years leading up to the Lovings' case. He also listed the sixteen Southern holdouts.

Warren may have been influenced by the *Perez* case, but he did not rely on its sweeping rhetoric.[46] Instead, he adopted the lens of history that Cohen and Hirschkop had presented. Warren quoted Judge Bazile's language about God's alleged intention to separate the races, and the Virginia Supreme Court's preoccupation with "mongrels" and "race pride" in *Naim*, apparently to undergird his ultimate conclusion that Virginia's miscegenation law was an instrument of "White Supremacy," he wrote with capital emphasis. "Penalties for miscegenation arose as an incident to slavery, and have been common in Virginia since the colonial period," he continued. "The present statutory scheme dates from the adoption of the Racial Integrity Act of 1924, passed during the period of extreme nativism which followed the end of the First World War." Warren then reasoned that Virginia's miscegenation law was motivated by "invidious racial discrimination" and was therefore unconstitutional.

He cited a series of Supreme Court precedents and stated that the court had "consistently denied the constitutionality of measures which restrict the rights of citizens on account of race." This statement was revisionist: Warren tried to put the best face he could on the court's checkered record, claiming a consistent legacy of equal protection against racism and leaving out the court's long history of sanctioning discrimination.[47]

One of the cases Warren cited favorably was decided in 1943. It involved a Japanese American, Gordon Hirabayashi, who intentionally violated a military curfew imposed on people of Japanese descent. In *Hirabayashi*, the court had said that distinctions of race were "odious to a free people" and then proceeded to uphold the race-based curfew anyway.[48] The court also betrayed Fred Korematsu in 1944, when it said that racial distinctions used to forcibly intern Japanese Americans would be "odious" and then upheld the internment. Korematsu had defied the internment order because he wanted to stay near his Italian American girlfriend.[49] In Korematsu's case, love did not conquer all.

Warren had been attorney general of California and part of the active chorus for internment of Japanese Americans. Perhaps he regretted it and wanted to ensure that the Equal Protection Clause actually would rout out such bigotry in future cases.[50] Warren cited *Korematsu* for the now well-established proposition that racial classifications will be subjected to the "most rigid scrutiny." For Warren, this scrutiny required proof of a purpose independent of invidious racial discrimination.

As governor, Warren had signed the law that repealed segregation of California public schools.[51] As chief justice, he seemed to be trying to steer the republic to eliminate not just the ideologies of the past but also the structures that flowed from them. His opinion in *Brown* suggested such an aspiration, as did another opinion he wrote that was issued two weeks before *Brown*. In *Hernandez v. Texas*, the court declared that it was unconstitutional to try a Mexican American man for a crime while not allowing any Mexican Americans to serve on juries. Warren offered a novel theory. A person singled out by the state for different treatment because of "differences from the community norm" is denied equal protection under the Four-teenth Amendment. So it was with Mexican Americans perpetually excluded from juries in Jackson County, Texas, so it might be today with any fresh brand of othering by the state.[52]

In *Hernandez*, *Brown*, and *Loving*, all unanimous opinions writ-ten by Chief Justice Warren, the court imagined a lot more than color blindness for the equality clause birthed by the Civil War. And so, in *Loving*, Warren was willing to name the white supremacist mean-ing behind the Racial Integrity Act and strike it and all other such laws down. It was a victory for seeing and naming an awful history and eliminating one plank in the architecture of separation.[53] It was easier for Warren to be forthright about Virginia's history, however, than to acknowledge that Virginia's way had once been that of nearly all of America or that the court itself had been complicit in reifying the structures of separation.

When the Lovings got the word that they had won, Richard told Booker, "I just stood there, frozen with happiness. For the first time, I could put my arm around 'Baby' and call her my wife in Virginia." They returned to Central Point, and Richard moved forward with long-held plans to build his bride a house. It was a simple struc-ture made of cinder blocks, each of which Richard laid himself. He built their castle on Passing Road, not far from his parents' and his in-laws' homes.[54]

In Central Point, the Lovings were happy and supported by neighbors and friends. Perhaps the people who burned a cross on their yard were outsiders. Richard told a reporter that they endured hostile stares only when they ventured beyond their hometown. "It makes me want to ask them what the hell they are staring at," he said.[55]

They enjoyed eight more years together, until a drunk driver broadsided the car Richard was driving, killing him instantly and causing Mildred to lose her right eye. Mildred died in May 2008 as Barack Obama, a child of an interracial marriage, was clinching his nomination as Democratic candidate for president. By then, there were over 4.3 million interracial married couples in the country.[56]

PART THREE

· · ·

After *Loving*

CHAPTER SIX

2017

*Interracial Intimacy and the Threat
to and Persistence of White Supremacy*

In 1967, Sidney Poitier appeared in three box office hits dealing
with race, including *Guess Who's Coming to Dinner?* It was everybody's favorite protest movie, released six months after *Loving*
was decided. Young woman, Joanna Drayton, meets older man, John
Prentice, on a holiday in Hawaii, and they fall in love. Ten days later,
as the movie opens, she is bringing him home to meet her wealthy,
liberal parents in San Francisco. She announces their engagement
and is surprised that her parents, who taught her antiracism, have
misgivings about her marrying a black man. By the final scene, Spen-
cer Tracy, who plays Joanna's father, is preaching to Prentice's black
father about love being the only thing that matters, and the would-be
in-laws and interracial couple prepare to sit down to dinner together.

Although the movie was light-years past *The Birth of a Nation*
in its depiction of a black man honorably pursuing a white woman,
Poitier's character, Prentice, was neutered. He was allowed to kiss his
fiancée on-screen only once—in a taxi—and was scripted as impossi-
bly perfect and nearly asexual, a widowed doctor who saves African
children with his research. In one scene, Joanna's mother asks her

directly if she has slept with Prentice. Joanna tells her she was open to premarital sex but saintly Prentice insisted that they marry first and only if her parents agreed to the marriage.

Fast-forward to 2017, and very different cultural fare can be found if one wants to view it in an atomized media market. On large and small screens, a black man is allowed to touch and be intimate with a white woman. The bugaboo, the mere suggestion of which once got black men lynched, may now be a marketing ploy to draw eyeballs. This is not civil rights progress so much as one cultural indicator of a new frontier we have entered. In real and fictional worlds, the state no longer polices whom one is allowed to love, and social barriers to interracial intimacy have fallen dramatically. Most politicians have stopped dog-whistling about interracial sex, although President Trump launched his candidacy by casting Mexican immigrants as rapists. Modern dog-whistling is usually about the issue that underlay miscegenation debates for three centuries: the whiteness of the nation.

White supremacy, invented by slave-owning conquerors of yore to get and retain what they wanted, still exists as the subtext of modern American politic divides. The year 1965 was pivotal not only in unleashing the Voting Rights Act, but also in implementing dramatic immigration reform via the Immigration and Nationality Act. A country that desired to be the world's leader decided to eliminate both preferences for northern and western European immigrants and extra restrictions on people from places replete with color. President Johnson advocated and signed both laws and correctly predicted a white backlash.[1]

Fear about the erosion of white dominance—and the stoking of that fear—explains how people can be motivated to vote against their economic interests and how a billionaire class can replace a planter class in ways that hurt working and poor people of all colors. As the Lovings were fighting their court battles, Richard Nixon's Republicans formulated a Southern strategy that became a national strategy for harnessing white resentment about the changes wrought by the civil rights movement. For decades, both Republicans and Democrats followed this playbook, participating in a cynical, race-coded, "super-predator" politics that, among other things, over-incarcerated high school dropouts of all colors. Like lawmakers of old who squashed rebellions, modern elites also decimated programs and contexts for building solidarity among struggling people. They busted unions and privatized and defunded schools, for example, while also contributing to a toxic polarity in which many struggling white people direct their anger at immigrants and people of color rather than vulture capitalists or the corporate lobbyists that fund both political parties.[2]

Meanwhile, some white people are on a journey of acquiring cultural dexterity through intimate connections and proximity with people of color. The individuals who intentionally decide to walk this road are less likely to fall for dog-whistling and are critical to disrupting ancient racial scripts. Bill Zavarello is such a person. Admittedly, he is a close friend. Were he not, I doubt he would have trusted me enough to spill his guts, for attribution, about his process of acquiring dexterity and becoming an ardent integrator.

Like me, Bill was born in 1961. Unlike me, he grew up in overwhelmingly white, Catholic, and Protestant suburbs of Cleveland. His family members were liberal Democrats. His parents looked up to Martin Luther King Jr. Although his parents understood racism and taught Bill that it was bad, they had no close black friends. There were only three black people at Bill's high school—all football players. He was exposed to a lot more color when he left home to attend Northwestern University.

For a selective school in the early 1980s, Northwestern may have been ahead of its peers in recruiting a critical mass of African Americans. College was the first time that Bill was exposed to that much blackness. He was curious about people from different walks of life—black, Jewish, anyone who diverged from what he already knew—and intentionally sought them out. "I remember sitting down with a black person over dinner or lunch, trying to be open about race, to mixed effect," he recalls. "I didn't know what I was doing. But I knew there was something I needed to know. Out of this experience, I started to get to know and genuinely care about black people."

The next step was trust. "For the first time in my life," he says, "sometime in the middle of my college experience, I had black friends." A white friend who was a musician turned Bill on to jazz and R&B. The music changed everything for him. Soon he had a thirst not just to be around black people but also to understand black culture. He started taking courses in black studies, one of many academic departments born of student protests in the late 1960s. Bill began to have not just black friends, but close black friends. He and one friend became so inseparable that others nicknamed them "Salt and Pepper." He became friends with one of the most militant black men on campus, the president of the Black Student Union. He and Tony would drink and philosophize in Bill's dorm room or Tony's, listening to Earth, Wind & Fire. Tony was the first person to tell Bill: "You need to go to a black frat party. Experience what we experience when we are the only one in the room."

Bill did go to a party with Tony. "And for the first time in my life, I found myself the only white person," Bill recalls. "It felt unusual and uncomfortable at first. But I never felt shunned in those experiences. I would sit at the black table in the cafeteria." In a weird way, his white friends were impressed that he had mastered blackness to such a degree.

Tony changed Bill's life in other ways when he encouraged his white friend to apply for a job with a progressive black congressional representative. Bill landed instead with Representative Barney Frank. The next big step in his journey was coming to "Chocolate City" in 1983. Back then, the nation's capital—which Hamilton, Jefferson, and others "in the room" had located on the Potomac River to soothe the agrarian South—was 70 percent black. Bill has lived in the District of Columbia ever since, later serving as legislative aide to Representative Maxine Waters, a fierce African American progressive.

For Bill, the district was also a place for higher learning. He recalls stopping at a gas station in Northeast DC shortly after arriving in the city and being afraid. "I learned that city life was black life." All of the political and cultural institutions that seemed to matter locally were black—the mayor, the city council, the radio stations that everyone listened to, all chocolate. This dominance of blackness was new, and again he found himself in situations where he was one of the few white people. He started a group house with a black friend. "Now I was smelling chitlins. He was a good cook," Bill says of his housemate.

Bill and his two black and one Latino housemates called themselves "the Rainbow Coalition." By then, Bill was "all in" to the black world, and their house was filled with the tunes of Luther Vandross, Marcus Miller, Al Jarreau. His girlfriends in college had been white. Crossing the color barrier in romance was the next leg of his journey.

Bill frequented a record store in Anacostia, then and still an overwhelmingly black neighborhood that boasts Frederick Douglass's last home. He developed a crush on a dark-skinned black beauty who worked at the register. When he worked up the nerve to ask her for a date, she did not know how to respond. There were too many cultural chasms of race and class between them. What he was asking for just wasn't done in that time and place, and so they never got past a few phone calls.

In time, dating women of color became a normal experience for him, although he has been open to people of all backgrounds. He had a civil union with a woman who self-identified as both black and multiracial. He was also in a long-term relationship with an olive-complexioned Jewish woman who was racially ambiguous, meaning people who observed her often desired to know but could not pinpoint her ethnic heritage.

As a white guy in a then chocolate city, being seen with attractive women of color either as dates or just as friends, he often experienced resentment from black men. In Ohio, his experience was totally different. "What are you doing with her?" was often the explicit or implied response from white people when he took someone home with him. As time marched on, any negative reactions he received became more nuanced. By the 2000s, he sensed that the cultural protectiveness in DC was more about the beauty and voluptuousness of his civil union partner and the incredulity of brothers that she would be with "an average white boy."

In 2016, when I interviewed him, he was dating a black woman with dreadlocks; he had met her online. They had recently spent a weekend in Lancaster, in politically conservative Pennsylvania Dutch country, and had experienced no problems there. Everyone they encountered, including the owner of the cottage they had rented online, was quite friendly, he says. "It has changed in DC too, but we still get looks. There is still a cultural protectiveness." Black women have always been suspicious of his motives but much less so than in the past, he says. "They want to know that I am genuinely interested in them as a person and not just acting on some fetish."

He shares some of the challenges he has faced: "When you are open to dating black women, people say things like 'You want to be black,' or 'You think you are black,' or 'Bill is confused,' but none of those things are true. I know damn well I am not black, but I like black. And when I am really cynical, I will admit that I am not trying to get my ass beat by cops. I know I get to escape some things that I don't want to go through. I admit, whiteness has privileges." He offers the example of a cop once pulling him over for driving while intoxicated and telling him to go sleep it off.

He adds that his former partner says he is "black by persuasion" because there is so much about blackness that he enjoys. But Bill distinguishes carefully between liking black and being black. He is around black people daily in his work and social life, and his cultural references are now quite similar to that of many African Americans. Because his dexterity has become highly attuned, there are days when he finds it easier to relate to a black person than to a white person. The people he is drawn to are more likely to be people of color, and his dating patterns reflect that reality, although he still goes out with white women or anyone else he connects with. His father doesn't understand it, he says, not because his father is racist but because he is not dexterous. "I am so different from almost all of the white people he knows," Bill says of his father.

Other whites in his network take advantage of his dexterity. They come to him with questions they might be afraid to ask a person of color. Sometimes he feels like an interpreter for them of things that happen on the racial landscape. He obliges although he believes everyone must struggle to learn and unlearn.

"The thing about antiracism is that it takes work," Bill concludes. "You don't get to declare yourself unprejudiced. You have to unlearn. And that is true with black people too." He is speaking of the pervasive messaging that values some people, devalues others, and can lead to self-hatred. The ultimate payoff from doing the work Bill alludes to is trust, a space in which two people—Bill and I, for example—can talk about the hard things and there is no white guilt on his part and no filtering on mine.

I offer his example not to suggest that it is common—indeed, people like Bill are rare—nor to suggest that all white people should follow his path. I offer it to show that dexterity born of intimate relations with racial others can be acquired and is being acquired, to varying degrees, by those willing to try.

Segregation is the backdrop that inhibited Bill in childhood and others more recently from having daily contact with people of different races. Most people hew to their tribe when choosing whom to love or befriend. Physical segregation in neighborhoods and schools exacerbates that likelihood. And physical segregation, like the vanquished regime of antimiscegenation, is also a legacy of our nation's multicentury effort to construct and insulate whiteness. The history of orchestration and intention behind physical segregation is beyond the scope of this book but has been told by many.[3] Suffice it to say that the architecture of separation endures, and modern tools like exclusionary zoning and zip code profiling by investors enable current masters of the universe, and others with choices, to insulate themselves from populations they do not want to deal with. A serious lack of dexterity for dealing with out-groups ensues, along dimensions of race and class.

Robin DiAngelo, an antiracism scholar and educator, coined the term *white fragility* to describe "a state in which even a minimum amount of racial stress becomes intolerable, triggering a range of defensive moves."[4] Segregation fuels white fragility. Most whites in America live in majority-white settings. The average white person lives in a neighborhood that is 77 percent white.[5] For segregated whites, their social environment "protects and insulates them from race-based stress," DiAngelo writes. Such insulation "builds white expectations for racial comfort while at the same time lowering the ability to tolerate racial stress. . . . Racial stress results from an interruption to what is racially familiar."

She offers a litany of examples that can trigger stress in a "fragile" or nondexterous white person. Among them: people of color speaking directly about their racial perspectives; receiving feedback that one's behavior had a racist impact; an acknowledgment of racial inequality in America; being presented with a person of color in a leadership role; being presented with information about other racial groups, say, through multicultural education; or watching a movie where a person of color drives the action in a nonstereotypical way. Whites that "have not had to build the cognitive or affective skills or develop the stamina that would allow for constructive engagement across racial divides," she writes, are often at a loss for how to manage the frequently unconscious stress such situations may induce in them. And so they may respond with anger, fear, guilt, defensive argumentation, silence, or a departure from the situation, among other behaviors designed to restore white racial equilibrium.

We don't like to admit that the ideology of white supremacy, constructed and reified for centuries, is still with us in the expectations that many whites have. In a social world in which whiteness is central, where white people have the luxury of thinking of themselves as individuals and never in racial terms, seeing or talking about race is unnecessary and often forbidden, except for intratribal talk about the problems of others. In this sense, people who profess themselves to be color-blind are disingenuous or deluding themselves.

DiAngelo argues that many whites develop a sense of entitlement to remain central and racially comfortable. They can also develop an arrogant belief that their successes are individually earned and be angrily dismissive of other racial perspectives: "The history of brutal, extensive, institutionalized and ongoing violence perpetrated by whites against people of color—slavery, genocide, lynching, whipping, forced sterilization and medical experimentation to mention a few—becomes profoundly trivialized when whites claim they don't feel safe or are under attack when in the rare situation of merely talking about race with people of color."

So if a black friend shares an experience with racism, accepting it as truth may be shattering to a white person's worldview. White people in that situation will often assert their own identity as racially tolerant and may dismiss what their friend is saying, "rather than recognize or change their participation in systems of inequity." When whites do this, DiAngelo concludes, they "invoke the power to choose when, how, and how much to address or challenge racism."[6]

Now consider how this pattern is disrupted when a white person
has developed a love relationship with a person of color. Ardent integrators, someone captured by the power of love, don't have the luxury of invoking that choice if their partner has a different perspective
and they want the relationship to thrive. Love, whether accidental,
romantic, or platonic, may be one of the few inducements to doing
the work of unlearning or of accepting the loss of centrality of whiteness. Love, not mere exposure, can make people do uncomfortable
things, like going home to meet a black lover's family and being the
only white person there.

MARRIAGE AND COHABITATION

I begin discussion of the current status of interracial intimacy in
America with marriage because of the centuries of fuss and fury over
it, though it may be the least impactful form of cross-racial intimacy
in terms of spreading dexterity since relatively few engage in it. More
people marry interracially than in the past, but these unions are a
distinct minority of all marriages. Moreover, fewer people are marrying at all, particularly fewer working-class people. Marriage, and
the picket-fence connotations that came with it in yesteryear, is becoming a luxury of the college educated.[7] In 2010, only 48 percent of
American households were married, down from 78 percent in 1950.[8]
Still, from the lens of history, supremacists lost the battle for white
racial purity in nation and marriage. Ten percent of all marriages
were interracial or interethnic in 2010, up from 7.4 percent a decade
earlier.[9] Three years later, 12 percent of newlyweds married someone
of a different race, and 15 percent of newlyweds married someone of
a different race or ethnicity.[10]

History influences current trends. As whites have never been restricted from marrying Latinos in the United States and there is a
long history of mixing between them in the states that used to be part
of Mexico, marriages between non-Hispanic whites and Hispanics
make up the largest group, more than one-third of "interracial" marriages. These marriages are concentrated in the Southwest. Meanwhile, marriages between blacks and whites make up the smallest
group of interracial marriages, accounting for 1.7 percent of all new
marriages in 2008–2010.[11]

The state with the highest percentage of black-white interracial marriages in the country is Virginia, where 3.3 percent of newly married couples cross the line that generations of supremacists tried so hard to maintain.[12] There is some poetry in Virginia's being first, but there is also a logical explanation. The highest concentrations of interracial marriage in Virginia and elsewhere are near military bases. The American military integrated its units in 1948, stopped "asking and telling" in 2012, and, unlike the retreats and defeats in desegregation in other realms of American life, has continued to fight the battle of integration. Not surprisingly, men and women who serve in the military marry interracially at higher rates than do civilians.[13] Jack McCain, son of conservative Republican senator John McCain, proudly posted pictures of himself and his black wife, Renee Swift, after trolls objected to an online ad from a clothing retailer featuring an interracial couple. Theirs is a mixed marriage in other ways: a Navy lieutenant married to an Air Force Reserve captain. The couple met while both were serving in Guam.[14]

In the 1950s, 0.1 percent of marriages of whites involved a black female and a white male and the same percentage of marriages among whites were between a white female and a black male. By 2000, those percentages had roughly doubled for marriages between white men and black women and quadrupled for marriages between white women and black men.[15] As mentioned, whites are the least likely to marry outside their race, but the trajectory is rising. In 1980, only 2.6 percent of white newlyweds married out, by 2008, 5.9 percent did, and by 2013, 7 percent did.[16] American Indians (58 percent), Hispanics (39.6 percent), Asian Americans (28 percent), and African Americans (19 percent) out-marry at higher rates. Overall, 15 percent of new marriages cross boundaries of race or ethnicity, although rates of intermarriage are higher among Asian American women (37 percent) and black men (25 percent) than Asian American men (17 percent) and black women (12 percent), respectively.[17]

Given the declining rates of marriage, an accurate take on where we are with long-term interracial relationships should include unmarried cohabitants. According to the US Census Bureau, 19.7 percent of cohabiting partners were interracial or interethnic in 2015.[18] While most people cohabit within their own race or ethnicity, one of five cohabiting couples crosses racial or cultural boundaries, although rates vary among races and sexes.[19]

In the market for long-term partners, the United States remains an outlier in terms of the prominent racial barrier between those with visible African ancestry and those without it. Canada, France, Germany, Great Britain, and the Netherlands, for example, all have higher rates of unions between whites and second-generation immigrants of African descent. The boundary between Muslims and white Europeans in European countries, however, is similar to the white-black racial barrier in the United States.[20]

Canada, which never adopted antimiscegenation laws against Afro-Canadians or had much African slavery, provides a pointed contrast. The Great White North is not particularly white in terms of the market for romance. In a comparison of married or cohabiting couples aged twenty-five to thirty-four in metropolitan areas, one study found that 62 percent of black men and 49 percent of black women in Canada have a white partner, compared with 16 percent of black men and 7 percent of black women in the United States.[21]

Interracial love and changing cultural acceptance have been pronounced for same-sex couples. Same-sex relationships are twice as likely to be interracial than opposite-sex ones, with about one in five gay or lesbian couples being interracial or interethnic.[22] *Loving* inspired litigants in the fight to legalize same-sex marriage. Activists believed against the odds and created a movement. The issue was engaged in courts, legislatures, and voting booths across the country for two decades. The Hawaii Supreme Court held in 1993 that the state needed a compelling reason to deny same-sex couples the right to marry, and forces of opposition gathered. By 1996, voters in twenty-five states agreed to amend their state constitutions to limit marriage only to heterosexual couples, and Congress and President Bill Clinton denied federal recognition of same-sex marriages when they enacted the Defense of Marriage Act in 1996.

Leaders in the movement for marriage equality chose to be hopeful and had faith in the rightness of their vision and their strategy to persuade enough Americans. They created a playbook inspired by their analysis of the lead-up to *Loving*: thirty-four states allowed interracial marriage by the time the Supreme Court took up the issue and finally got right what it had gotten wrong in prior cases. The movement's goal was to win enough states and public opinion to persuade the Supreme Court to do the same for same-sex marriage. Movement leaders filed lawsuits in states and launched a campaign of direct education in which millions had conversations to change hearts and minds. Despite being told constantly that they could not win (and they did lose, repeatedly), folks in the movement kept trying and learned how to win. In particular, they learned that connecting the personal stories of love and hardship of same-sex families to core American values was the key to changing minds.[23]

In 2007, when advocates for marriage equality asked Mildred Loving to support their cause, the reluctant agitator allowed this statement to be read on her behalf on Loving Day 2007, the fortieth anniversary of *Loving*:

> I believe all Americans, no matter their race, no matter their sex, no matter their sexual orientation should have the same freedom to marry. Government has no business imposing some people's religious beliefs over others. . . . I am still not a political person, but I am proud that Richard's and my name is on a court case that can help reinforce the love, the commitment, the fairness and the family that so many people . . . seek in life. I support the freedom to marry for all. That's what *Loving*, and loving, are all about.[24]

Law and popular opinion were in dialogue, the one influencing the other. As dominoes fell in particular states, with courts or state legislatures legalizing same-sex marriage, people adjusted to the idea. In 1996, only 27 percent of Americans approved of same-sex marriage. By 2015, the number had grown to nearly 60 percent.

Attitudinal change seemed to accelerate in 2010, approaching the outer reaches of a geometric progression toward the inevitable—acceptance by a dominant majority. Women, younger people, college graduates, single people, and non-Southerners were more likely to adopt modern, inclusive definitions of a family than were men, older people, the less educated, married people, or Southerners. People living in large cities tended to be more accepting than those in rural areas.[25]

Above all, acceptance spread as straight people had *conversations* with someone who was openly gay or lesbian or a straight ally of the cause. One study found that a single twenty-minute conversation with a gay canvasser produced a large and sustained shift in attitudes toward same-sex marriage for residents of Los Angeles County. The magnitude of the shift for the person who answered the door was as large as the difference between attitudes in Georgia and Massachusetts on this subject. Follow-up surveys showed that this change in attitude persisted up to nine months after the initial conversation. The study also showed strong evidence that people transmitted their change of opinion to others living in the household. In a follow-up experiment, researchers found that contact with a canvasser of color coupled with discussion of issues pertinent to the canvasser could also produce a cascade of opinion change.[26] If twenty minutes with a stranger can have such an impact, imagine the influence of actually knowing and caring about a gay or lesbian person.

Skirmishes about same-sex marriage ensued after the Supreme Court's landmark *Obergefell v. Hodges* decision granting same-sex couples the right to marry, mainly in Southern states. But the Constitution is now on the side of gay and lesbian couples that wish to marry, as are a majority of Americans. Those who resist are forced to adapt or accept being on the wrong side of history. This process of exponential growth and spreading of one kind of tolerance, of a concept once strange becoming ordinary, continues and offers hope that other dimensions of empathy will expand with increased intergroup conversation and engagement.

About one-quarter of Americans have a close relative married interracially. This figure does not correlate with income or education; exposure is happening among families of all socioeconomic levels.[27] Although most people do not choose partners outside their race or ethnicity, the nation has grown much more tolerant of other people's desires. In 1987, when Gen Xers were quite young, only 62 percent of them approved of interracial dating. Twenty-five years later, 92 percent of them did, as did 95 percent of millennials.[28] In a 2011 Pew Research Center survey, 89 percent of respondents said that cross-racial marriage was a change for the better or made no difference at all, compared with 11 percent who said it was a change for the worse.

For the most part, older citizens were the ones objecting, while 61 percent of eighteen- to twenty-nine-year-olds said that people of different races marrying each other was a change for the better.[29]

As with same-sex marriage, younger people who were not inculcated in rigid regimes of the state have a different worldview than their grandparents have, although reported attitudes may differ from implicit biases that flash through people's heads when they observe an interracial couple. That is, what people say and what they think may be different.[30] When it comes to nonblack people's attitudes toward black people (the group that, frankly, all nonblacks have the most reluctance to integrate with), opinions have improved and younger generations are also more open-minded. According to a 2009 Pew study, most Americans were "fine" with a family member marrying an Asian American or a Hispanic (75 percent and 73 percent, respectively), but were slightly less so (66 percent) if the theoretical spouse were black. Among eighteen- to twenty-nine-year-old whites, 88 percent were fine with the prospect of a nonwhite in-law, compared with only 36 percent of whites sixty-five and older.[31]

In the future, many more people will act on the openness they profess in opinion polls, because they will not be burdened by the cultural conditioning that their parents and grandparents endured. By 2020, more than half of children in the United States, those under age eighteen, will be Hispanic, black, Asian, or some other nonwhite group.[32] Many children in this country already have a close relative who is married interracially. People who attend diverse schools, for example, are more likely to date interracially.[33]

According to one study, interracial couples (and students who attend well-integrated schools) serve as associational brokers that create connections between different racial and ethnic groups.[34] Whites who live integrated lives tend to be less prejudiced, and those with reduced prejudice, in turn, have a similar worldview to many people of color, that is, they support policies designed to reduce racial inequality.[35] People who attend racially diverse churches, for example, are more willing than those who attend homogeneous congregations to talk about racial issues, to attribute racial inequality to systemic factors, to support policies to help disadvantaged minorities, and to support interracial and same-sex romantic and family relationships.[36]

In sum, the culturally dexterous share a certain headspace that rejects both supremacist thinking and a color blindness in which whiteness is the unspoken norm for all of humanity. Those who think of white people in monolithic terms miss this nuance.

A study of whites married to blacks and other people of color, for example, documented increased understanding of racism. Whites married to blacks were likely to readjust how they conceptualized racial issues, and those married to nonblack people of color were likely to experience a shift in their thinking about immigration.[37] A friend shared a story with me illustrating this phenomenon.

A black man married to a white woman was stopped for "driving while black." Police searched his car, found "a suspicious white powder," and arrested him. His wife saw police officers as good people who serve and protect. She could not imagine them arresting someone with no grounds and asked her husband when she met him at the jail whether he had a drug problem. He exploded, "You *know* me, and you are suspicious? I don't even drink. Of course I have white powder in my car. I'm a contractor!" With the prodding of a costly lawyer, the police offered to clear his arrest record only if the family signed an agreement not to sue the department. The wife came to reinterpret the incident through her husband's lens. It occurred long before the Internet age of viral videos of police shootings of unarmed black men and sent her into months of depression, seeing America through a black man's eyes and now feeling that the police were a threat to her family.

MIXED-RACE PEOPLE AND THE DECLINE
OF THE ONE-DROP RULE

The greatest cultural influence of interracial marriage may be the children these unions produce, although plenty of unmarried interracial couples are also procreating. In 1970, only 1 percent of babies living with two parents were biracial. By 2013, their share had risen to 10 percent. The US Census Bureau projects that if current trends continue, the multiracial population in the United States will triple by 2060.[38] The bureau suggests that these trends may accelerate, so that multiracial people will be the fastest-growing population in coming decades. Pew researchers estimate that 6.9 percent of all US adults have at least two races in their background, including themselves, their parents, or their grandparents. Although this estimate accounts for adults, nearly half of multiracial people in the United States today are under age eighteen.[39] Considering children and adults and projected trends, by 2050, as much as one-fifth of the US population may be multiracial.

How mixed-race people identify themselves varies greatly with the mixture. According to Pew's estimates and survey, about half of mixed-race people in the United States are Native American and white, and only a quarter of them identify as mixed. They appear white to most people, and the vast majority of them self-identify as such. The next-largest mixed-race group is Native American and black, only a third of whom identify as mixed. Most people see this group as black, and most black-indigenous people apparently identify as black. Because these two, partly Native American groups make up 62 percent of all mixed-race adults, and few of them see themselves as mixed, it is not surprising that in the aggregate, only 39 percent of adults with a mixed racial heritage identified themselves as multiracial in a 2015 Pew survey.[40]

Something entirely different appears to be happening with people of black-white and Asian-white heritage. Seventy percent of Asian-whites and 61 percent of black-whites informed Pew that they saw themselves as multiracial. And they self-identified this way, despite acknowledging that large majorities of people probably see them as only one race.[41] An insistent cohort of mixed people has emerged with their own identity apart from categories preordained for them. Dual heritage. Mixed heritage. Mix-d. Hapa. Halfrican. Blewish. Blexican. Mixed people have created new words and phrases to define themselves. And yet, black-white people are more likely than other multiracial folk to see their racial background as an important part of their identity. A majority of them say they feel more in common with blacks than whites and that they feel more accepted by black people than by whites, both in the world and in their extended families.[42]

Multiracial people are not by definition sophisticated about, or interested in, issues of race or racial identity. Journalist Jenée Desmond-Harris, daughter of a black man and a white woman, writes that some multiracial people are the product of a parental philosophy that race should be deemphasized. She also says that biracial people are often forced into thinking about race because of the reactions of others to their racial ambiguity and suggests that it is common to develop special insights from being immersed in different cultures.[43] Like other people of color, multiracial people differ in their degree of interest and experience with race. Many people of color and many mixed-race people gain dexterity simply by living in a country where whiteness is so dominant. They necessarily acquire something akin to the "second sight" or "double consciousness" Du Bois wrote of in *The Souls of Black Folk*. The skill of code-switching, of traversing between cultures, of adjusting one's way of being in majority white spaces and reverting by degrees in other realms to something else— all these practices are forms of cultural dexterity that people of color often acquire.

White mothers of biracial children were in the vanguard of the movement that led the US Census Bureau to allow humans to check more than one box for race in 2000. That year, only 2.4 percent of Americans checked two or more boxes for "race," a category that included five choices: American Indian or Alaska Native, Asian, Black or African American, Native Hawaiian or Pacific Islander, or white. Hispanic origin is labeled an ethnicity on the census, although two-thirds of Hispanics say it is, at least in part, their race.[44]

Mixed people are part of the demographic explosion that is projected to render half of the population nonwhite, non-Hispanic, by 2043.[45] With the freedom to check more than one box for race and the overlay with ethnicity, the potential number of ethnoracial groups tracked by the census is up to 126.[46] The census bureau is currently experimenting with the idea of dropping the word *race* and allowing people to check any "category" that applies to them in a menu that includes the aforementioned five racial groups, along with "Hispanic, Latino or Spanish," "Middle Eastern or North African," or "Some other race, ethnicity or origin."[47]

The mixed descendants of ardent integrators are adding their voices to the American story. Renée Landers, a law professor, has written of her experience as the child of an African American father and a white mother. She was born in 1955 and grew up in a transitional neighborhood in Springfield, Illinois. A railroad track separated the neighborhood from the Old State Capitol Building, where Abraham Lincoln delivered his "House Divided" speech. As she came of age, the neighborhood morphed from middle class and integrated to majority black and economically fragile. Her mother insisted that she write "other" on any official form asking her race because neither black nor white accurately described her.

Despite her mother's entreaties, Landers and her sister formed identities as African American, largely because that was the way the world saw them, she tells me. In a 2012 essay, she argues that *Loving* had not altered "settled societal expectations and practices," one of which was an insistent consciousness of categories and "a collective resistance to the erosion of racial boundaries." When she arrived as a freshman at Harvard-Radcliffe, for example, she was assaulted nearly daily with questions about her race or ethnicity. "What are you?" was the persistent question strangers felt entitled to ask her and other racially ambiguous people well into the 1990s and 2000s.[48]

In a follow-up interview in September 2016, I ask her if the questions have abated. She says they had. When Landers is out with her husband, who is white, she says she doesn't notice looks much anymore. The last awkward comment about her family, she remembers, was when her son was fifteen, about five years before we spoke. "Wow, your family is certainly a walking United Nations," a man had remarked at her son's piano and pennywhistle recital at a suburban music school. Today, interracial pairings seem to be a nonissue among the highly educated people she is usually surrounded by, she says. She lives and works in the Boston metropolitan area.

Her son Nelson, a senior at Harvard, is not assaulted with the "What are you?" question. In his time at Harvard and at a prep school before that, he was never asked the question, although he did have conversations with black students wishing to affirm the African American heritage they correctly discerned in him. Nelson's wildly curly hair and perhaps sharing a first name with Nelson Mandela signal blackness to those with an attuned radar. Most whites experience him as white, he tells me. Depending on the circumstances, he could be white, black, or mixed. His black classmates did not have a problem with his identity as biracial. Nelson's experience, and that of other mixed-race people he has spoken to, he says, is that complicated identities can emerge from the varied reactions they receive from others. A close friend of his is part Asian and part Hispanic and strongly identifies with both cultures. "It is a lot more common [than in the past] for people to accept a degree of racial ambiguity," he tells me, although he admits that some of this tolerance may reflect the highly idiosyncratic diversity of Harvard's campus.

Nelson's observations are consistent with what multiracial people said in the Pew survey. Only a quarter of multiracial adults reported that others are often or sometimes confused about their identity. This happens most for those who are white and Asian American (44 percent); white and black (34 percent); and white, black, and Native American (40 percent).[49] More people, it seems, have learned to stop demanding to know. The mind may desire simplicity, but as hearts and libidos broaden the human spectrum, adherents of one-drop-ism are forced to accept the identities others choose for themselves. Historically, mixed-race people were assigned monoracial identities, typically that of the lower-status group in their heritage. Black-white people in particular faced a great deal of social pressure to identify solely as black.[50]

Mildred and Richard Loving's surviving child, Peggy Loving Fortune, self-identifies as "full Indian," but if students at the school she works at as a teacher's aide ask, she says she is a "rainbow." She married a mixed-race man. Their son strongly identifies with his Rappahannock heritage and performed a ritual of his tribe at the funeral of his uncle, Donald.[51]

I watch Peggy Loving Fortune in a documentary. She speaks wistfully of her deceased parents, and when I close my eyes, I hear an African American's soulful vocal texture and cadence. Her very pale skin and straight hair do not accord with the phenotype associated with blackness. That she identifies as Indian and not African American likely reflects both this reality and her mother's strong identity as Indian.

Some, however, are militant about their one-drop-ism. A biracial law student tells me she stopped participating in the Black Law Students Association (BLSA) because she got tired of being criticized by one of its members for refusing to disavow her white mother and self-identify solely as black. At a BLSA meeting, black folks are in charge, and here, as in any other given homogeneous context, the dominant group decides what the social boundaries will be, sometimes in ways that are quite stark. A white friend who moves in black and Hispanic circles tells me that he could offer five hundred examples, some funny, some not, of being singled out for his whiteness. The lowest common denominator of any homogeneous group often defines the boundary, he says, empowering any objector to criticize a person who does not conform to the dominant norm. Though his white skin has thickened, he says he has learned not to put himself in situations where he might be ridiculed. Relationships with others who vouch for him and trust are his entrée to the black and Latino planet.

Regarding one-drop-ism still extant in the African American community, I understand it. A people oppressed by the rule for centuries embraced it as black became beautiful. For some, one-drop-ism celebrates the excellence, creativity, love, and genius on our side of the line. Tiger Woods, when he was winning and not embarrassing us too much in his philandering pursuit of blondes, was black to us, despite his "Cablinasian" selfhood. One-droppers are also realists, ever cognizant that in certain situations, they, or Tiger, could be just a nigger confronting the barrel of an unhinged cop's gun. They point to enduring segregation and othering of black people. Or they fear that we will be pushed down below a new black-nonblack hierarchy in which lighter people, from pink to brown, really do get to be citizens and African Americans remain denigrated.[52] Whether animated by fear of loss of a culture or of allies, one-droppers cannot blind themselves to the complexity that is emerging. Everyone with a racial ideology in America is being forced to contemplate disruptions that ardent integrators are bringing about, and all of us have to work at adjusting to difference.

ACCEPTANCE AND CHALLENGES

A student of mine tells me a story of a friend who is militantly black but who has a white lover that might even qualify as a boyfriend. The story mirrors the script of a recent movie. This militant black girl is ashamed to bring her white boyfriend around because he does not fit her ideology. She can barely stand her own dissonance, sleeping with the guy at night, agitating against antiblack racism in daylight, upset that the new Jim Crow has disappeared a million black men and limited her probability of snagging a black prince.[53] Reduced numbers are not her only problem. Although most straight "brothas" still prefer "sistahs," the more affluent a black male is, the higher the likelihood that he may date or marry outside his race.[54]

If we are honest, this new trend breaks many black mothers' hearts. She worked so hard to groom a fine young gentleman and hopes he will uplift the race. If he brings home a nonblack partner, one strain of that dream dies. A stratospherically successful black male speaks openly to me of what boxer Jack Johnson said of "colored" women in his biography. For the black man who believes that everyone wants him, black females are perceived as high maintenance and nonblack women can be a lot more accommodating, this black man tells me. This is a lightning-rod claim, but now that social barriers to dating and marrying black men are coming down, this is part of the market dynamic that black females must contend with. Law professor Ralph Richard Banks advises black women to date outside their race to expand their options and perhaps to inspire some black princes to get over themselves.[55] Some sisters are waking up to the wisdom that the only criterion that really matters in love is that their partner cherishes them. The Internet swells with videos celebrating interracial love. In them, I sense that the uploaders are sending a message that black women in particular are beautiful and should be valued, that they can and do find loving partners of whatever color.[56]

Many people adapt. In my own extended family, a cousin, an African American man, married a Jewish woman. Most likely, a husband of another race is not what her parents would have chosen for their daughter, but the love they have for her helped them support her in her happiness and embrace her husband. When a beautiful, brown grandchild came along, they were just as over the moon as any other grandparents. It is a happier narrative than that of many interracial couples of past decades, when a marriage or pregnancy created by a pair of different races became a cataclysmic event. Hettie Jones describes how her father disowned her after she married

LeRoi Jones, later Amiri Baraka, in 1958, the same year the Lovings married. For the crime of marrying a non-Jew and a black man, she was dead to her father. And the marriage did not survive a 1960s black consciousness that put pressure on Baraka and others to disassociate from whites.[57]

I am not suggesting that interracial marriage or mixture in families is now easy or that the world fully accommodates these families. Divorce rates remain higher among interracial marriages than same-race ones.[58] Angela Onwuachi-Willig, a law professor, and her husband, Jacob Onwuachi-Willig, describe "the daily microaggression of having our status as a family assumed away," for example, by a grocery store cashier who looks at a black woman, white man, and children with skin tones in between and still asks, incredulously, "Is this together?" when ringing them up. In public spaces, a stranger would frequently accost one parent or the other with "Is that your child?" They constantly had to plan where to eat, play, or stay in hotels to avoid discrimination and had difficulties locating welcoming integrated neighborhoods in which to live.[59] In 2009, when their essay was published, the Onwuachi-Willigs lived in Iowa. They have since relocated to northern California.

While the challenges are real for interracial families, the ranks of people who accept them with a smile are growing exponentially. Like everyone else with the luxury of mobility in housing markets, people sort by race, income, ideology, and mind-set. With effort, pluralists find one another, although there are trolls in the woods of every state.

MEDIA PORTRAYALS AND INTIMATE VIRTUAL CONNECTIONS

The families I have described are not unlike that depicted in a Cheerios cereal commercial in 2013. A biracial girl with a mop of golden curls and adorable fat cheeks asks her white mom innocent questions about the heart healthiness of Cheerios, then takes what she learns and dumps Cheerios on her sleeping black father's heart. The commercial ends with a single-word sentence brought to a close with a Cheerio period, "Love."

The trolls came out on YouTube, posting nasty comments of "racial genocide" and worse. General Mills, maker of Cheerios, closed

the comment section, and much of the discussion about the controversy focused on the reactionaries. But before comments were closed,
those who clicked an upward thumb to signal their approval of the
ad outnumbered those who disliked it by about nineteen to one.[60]

A year later, General Mills aired an ad during the Super Bowl. In
the commercial, the same father gingerly uses Cheerios to explain to
the same moppet, Gracie, that a baby brother is on the way. Gracie
looks at her father and visibly pregnant mother, then advances another Cheerio on the kitchen table to insist, successfully, that this
family lineup will also include a puppy. Again, more people laughed
and approved than those who choked on hate. Nonfragile, emotion-
ally secure people move on.

Multiracial families have become de rigueur in advertising for
companies that wish to convey that they are open to all customers
or to signal hipness to their brand. Or the companies are playing
racists like a fiddle, benefiting from the free viral publicity their intercultural ads sometimes create when trolls object. The world they
depict—happy, laughing people of different colors and hair textures
having a party, raising glasses as they wear cool stuff, inhabit mod
furnishings, eat from neon plates—is idealized, but some people are
buying it. It is hard to know whether this trend is the beginning of a
new normal or a marketing fad. The Cheerios ads and other unam-
biguous depictions of interracial families are a clear departure from
what was standard even five years ago.[61]

Viewers can now see many interracial couples in dramas and sit-
coms, and this may have contributed to the transformation in public
attitudes about such couples. We have traveled far from 1968, when
Captain Kirk boldly went where no white man had gone before on
television. According to the camp script for episode 65 of *Star Trek*,
sadistic "Platonians," who modeled themselves on Ancient Greeks,
controlled the minds of members of the starship *Enterprise*. The Platonians made Captain Kirk and Lieutenant Uhura kiss against their
will, and they breathlessly suffered through it. It was the first time
on American TV that a white and black person kissed in prime time.
Originally, Spock was supposed to kiss Uhura, but the actor William
Shatner insisted that he wanted to do it. So that studio executives
would be forced to air the kiss, Shatner purposely crossed his eyes in

the tandem, non-kiss version the director shot. The then small band of Trekkies loved this lurch to a new frontier. Others were scandalized.[62] In the South, where miscegenation laws had just been struck down by *Loving*, NBC executives considered blacking out the kiss but ultimately aired it.[63]

By the 2000s, viewers were experiencing an explosion in portrayals of interracial couples on television. A five-week content analysis of shows on major networks in 2004 found that 21 percent of shows portrayed an interracial liaison.[64] That was a year before Shonda Rhimes aired her first multiracial hit show, *Grey's Anatomy*, in which residents and surgeons of different colors and sexualities save lives at a fictional Seattle hospital, depend on one another, and have a lot of sex. The show, currently in its thirteenth season, was groundbreaking primarily because it reflected the lens through which Rhimes, an African American, sees. In her world, successful people of color run things and are three-dimensional, sexual beings.

There are several dimensions of interracial intimacy reflected in the six successful television shows produced by ShondaLand, Rhimes's production company. Four of these shows still air, with impressive ratings and loyal audiences. In ShondaLand, interracial couples are common and some are married: Korean woman and black man; mixed-race black man and white Christian woman; Latina and white man; Latina and white lesbians; black woman and white, wheel-chair-user man; black woman and white man who is president of the United States; black man and white woman; bisexual black woman and white lesbian—the list and combinations go on. Two popular characters, Olivia Pope of *Scandal* and Annalise Keating of *How to Get Away with Murder*, are African American female leads who order their minions of different colors around and drop their panties with white and black lovers a lot more frequently than their real-life or TV mothers would probably prefer. Interracial sex is so common in ShondaLand that any regular watcher surely is inured to it.

Beyond interracial sex, in ShondaLand, people of different colors and sexualities live together, struggle through crises together, argue, eat meals, get drunk, and cry together. For ten seasons, Dr. Cristina Yang, a Korean American, was the "person" of Dr. Meredith Grey, a white American, and vice versa. On air, they shared an emotional intimacy that was as deep as sisterhood, understanding and tolerating each other's irritating neuroses. What characters in ShondaLand did not do was discuss race or racial challenges, at least not directly—a criticism raised by commentators on the interracial relationships that are depicted in television.[65] Rhimes answers that she wanted to make her statement by "making a television show that I wanted to watch and part of that was putting people of all colors in it so that you saw people like you on television."[66]

Another criticism of *Grey's Anatomy* and other shows like it is that interracial relationships are often depicted as hypersexualized, deviant, or dysfunctional. Critics and interracial couples argue that there are "virtually no representations of happily married middle-class interracial couples raising their two children in the suburb."[67] This is a fair point, but most shows with interracial casts are marketed to younger people for whom marriage and suburban child-rearing are increasingly alien lifestyles.[68]

I suspect we will eventually enter a phase of maturity in which depictions of interracial couples are so varied that some get to be mundane. ShondaLand changed the way many small-screen content producers think about casting. American popular culture increasingly depicts a multiracial pluralism. We are not where we should be in the representation of myriad racial and cultural experiences, but diverse representations are increasing and perhaps accelerating. Many outlets feel pressure, as they should, to reflect people who had been here for centuries or a while, contributing to the American story—people who are no longer willing to hide in plain sight.

The explosion continues, with more variation in presentations of interracial couples and less insistence that one of the partners always be white. An article about interracial couples depicted on television and streaming services in 2015 mentioned nineteen shows and highlighted favorites. The hugely popular African American character Cookie of the hip-hop drama *Empire* has a Latino boyfriend, and fans are hoping that her black gay son, Jamal, gets back together with his Latino lover. *Empire*, conceived and produced by Lee Daniels, who is black and openly gay, also pushes the envelope in normalizing gay and bisexual liaisons of all flavors. It is the top-rated show for the Fox network. In *Master of None*, a show that itself deals with issues of representation of South Asians, the character Dev, after dating many white women, falls in love with Rachel, played by an actress of Latina and Tunisian descent. In other shows, characters paired with whites include a Chinese American, a Filipino American, a Vietnamese immigrant, and, in a sci-fi drama about global characters who share a psychic connection, a black trans woman. The interracial relationships on television vary from innocent first love and a cartoon aimed at children, to nonsexual, unconsummated flirting, to soft porn.[69]

Whatever critics may think of these shows, the depictions help spread dexterity. Social psychologists have documented that extended contact with fictional black-white interracial couples portrayed in media was associated with more positive attitudes toward black people and interracial relationships.[70] Similarly, social psychologists have validated a phenomenon labeled *parasocial contact*, in which a viewer, exposed to a positive portrayal, fictional or otherwise, can develop such a level of emotional intimacy or affective ties with a member of a minority group that he or she becomes less prejudiced. Coming to know and like a fictional character or, say, a black president of the United States through years of parasocial contact can be particularly transformative for a viewer who has limited real-world contact with a minority group. Exposure to gay characters on television has been shown to reduce prejudice toward gays, for example.[71]

In contrast, many, though not all, who opposed our real-life black president, Obama, seemed to exhibit the fragility DiAngelo theorized. Perhaps nothing in US history upset white centrality more than an African American rising to the presidency. The accusations that he was born in Kenya, that he was a terrible student at Harvard when he graduated magna cum laude and was president of the law review, the "you lie" disrespect at his health-care speech to Congress, the epic obstruction and vilification of him, this and more seem of a piece with the defensive, angry efforts to restore white equilibrium that DiAngelo describes. Meanwhile, Obama's supporters empathized with him as he faced obstruction, time and again. Through him, blackness was humanized. Many developed an intimate parasocial relationship with a black man for the first time in their lives.

They would testify online to the love or admiration they felt for him, and by the end of his time in office, many had grown quite comfortable calling obstruction of him racism.

DATING AND MATING

People of a certain age use the term *dating* to describe the rituals of courtship. It may not be an appropriate word for the highly varied mating rituals of teenagers and young adults. Some do date in the traditional fashion associated with the word. Others hang out in groups, content to avoid the social pressure of a one-on-one encounter, or the awfulness of a dinner with an inept conversationalist. Others experiment with hookups and casual sex. Most single people under age thirty probably have had experiences along this spectrum and have strong opinions about whether the economy and technology degrade or enhance their possibilities. For all the criticism of them by older generations, millennials do form relationships and are more open to crossing racial and ethnic boundaries in romance and sex than their elders are.

This phenomenon appears to transcend class. Among adolescents, for example, socioeconomic status seems to have little effect on whether one will date interracially, except in the case of Hispanics. Hispanic teenagers of higher socioeconomic status are significantly more likely than their poorer counterparts are to participate in interracial dating.[72]

Men are more willing than women to date interracially. In a survey conducted in 2008, about half of white men said they are willing to date and marry black women, compared with 38 percent of white women who said they were willing to date and marry black men.[73] Studies about online platforms are a window onto the extent of interracial dating. Nearly four in ten singles in America in search of a partner use dating websites or mobile applications.[74] Social scientists have studied the website OkCupid because it released data regarding interracial interactions on its site. The proportion of members who said in their profiles that they preferred to date only people of their race declined from 43 percent in 2008 to 33 percent in 2014.

Indicating openness to interracial contact is one thing, but actually having such interaction is another. In contacting and rating others on the site, most men and women preferred members of their own race, and this underlying behavior did not change between 2008 and 2014. Whether black, white, Asian, or Latino—the only categories measured—all groups most preferred their own. A survey of data from Match.com and DateHookup.com found nearly identical results.[75]

In the United States, black men and women received the lowest rankings from nonblack members of OkCupid and roughly 75 percent of the attention white members experienced. As with interracial marriage and cohabitation, the story differed in other countries without a long history of black slavery and antimiscegenation laws. In the United Kingdom, OkCupid's black members receive messages from white members at about 99 percent of the frequency that whites do. In Japan, that number is 97 percent; in Canada, 90 percent. Multiracial people who indicated they had some white heritage fared better in the United States than those indicating they were solely black, Asian, or Latino. This "bonus effect" for multiracial daters has been found on another, unnamed website.[76]

OkCupid members are generally reluctant to initiate cross-racial contact by sending a message to a user of a different race. But if a member *received* a message from a user of a different race, the recipient was much more likely to send a cross-racial message of his or her own. The authors of this study speculate that one reason people resist cross-racial encounters online is fear of rejection from members of other races. At least in the short term, their horizons appear to expand when someone of a different race reaches out to them. This effect was observed with all of the groups studied, but the effect was particularly strong for Asian women and men and black women.[77]

In the dating cybersphere, whites show the strongest disinclination to contact users of other races. In one study, 85 percent of whites' messages went to other whites while only 3 percent of their messages were sent to blacks. Only 45 percent of messages sent by black men and women were sent to other blacks, while 37 percent of their cross-racial messages went to whites. Black males were the least likely to adhere to their own race, whereas white women displayed the strongest same-race affinity.[78] Whether out of sheer in-group preference, fear, or lack of dexterity, most members of these dating sites still date within their own race, even as acceptance of those who cross boundaries spreads.

Numerous websites and mobile apps cater to people intentionally seeking partners of a different race or ethnicity. Those who have that preference may go directly to interracial dating websites like Afro-Romance.com, which boasts eighty thousand members; four other sites have between ten thousand and twenty thousand members.[79] Although these numbers are dwarfed by the membership of general-ist dating websites, the growing market of interracial daters was un-fathomable before *Loving* was decided. A survey conducted in 2000 found that nearly one-fourth of college students reported having dated interracially and almost half expressed an openness to become involved in an interracial relationship.[80]

And so interracial intimacy and its multiplier effects accelerate on varied fronts, including dating. What was true even five years ago doesn't accurately describe the here and now. As I write this chapter, it is becoming outdated. Norms for intimacy—parasocial, between sheets, and among friends who used to be strangers—are changing rapidly, as are standards of beauty. Whiteness is no longer the defin-itive archetype for what is alluring or desirable. Lupita N'yongo, a Kenyan-Mexican actress, won an Oscar for her sensitive portrayal of an oft-raped slave in *12 Years a Slave* and a Tony for her part in the Broadway drama *Eclipsed*, which featured an all-black, all-female cast. Lupita, of short natural hair and silky ebony skin, was declared the most beautiful woman by *People* magazine and was the new face of luxury cosmetics for Lancôme, Paris, in 2014.

Naysayers who have made careers critiquing the color line and its many manifestations will point to the hordes of intolerant folks who still see black as ugly as evidence that I overstate my case. My claim is modest but potentially radical. Through intimate experience, an emerging class of whites has come to value, and sometimes even love, black people and other people of color. They are not disman-tling white supremacy so much as chipping away at it.

Hooking up, on the other hand, is intentionally devoid of emo-tional intimacy. Interracial sex, like any sex, does not necessarily come with commitment or caring by the people engaging in it. That said, with the fear of black male sexuality apparently dissipated, something new is going on, especially among the young and libidinous.

A white gay friend of mine who is in a long-term relationship with a black partner tells me that he believes many whites now feel compelled to try interracial dating or sex, "just once, nothing serious," he jokes, perhaps because it was off-limits for so long. A black female college student tells me that there is a pronounced hook-up culture at her very diverse university and that interracial liaisons are part of the menu of sexual exploration. "I had my first black guy last night," she recalls one of her white sorority sisters telling her.

I am amazed that this black student is a member of this traditionally very white sorority. I attended Vanderbilt in the early 1980s and my (admittedly stereotypical) image of this sorority is a blond woman from Texas wearing pearls and preppy clothes and thoroughly ensconced in an all-white social world. That she might be hooking up with a "black guy" or that the sorority now accepts black sisters or that some "sistahs" are joining this group instead of, say, Delta Sigma Theta, a venerable black sorority, makes my black boomer head spin. An Asian woman student at Harvard writes of white males with "yellow fever," who objectify and fetishize Asian women and their bodies and seek them out for dating and sex.[81] The Google images that accosted me as I searched the Internet for social science on interracial sex at colleges made me blush and long for more circumspect times. The interracial sexual revolution has been posted, for all to see.

CHAPTER SEVEN

More Loving

Families and Friendship

A parent adopts transracially and has to see and internalize systemic institutional racism and must sometimes accept the helplessness of not being able to do anything about it. Sharon Rush, a law professor at the University of Florida, wrote of this awakening. It took years "of living in an intimate mother-daughter relationship with a Black child for me to uproot my own White liberalism," she writes.[1] She means the tendency of whites "of goodwill," as she phrased it, to believe that they themselves are not prejudiced and therefore to be much less willing to entertain the possibility that racism may be operating in themselves or other people in any given situation.

She began to keep a journal, writing down the stories that boggled and depressed her. A liberal academic who wrote about race and actively fought for racial equality had no idea how pervasive racism was until she began parenting Mary, a biracial African American girl. Rush published the stories in a book in hopes that the world would see, internalize, and ally with children of color.

In one episode, a softball coach surreptitiously held Mary back at the start of a footrace against a white teammate and invited the child to quit the team when she challenged him on why he did it. A white woman in an airport waiting area accused Mary, then age six, of stealing her purse when the woman had left it with the ticketing agent. At Mary's public school, the principal was white, as were almost all the teachers and staff. The main representation of black adults was the janitors. Rush was appalled as she thought about what messages this would send to her daughter. She soon learned how few allies Mary had at the school.

Rush soldiered through a Kafkaesque ordeal to get Mary placed in the gifted class. She paid for a private firm to test Mary, as the school recommended. Yet even after Mary met the advanced IQ threshold on the standardized test, the school insisted on observing her for six weeks and seemed to add more procedural requirements at every turn. No one within the school advocated for Mary. Rush was on her own and only after she invoked her child's right to a formal hearing did Mary finally become the only black child to be placed in the gifted class to which she was assigned.

The new teacher greeted Rush coldly, but Mary liked the more challenging work. When Dinosaur Day arrived, the proud families were invited to watch the children make presentations about the particular dinosaur they researched. When Rush and her own parents arrived, she was alarmed to find Mary seated in a corner by a storage closet, literally segregated from the rest of the class by a four-foot laboratory desk that made it impossible for the others to see Mary and for Mary to see the rest of the class. Rush confronted the teacher, asking whether her daughter had been placed there as a punishment for something she had done. The teacher invoked space limitations as the reason. Rush could see from the available space in the room that her answer was disingenuous. She did something she had never done before in her years of parenting Mary when questionable incidents arose. She told the teacher that isolating her daughter was "cruel" and "racist." The teacher deflected, became upset, but ultimately moved Mary next to other children in the classroom, where the child desperately wanted to be.

Mary's grandfather was also incensed. "Well, I guess they still have segregation here in the South," he said when they returned home. "What was her teacher thinking about treating her that way?" The older man and woman, who were normally quite temperate and judicious as grandparents of a black girl, vented their anger for days, telephoning their other daughters to relive the awfulness. The silver lining in the experience, Rush notes, was that her supportive parents had witnessed firsthand an incident that was similar to others she had reported to them and they finally internalized their granddaughter's pain.

"The racism hurt them directly," Rush says, "[and] helped my parents understand in a different, much deeper way what their granddaughter goes through on a daily basis. . . . [W]hen White people feel some of the pain of racism, I believe that they become stronger allies in the struggle for racial equality. I wish we had more allies . . . my heart ached for my daughter and all the children of color in this world."

Rush developed coping skills that remind me of what black strivers and agitators do. She moved her daughter to a racially diverse university laboratory school and again had to advocate for her daughter to become the one black child in her gifted class. Through years of effort, Rush learned to live with awareness of race and its pernicious effects without allowing this knowledge and experience to depress her daily. She turned to spirituality and continued her activism for her daughter and other children. She also willed herself to remain hopeful. She called on others to develop an authentic interracial relationship built on empathy, in which both parties have equal dignity and are valued for who they are racially or ethnically. If they are lucky, they will experience the transformative love Rush describes in her journey with her daughter. In these relationships, she concludes, whites might also gain a place of trust where they can talk about race, ask questions without judgment, and join the struggle for racial equality.[2]

Rush's awakening and the events she shared occurred in the 1990s. She and Mary and families like theirs probably have more allies now even as racial discrimination continues. For all the controversy that has surrounded it, transracial adoption has become normal—that is, accepted—in American culture. White adoptive parents tell stories about receiving cheers or blessings from African American strangers for adopting a black child domestically.[3] Responses vary, but overall black public opinion supports it, as do most Americans.[4]

Such general acceptance was not always the case. Before 1950, domestic transracial adoption was quite rare in the United States. During the American Indian Movement, indigenous nations protested transracial adoption of Indian children. They repudiated a social experiment in which whites became parents to about seven hundred Indian children between 1958 and 1967. Congress responded by enacting new federal protections to give first priority to tribal custodial arrangements. As the Lovings were fighting to add themselves and other ardent integrators to the institution of American marriage, indigenous nations were fighting to keep their people and sovereignty from being dissolved into the so-called melting pot.

Like the Lovings, black people in the civil rights movement fought to be included, and in the zeitgeist of integration, some whites opened their minds to new possibilities. By 1971, some 35 percent of adoptions of African American children were transracial. Because housing was segregated, when a well-meaning white family adopted a black child, the adoptive parents often brought him or her into their white environment and continued with their usual practice of not thinking about race. For the child, it was classic assimilation to a white, middle-class culture, and parental love was not enough to overcome inevitable challenges.

As adults, transracial adoptees of that era told interviewers that they suffered racism, lacked ethnoracial role models, and felt disconnected from the racial or ethnic community of their birth.[5] Robert O'Connor was raised by a white family in Rush City, Minnesota, a small town with few other black people in it. He became an academic who studies transracial adoptions and told a *New York Times* reporter that he felt awkward around other blacks as a youth. He didn't understand black fashion and music, even as they were ascending in American culture. He was mystified by black cultural traditions like playing the dozens, in which trading insults is an oral art form. "I always felt like I had this 'A' on my forehead, this adoptee, the people could see from a far distance that I was different," he says.[6] It may not have been every black adoptee's truth, but it was his and that of others. Children of other races and ethnicities with dark skin placed in a white family and very white environs also reported problems.[7]

Famously, in 1972, the National Association of Black Social Workers (NABSW) took a "vehement stand against the placement of Black children in white homes for any reason." The association and other critics of the practice were outraged at the forced racial assimilation involved and the idea that white people, who never had to endure antiblack racism, would be raising children without teaching them these skills. Dashiki-wearing, Afro-ed black folk of that era affirmed the blackness that America had devalued for centuries. Other groups, like the National Urban League, also supported race matching in adoption. Adoption scholars and agencies concurred and many would-be parents turned to international adoption. As transracial adoption of black children plummeted, international adoptions accelerated nearly 200 percent after the contretemps. Because half of the children languishing in foster care were black, critics of race matching began to gather force to change adoption policy.[8]

In 1994, the NABSW reaffirmed its view that transracial adoption was not in the best interest of black children. The association underscored its original position that not nearly enough was being done to preserve black families and eliminate barriers to black families in the adoption process. It sanctioned transracial adoption only as a last resort. That same year, however, the NABSW lost that policy battle when Congress passed the Multiethnic Placement Act (MEPA), largely in response to the frustrations of white parents trying to adopt black children domestically. With the exception of Native American children, the act, as amended in 1996, requires *color blindness* on the part of any adoption agency that receives federal funds. As with *Loving*, another legal barrier to interracial love was eliminated. Social barriers are also eroding, although in the adoption market, like the dating market, black Americans sit at the bottom of a still-extant racial hierarchy.

Transracial adoption of African American children has increased only moderately since MEPA was enacted. In the 2000s, adoption of black domestic youth declined slightly even as adoption rates rose for Hispanic, white, and multiracial children born in the United States. African American children are the least likely to be adopted; other children are seven times more likely to attract interest.[9] Some of this discrepancy may be due to the large number of older black children in foster care. In 2015, nearly one hundred Canadian, Dutch, Irish, German, and English citizens came to America to adopt black children.[10] Whatever forms of othering may be going on in their countries, they are not infected with American antiblack bias that coursed from Virginia's legal codes in the seventeenth century through the supremacist regimes of later ages to the subconscious of far too many Americans in the twenty-first.

Some whites interviewed by researchers about the lack of willingness to adopt African American children frankly admitted that while they were open to adopting a child of color, they perceived domestic black children as "too different" both physically and culturally. For some, it was pure stereotypical devaluing of American blackness and an acknowledgment of antiblack prejudice in their own extended family. Others perceived African American culture as more foreign and inaccessible to them than, say, Chinese, Korean, or Guatemalan culture. They either devalued black American heritage or were mystified at the prospect of learning and socializing a black child to it. As half of the people in this study came from Vermont, I understand why they might have found black Americans foreign. Others lacked confidence that they had the seemingly supernatural powers required to raise and protect a black child. They looked out on American society and shuddered at the potential obstacles that their hypothetical black child would face and the cultural chasms they would be forced to bridge. It was just too much to contemplate, more work than they were willing to take on. These largely white, college-educated people knew full well the long, deep, seemingly inexorable problem of black-white relations in the United States and, like the NABSW, doubted their cultural competence. Or they simply wanted to avoid that miasma.[11]

Meanwhile, American pilgrims fly to African countries in the sincere though sometimes misinformed belief that they are adopting a destitute orphan.[12] In the mid-2000s, when evangelicals, including megachurch pastor and author Rick Warren, launched a movement for worldwide adoption of orphans, parishioners answered the call. As many as a thousand churches participate annually in national Orphan Sunday. The faithful attend adoption conferences and take seriously a new theology that likens the adoption of babies to God's adoption of Christians. Other motivations also propel the movement. Some leaders and parishioners believe that this adoption movement is the perfect complement to their anti-abortion views. Others see it as a means for spreading the gospel globally, embodying their evangelical mission. Some pastors cast the movement as a means of racial reconciliation. In a resolution encouraging adoption, the evangelical Southern Baptist Convention suggested that this new "adoption culture" reflected "a gospel of oneness that is determined not by 'the flesh,' or race, or economics, or cultural sameness" but by Christian spiritual unity.

Russell Moore of the Southern Baptists has equated the orphan adoption movement with the civil rights movement and acknowledged that his denomination had been on the wrong side of history in the 1960s. He advocates adopting transracially as a means for his denomination to atone for its past failings and to diversify historically white evangelical churches. Critics point out the ironies of "mass adoption of black children into white churches that, just a generation ago, defended segregation." Author Kathryn Joyce argues that many Southern Baptist churches import diversity solely through adoption of children from other countries, with little effort to attract adults of color to join their congregation or to directly challenge systemic racism their children may face.[13]

Perhaps because of the orphan movement, adoption of children from Africa has increased dramatically, rising from 1 percent of international adoptions in 1998 to 30 percent by 2012.[14] Ethiopia rose to become the second-most popular country for international adoptions, behind China in 2009, after Guatemala closed its door to international adoption. This trend upends race scholars' claims that America will always place dark black bodies at the bottom of racial hierarchy.[15] Perhaps it would be more accurate to predict that black Americans will remain at the bottom of the racial hierarchy in American adoption for the foreseeable future. And yet adoption of black American children might rise in the coming decades as more people get used to seeing others do it, as younger generations feel less cultural distance from African Americans, and as adopting parents wish to take advantage of the often cheaper expense and shorter wait times for adopting black children domestically.[16]

Celebrities like Sandra Bullock and Charlize Theron, both of whom have recently adopted black children domestically, may also be popularizing this choice.

With many countries tightening controls on adoption, international adoption has declined by more than 60 percent in recent years, perhaps explaining the rise in domestic adoptions of Hispanic and biracial children. In 2004, 26 percent of these children were adopted transracially, almost all of them by white parents. In 1998, that number was 14 percent.[17] As with other forms of interracial love, we are on a trajectory to something new. An emerging class of ardent integrators is diving into cross-racial parenting, and acceptance by society of multiracial families of choice is easing their journey.

Today, transracial adoption is part of our everyday existence. One can spy a pale adult holding the hand or small body of a black, brown, or yellow cherub not only in a dense metropolis but also in many Southern Baptist churches. The phenomenon transcends red- and blue-state mind-sets, and although religious and personal reasons for it vary greatly among adopters, those choosing transracial adoption often invoke the word *love* as the potent emotion involved.

According to the 2010 census, about 28 percent of all adopted children in the United States are placed with a parent of a race different from their own, up from 17 percent in 2000. About 10 percent of adopted children are in a Hispanic/non-Hispanic pairing. Four in ten adoptions in America cross boundaries of race, ethnicity, or culture. About seventy thousand black and forty-two thousand black-white biracial children are living with a nonblack parent. The combined numbers of children with African or African American ancestry placed with nonblack parents are only slightly lower than the number of Asian children living with a non-Asian parent.[18]

Younger families, lesbians, and people who perceive their own neighborhoods as more diverse than others are among the nonblack people who are more likely to adopt an African American child. People who give child-centered reasons for adoption as opposed to adult-centered reasons are also more likely to adopt transracially. Some lesbian adopters who have experienced family rejection or othering because of their lesbianism have informed researchers that these experiences led them to seek out children perceived as undesirable by society. Same-sex couples are more likely than opposite-sex couples are to adopt transracially, in part because the couples themselves are more likely to be interracial. One study involving 106 families found that most same-sex couples adopted transracially while most opposite-sex couples did not.[19]

Walking down Fourteenth Street in Washington, DC, I observe a white gay couple with their black princess daughter. She sports manicured braids and an impressive outfit. This princess and her two dads look like a happy, well-adjusted family to me. They remind me of another family at my children's school, also white gay dads raising a black daughter. They smile a lot and seem to bring a bemused spirit to the adventure of parenting. In them, I sense a child-centered effort to bridge cultural differences. Such race consciousness bodes well for them.

When a new biracial or multiracial family is created through adoption, whether the parent is ready for it or not, the adult should have racial dexterity or be willing to acquire it. Social science research suggests that color blindness is a recipe for damage.[20] Eventually, parenting and loving a son or daughter of a different race forces the adult to see race and racism.

A clerk at a McDonald's calls security when a black teenager reaches into the purse of his white adoptive mother. A black third-grader cries when looking at congratulation cards sent to her white mother when she was adopted. The mother had never noticed that all the children on the cards were white until her daughter exclaims, "Was I supposed to have been white?"[21]

An evangelical pastor says that the biggest challenge he has at his church is mothers coming to him for advice on how to deal with racism in their extended families and elsewhere against their children. Some are waking up to the reality that their Ethiopian son could be Tamir or Trayvon and are grasping for emotional support and other resources to deal with it. Moore writes of their difficulties: "I've seen young couples in tears on the couch in my office, asking how they can love their first child and honor their father and mother at the same time. I've seen family members of every race and every region of the country turn up their noses at the idea of a niece, nephew, or grandchild of another ethnicity, usually with some highly spiritual rhetoric."[22] Dan Cruver, of Together for Adoption and a leader in the orphan adoption movement, is white and himself the father of two black boys. Cruver posts an interview with the African American pastor of a robustly multicultural congregation. The questions are pointedly race conscious and must be born of his own experience and those of other adopters. He asks J. B. Watkins of the St. Roch Community Church in New Orleans about the importance of white parents connecting their black children to the black community, how different-race parents can help their adopted children deal with racism, and the problems for transracially adopted children with living in a "nonintegrated" neighborhood.[23]

The white mother of a Vietnamese-born daughter learned how difficult it can be to convince a brown, almond-eyed girl that she is pretty. Her daughter liked dolls with blond hair and blue eyes. She told the *Washington Post*: "When she draws herself, she gives herself red hair and blue eyes. . . . No matter what we do to show her that beauty comes in all shades, she's already picked up that it's best to be white and blond. It breaks my heart." Among the strategies to counter this perception, the family hired a Vietnamese babysitter and filled their home with books and toys that celebrate nonwhite cultures. They also enroll their daughter annually in a Vietnamese culture camp, where she can immerse herself in the customs of her birth country and meet other Vietnamese adoptees who relate to the multiplicity in her life.[24]

Other parents who adopt transracially are taking the advice of adoption counselors to create a community that looks like their multiracial family, one with adult friends as well as children of their child's heritage. One couple going through the adoption process considers moving to a neighborhood with more black professionals and joining a more integrated church. Others maintain a relationship with birth mothers. Another family bonds with a black family that adopted the siblings of their child. Other families adopt additional children that have the racial heritage of their first child.[25]

A friend of mine—I'll call her Sharon—is a white adoptive mother of two African American children. She is European American, the daughter of a Swiss father and an American mother, and is married to a white Spaniard, whom I will call Juan. After having a biological son, they decided to adopt to expand their family, telling the agency they were open to adopting a child of any color. One day, the phone rang. The agency said that a biracial baby boy, the son of a black mother and a white father, had been left with the agency unexpectedly on a day when the mother got overwhelmed by her inability to get formula for him. Sharon and Juan took him in, and through some nervous days, the birth parents approved of them. Their son, whom I'll call Thomas, is a red-brown boy who looks like his African American birth mother. Later, Sharon and Juan were motivated to adopt another African American child, a girl, because they didn't want Thomas to feel isolated. My own sons and their sons are playmates, and our families have spent many happy hours together—adults sharing meals and laughs about the challenges of parenting as children tear through our homes. Regular sleepovers between our families give one set of parents a retreat from exhaustion.

Our closeness enabled honest sharing, often about what to do with curly African American hair. Sharon once confided that she felt utterly unprepared to answer young Thomas's innocent question, "Mommy, why were all the slaves black?" The questions persisted. Thomas envied his older, white brother and even ventured that the big brother was "so lucky" to be white. Slavery, a subject covered at Thomas's very diverse public school, was perhaps his first awakening to a profound difference about blackness in this country. He gets embarrassed and uncomfortable when the subject of the Civil War and slavery arises. As the mother of black sons, I have had similar dilemmas about how to explain slavery and the many sad stories that suffuse African American history. I share my rhetorical strategies with Sharon, the little black lies I told my sons when they were young—"That was in *old* times. It's much better now."

Having Barack Obama as the first and only president my sons ever knew helped present a fairy-tale version of American progress to them. That and our keeping the radio and television off most of the time enabled them to have a childhood and believe the shibboleths that we would like to be true for America. I tell Sharon how my husband and I deprogrammed one of our sons who, at age three, claimed he was not black but "honey" and clearly thought there was something wrong with black. We bought picture books about inspiring black men, Matthew Henson, Muhammad Ali. Ali's poems and "I am the greatest" self-love helped more than any other role model did. Barack Obama. Martin Luther King Jr. Langston Hughes—his I, too, singsong rhymes resonated at age four, five, and six. We read about Bass Reeves, a black deputy US marshal I had never heard of. He escaped slavery, lassoed bulls, and was very good at finding and, when necessary, shooting outlaws in Native American territories.[26]

My husband and I talked to our sons a great deal about the proud, striving people they descended from, the fact that their grandparents and great-grandparents were involved in the fight for black freedom. We also never missed an opportunity to point out the accomplishments of their parents and ancestors. Our boys head off to school in shirts emblazoned with their parents' alma maters—Harvard, Vanderbilt, Berkeley. It is cheap elitism, a guerrilla tactic that works, even for my black husband, who notices how much better he is treated, how fewer women cross the street to avoid him, when he wears the crimson *H* on his chest. As we read to them and shared, I tell Sharon, eventually I saw a smiling confidence, even a sense of superiority about being African American emerge in my sons.

They are ten now, and we shield them less from adult discussions about current racism. The "talk" about how to avoid getting shot by a police officer will come later, when they have lost the cuteness of boyhood. Sharon and Juan are very racially aware, and when the time comes, they will no doubt be capable of giving the talk to Thomas, in their own way as parents who love him with all their hearts. Above all, Sharon and Juan have fully absorbed the terror that parents of black boys in America live with—the dread that no matter what we do for our sons, someone who carries the insanity of supremacy in his head, the inability, say, to listen to a black boy's preferred music, will start shooting.

Juan tells me that through parenting black children, he has developed a strong affinity for African Americans and enjoys talking to the many he encounters who marvel at his "beautiful family" and pass on friendly advice. He is drawn to their spirit and, as a foreigner with an accent, relates to the outsider status he perceives is being assigned to his children. He has developed a genuine friendship, one of "love," he says, with Thomas's birth mother and grandmother and feels a powerful empathy for disadvantaged black people. "I never saw ghetto poverty before," he says. He is aware of the chaos and struggle in the birth mother's life. She gets a job, loses it, lands in jail, gets out, repeats, yet she is constant in keeping up with how Thomas is doing. "It is just not true that poor black people don't want to do better," Juan says, his voice rising. He speaks of the sheer deprivation of the neighborhoods his children's families come from and how clueless so many people are about what residents of ghettos face.

Sharon also shares with me a story about how her father was forced to evolve when he acquired black grandchildren. Initially, he resisted forming a relationship with Thomas. He suggested that they send only their biological son to visit his grandpa in Switzerland. When Sharon informed her father that she and her husband intended to adopt a second black child, he wrote a four page, single-spaced letter arguing against it, stressing the economic costs and pragmatic challenges of a third child. A year passed, and a girl-cherub joined the family.

This child uses her dimples and smile as a weapon against any cold heart. Eventually, Grandpa relented and agreed to go on a trip with the family to Disneyworld in Florida. By the end of the week, he had fallen in love and was constantly demanding to have his granddaughter sit on his lap. A space opened in his heart for her and then for Thomas. Before the trip was over, he began to talk kindly about Thomas. "You know, Thomas is a good-looking kid," he said. He now has a relationship with all three of his grandchildren. Sharon's mother, who is divorced from her father, had bonded deeply with Thomas, as she had lived with the family during his first year. She became and remains his fierce advocate, forever concerned about his welfare and perhaps favoring the child she perceives as most likely to face headwinds.

FRIENDSHIP AND CONTACT THEORY

One need not marry, live with, date, or adopt a person of another race to experience the transformational love that Sharon Rush prescribes or to acquire cultural dexterity. An intimate friendship will do. I don't use the word *friend* lightly. I mean it to convey closeness beyond the multitudinous contacts of social media or the polite mixing forced in the workplace or a school's parent association. As with lovers, only intimate friendships can create transformative understanding, although any amity between people of different subgroups is a beginning. An intimate friend has probably been invited into your home to have a meal. In 1973, only 20 percent of Americans said they had invited someone of a different race to dinner recently. By 1996, that number had climbed to nearly 42 percent and remained stable for nearly a decade. Then researchers stopped asking the "Guess Who's Coming to Dinner?" question.[27]

For the uninitiated, a common affinity, like music, a sport, or another passion, is the best route to moving past the emotional architecture of separation. A study of middle-schoolers in Los Angeles found that students of different races bond over nonracial similarities like academic achievement or social status. Black and Latino students were more likely to befriend within their race or ethnicity, but their likelihood of making a friend from another background increased with classroom diversity. And those in diverse classrooms who befriended students of another race felt less vulnerable.[28]

Decades of research on what social psychologists call "contact theory" suggests how interracial friendships improve US race relations. Most scholars trace the genesis of contact theory to the hypotheses of sociologist Gordon Allport, who posited that under some conditions, increased contact between different groups would erode prejudices toward out-groups.[29] In 2006, two researchers amassed the results of all the studies on intergroup contact conducted in the twentieth century. Combining the data of 515 studies with more than 250,000 subjects in thirty-eight nations, they found that 94 percent of the studies reported a negative relationship between intergroup contact and prejudices of many types. In other words, intergroup contact reduced prejudices for those exposed to a racial, an ethnic, or a cultural other. Beyond reduced prejudice, intergroup contact "reduced anxiety, individual threat, collective threat and ingroup identification . . . enhanced empathy, perspective taking, outgroup knowledge, intergroup trust, forgiveness, job attainment and satisfaction, and perceptions of outgroup variability."[30]

Among college freshmen in 2014, some 80 percent of those who frequently socialized with someone of a different race or ethnicity also said they were able to see the world from someone else's perspective, compared with only 59.4 percent of those who never socialized across color lines.[31] Such a skill is increasingly necessary but often lacking when one steps beyond chambers of sameness. Those who have racial others in their lives are more likely to be amused than stressed by such experiences. In America, avoidance and sorting have been a dominant response to bewildering difference. Ardent integrators disrupt this pattern.

Almost any form of cross-group relationship has been shown to deeply affect the attitudes of those in such relationships toward out-groups. Close, meaningful relationships across group boundaries are likely to reduce prejudice, ease anxiety, and enhance willingness to engage in future intergroup contact. When a common in-group like a sports team is formed and its members are induced to perceive themselves and others as part of it, attitudes toward former out-groups members improve and cooperation and prosocial behavior across former group boundaries ensue.

The ardent integrators who form cross-racial bonds transfer some of these benefits to the less dexterous people in their tribe. Intergroup attitudes can be improved merely by knowing that someone has a close friend from another group. Interracial relationships face social and physical barriers, including an anxiety-driven tendency to end such relationships before they can even begin.[32] Those who have had previous contact with other groups are more resilient in recovering from stressful intergroup interactions.[33] Practice makes one better at pluralism.

The one caveat to this consistent body of research on the effects of intergroup contact is that if the contact is negative, meaning it does not go well, prejudice can increase.[34] This complication may help explain why college campuses and millennials are such a cauldron of contradiction. Children are more segregated than adults in America. Among parents with choices, the arms race for the best neighborhoods and schools, and a long history of nefarious social engineering, fuel this contradiction.[35] Millennials, overwhelmingly, say they were raised to believe in equality and not to acknowledge racial difference. According to one MTV survey, only 30 percent of white millennials grew up in a family that talked about race. They paradoxically believe in both "color blindness" and celebrating differences. And being raised not to acknowledge race means they lack the tools to deal with it or talk about it when it arises. Many have been taught that even drawing attention to someone's race in a positive way is wrong. In a survey, a large majority of millennials reported that they did not have the tools for tackling bias in themselves or in others and they were hungry to have respectful, judgment-free conversations.[36] At the same time, this generation grew up in a culture where peers become popular by being rude online. In this sense, they have been labeled both tolerant and desensitized.[37]

And then we require youth to negotiate the architecture of separation cultivated for centuries and the toxic divisions adults have created. The lucky among these innocents arrive on a college campus, one of the few American spaces where people of different walks and ideologies must interact with each other. Some first-year students experience robust diversity for the first time in their lives. Not surprisingly, there is a racial architecture to friendship. The closest bonds still tend to be intraracial. For example, in a dining hall, a predominantly Asian, black, or white table can often be found. Interracial relationships can be more difficult to form, or they may be compartmentalized to the common experience that brought about the friendship—a sorority, a sports team, the school newspaper.

The black college student I introduced in the previous chapter—I'll call her Marie—tells me that while she loves her assigned sorority big sister, who is white, she relates better to the few other black women in her sorority chapter. They, too, come from affluent African American families and have long experienced negotiating selective, majority-white spaces. Marie has many white friends but feels some differences between herself and them. "They don't feel the difference," she says, "but I feel it." Even among her closest white friends, she says, "whites feel like race was long ago, and they don't feel comfortable talking about it." Her longtime white friends feel confident that they would see things the way Marie does, but Marie is doubtful. Even though she was born into economic privilege, she is very aware that race is still prevalent. Among her black friends on campus, she says, "everybody acts differently between white and black friends." She can open up a little more and there is more unspoken understanding between black students on her selective campus. At the same time, Marie feels a cultural chasm that she would like to bridge better between herself and black people of lower socioeconomic status.

At the high school she attended, Marie also felt differences. There was a socioeconomic range of students and she perceived an "us against the white man" attitude among some black students. They made assumptions about all white people and were unwilling to push out beyond the black space they inhabited within the school, she says. Black male athletes seemed to acquire the most cultural dexterity in the school; they could "flip the switch" and move among black people of all economic classes and also hang out with the white kids who admired them. Marie also concluded that it seemed much easier for blacks and Latinos to relate to each other than for blacks and whites or Latinos and whites to bond.

Marie describes a perception gap between many whites and non-whites—a difference that I describe in an earlier book as a distinct hurdle in race relations.[38] Whites are more apt to claim a color-blind identity and not perceive or be uncomfortable acknowledging issues of race. People of color are more apt to be conscious of how race operates in society. For a white person, becoming an intimate of a person of color and understanding how and why that person thinks about race may require a cultural shift that is challenging or uncomfortable. If friends cannot discuss race honestly, then the friendship has not transcended ancient color lines and is not (or not yet) truly intimate. Sharon Rush labels such friendships "disingenuous" or "inauthentic."[39]

An intimate cross-racial or cross-ethnic friendship should expand intercultural knowledge. A black friend tells me about a white guy in her acting class who balked at playing a scene in which he was supposed to touch her hair. "I know you are never supposed to touch a black woman's hair," he said, to laughter. A man who dates or befriends a black woman learns this. It may be a weave or a perm, or it may be natural. Whatever it is, it is hers. One has to cross inner concentric circles of intimacy to be allowed to touch it. Casual acquaintances and especially strangers should never invite themselves to explore its texture. It's a black thing, and it takes time to understand it.

Another form of cross-racial contact on college campuses is living together as roommates. Among the strategies, from wise to silly, that administrators have tried to help college students adjust to robust diversity is random dormitory assignments. Social scientists have documented the increased dexterity that comes with interracial living, assuming the experience is positive or neutral. But roommate disasters happen. While interracial roommate relationships are generally "less satisfying and involving" than same-race ones, they can produce benefits. In one study, "automatically activated racial attitudes and intergroup anxiety improved over time among students in interracial rooms, but not among students in same-race rooms."[40] In another study involving white first-year students at Stanford, those with a roommate of a different race were found to have more friends of the roommates' race. The relationships didn't transfer to races other than the roommate's race, but the general tendency toward "homophily" with one's own kind of people was disrupted for these students.[41] Another study found that white students with a nonwhite roommate showed less anxiety and less verbal tension when interacting with a black person, even when the other-race roommate was not black.[42]

Very diverse college campuses benefit the students who inhabit them. There is something to the idea of critical mass, although I have challenged selective colleges about the opportunity-hoarding ways in which they go about creating it.[43] When people of color represent less than 20 percent of a campus population, they experience significantly higher levels of discrimination than on campuses with populations more than 36 percent nonwhite. In other words, the more that white students are exposed to students of color, the less discrimination is observed on a campus.[44] The percentage of first-year students who support promoting racial understanding is growing. Those indicating that this goal is very important or essential rose from 33 percent in 2011 to 40 percent in 2015. In 2015, one-third of these young idealists were white.[45]

Each new cohort of young people is more diverse than the one that preceded it, and this diversity can be a source of friction as well as wonder. Youth, who are in direct competition for limited opportunity with an increasingly broad rainbow of global aspirants, negotiate a diversity that their grandparents were insulated from. To-day, a majority of babies born in the United States are children of color or Hispanic or both. Despite residential segregation, this demographic change raises the probability that youth will have contact with a person of another race or ethnicity, especially if they attend college. For some, that contact is not going well. The Southern Poverty Law Center reports that every year, more than a half million college students are targets of racist, sexist, or homophobic slurs or physical assaults.[46]

Growing rates of cross-racial contact among ever-more-diverse cohorts of the young may explain why more young whites have friends of a different race than do their elders. At the same time, cross-racial contact devoid of intimacy and perceived as zero-sum competition may explain why some millennials are no more racially tolerant than their parents or grandparents. White millennials, like older generations, are not monolithic. It is inaccurate, however, to cast millennials as intolerant because of the distinct minority among them that exhibit prejudice.[47] A majority of millennials are more racially tolerant than their elders and appear comfortable with the infinite variations of the human spectrum in contemporary American society, racially and otherwise. Gay, straight, bisexual, transgender, same-sex, opposite-sex. Interracial, international. Undocumented and documented immigrants. Six in ten millennials say immigrants strengthen our country, compared with a minority of people over age thirty who think so. But only a plurality of white millennials say that the country needs to do much more to redress racial inequality. Optimism is a choice and a necessary ingredient to spurring action. I am betting on the tolerant ethos of this ascending generation to dominate our future.

CHAPTER EIGHT

The Future

The Rise of the Culturally Dexterous

Not yet love. It is growing apace, but fear seems the impulse of the moment. Gerrymandering, voter suppression, empowering corporate money in politics, building walls and zones of exclusion, boxing out people who would be fine living in a smaller home or apartment, stopping and frisking, arming to the teeth, just in case— all of it is consistent with a society premised on fear.

The dexterous aspire to something greater and more humane. At its heart, the civil rights movement was about economic justice and combating racism. Six months after *Loving* was decided, the Southern Christian Leadership Conference announced a new campaign for poor people of all colors. Native Americans, poor whites from West Virginia and other environs, and urban and rural blacks and Latinos of the Southwest descended on Washington, presented demands to Congress and occupied the National Mall for six weeks in 1968. Their multiracial protest for decent housing, income, and jobs would be forgotten in the wake of assassination, of a Kennedy and a King. Politicians dog-whistled for five decades, destroying possibilities for a unifying consciousness among struggling people. In the absence of class unity, culturally dexterous people may be our only hope for disrupting hoary scripts.

Here is what could happen. It is not a prediction as much as a hope and a conjecture. Whether we can fix what is broken in this "country 'tis of us" is up to you, dear reader, and millions like you. A person overcome by fear or resentment probably will not have read much past the book jacket, unless he or she is doing reconnaissance. But you are still here, and that means our country still has a chance, a magnificent chance.

We are in a state of toxic polarity now, but I am optimistic because cultural dexterity is spreading. The tailwinds and the math suggest a future in which culturally dexterous people predominate in America. Here are my five speculations about the future, four positive trends and one negative caveat:

FIRST, INTERRACIAL INTIMACY IS POISED TO EXPLODE. With legal and social barriers to race mixing falling, the raw numbers of Americans who have an authentic friendship or a love relationship with a person of a different race or ethnicity or who know someone who does will continue to increase and accelerate. Media in its myriad, ubiquitous forms will continue to de-whiten and represent a fuller multiplicity of racial and cultural experiences, enabling parasocial relationships that humanize others. We are in a geometric progression toward something new.

SECOND, IMMIGRATION, DEMOGRAPHIC, AND GENERATIONAL CHANGE WILL TRANSFORM AMERICAN IDENTITY. By 2043, Hispanics and people of color, including multiracial people, are projected to be a majority of the US population. Well before then, a critical mass of culturally dexterous whites will have accepted and become comfortable with, not threatened by, this impending change. Currently, the whites who feel most threatened by this impending transition are older people, who will not live forever. The future may already be here. "American" will no longer imply whiteness or honorary whiteness but a multiplicity of hyphenated people committed to our self-evident, egalitarian values.

THIRD, GEOGRAPHY WILL CONTRIBUTE TO THIS CHANGE. The culturally dexterous class, including immigrants, is moving toward metropolitan areas, and it will be impossible to escape robust diversity in these dense, urbanized spaces. In the fifty largest US metro areas, 44 percent of suburban residents currently live in multiracial, multiethnic suburbs.[1] And younger whites are moving to cities that their parents and grandparents fled decades before. With proximity comes more opportunity for practicing pluralism and creating new norms of inclusion. In these spaces, the culturally dexterous will invest in public institutions that promote inclusive opportunity because they value diverse people and must make diversity work. Those who cannot adapt may retreat to monoracial spaces and very white states.

FOURTH, THE CULTURALLY DEXTEROUS WILL RESTORE FUNCTIONALITY TO POLITICS. Culturally dexterous whites and progressive people of color will form a coalition of the ascendant. With each passing decade, it will be much easier for this coalition to win in national elections, and candidates and political parties will feel the need to compete for the votes of tolerant people.

FIFTH, RACIAL AND ECONOMIC SEGREGATION WILL CONTINUE TO DO DAMAGE. Stereotypes about low-income people of color, particularly black people, will endure as long as hyper-segregated, high-poverty neighborhoods endure. No amount of interracial intimacy will ameliorate this problem if the architecture of segregation, including mass incarceration, has not been dismantled.

Ardent integration, immigration, demographic change, generational replacement, and increasing geographic diversity—all of these forces will have a powerful, cumulative impact on our future.[2] Because of these forces, the ranks of those who live with diversity and are forced to acquire dexterity will continue to expand, perhaps exponentially, in coming decades. Hence I believe my speculations about the future are more plausible than the idea that those committed, explicitly or implicitly, to maintaining white supremacy will forever dominate. Such destructive ideologues don't dominate now in national opinion polls. Most of them are adults who have more yes-terdays than tomorrows in their life ledgers. They will be replaced by growing swaths of dexterous people who explicitly recognize and reject racism. Even past history, as awful as much of it is, provides reason for hope and inspiration. The ardent integrators and radicals who fought for our professed founding ideals were unable in their time to stop supremacy from being embedded in law and the vast majority of American minds, but they reconstructed the Constitu-tion and kept the ideals alive, and each generation of radical patri-ots kept fighting.

For all his flaws, Thomas Jefferson was a most useful patriarch. He penned thirteen words that proved timeless, *the* core American value: "We hold these truths to be self-evident, that all men are cre-ated equal." That value is suffused in the fastest-growing populations in America—Asian Americans, Latinos/as, and multiracial people. Between 50 and 60 percent of these populations say they experi-ence discrimination or that discrimination is a problem, and they are clearly inclined to support if not fight for racial equality.[3] Culturally dexterous white allies also support this value and say they want to be part of this conversation, contributing to the flourishing of attitudes of openness and empathy.[4] For example, a recent Pew study found that 40 percent of whites—mostly young and Democrat-leaning—express support for the Black Lives Matter movement, compared with just 28 percent of whites who disapprove of it.[5] Maybe we al-ready have a critical mass of white allies, but our country is still captured by segregation, gerrymandering, voter suppression, and the post–*Citizens United* dark-campaign financing put in place by those fighting to hold on to the centrality of whiteness.

Since *Loving*, supremacy has been formally disavowed in law, but we still live with the structures and dog-whistled ideology of su-premacy. With spreading dexterity, more people are acquiring the skills to see, name, talk about, and influence others about the *sys-tems* of supremacy and racism that endure. As Bryan Stevenson, ac-tivist founder of the Equal Justice Initiative, has argued, the ideology of supremacy that was constructed to prop up slavery has been as damaging as slavery itself. He asserts that we need to talk about this ideology to change the narrative and get to the point where enough nonblacks are prepared to say, "Never again."[6]

My speculation is not about the future dominance of any particular political party but of an ascendant coalition that all candidates will be forced to compete for. Democrats for a century were the party of white supremacy, and both Democrats and Republicans supported a race-coded War on Drugs that filled American prisons with men of color and high school dropouts of all shades.[7] Today it is the Party of Lincoln that is captured by angry, resentful whites. Some of these white people traffic explicitly in white supremacy or nationalism. Some voted for Obama but are frustrated by a plutocracy that is not responsive to their economic plight. Others are fragile souls indoctrinated in a worldview that blinds them to facts. Many live in stagnant white communities where blue-collar jobs that paid decent wages have disappeared and where the global information economy never arrived. They have bought the myth sold to them by people trawling for ratings and votes—the story that immigrants and people of color are the source of their problems rather than technological disruption and exploitive, outsourcing, tax-evading corporations.[8] White power, expressly and implicitly, has always been about segregating insurgent whites from people of color to insulate elites from economic demands. So it was with landed planters who wanted to avoid another Bacon's Rebellion. So it is now with plutocrats who prefer to stoke a race war to avoid even modestly redistributive economic fairness.

It is stupid, how trapped this great country is by the architecture of division. As Stevenson also says, though, "there is . . . power . . . in understanding brokenness."[9] Understanding helps foster seeing. In a rich country where even a debate about how to fix crumbling infrastructure can be stymied by racial resentment, allies are connecting the dots.[10]

What happened in California suggests how we might move beyond brokenness. Consider the theory of change developed by architects of the movement for same-sex marriage. Their strategy was informed by Malcolm Gladwell's idea of a tipping point—"the moment of critical mass, the threshold, the boiling point" that brings sweeping change.[11] Those fighting for the freedom to marry focused on convincing a critical mass of people and states, *not everyone*, of the rightness of their cause, and in doing so, they ushered in broad social acceptance of same-sex love.

I believe that we will reach a tipping point in race relations—a point when a critical mass of culturally dexterous whites accepts the loss of centrality of whiteness. In other words, a critical mass of people not fragile and fearful about demographic change, not ruled by their anxieties, able to assess candidates and policy debates according to facts instead of an entitled or a supremacist worldview. Such a tipping point, coupled with a confluence of other forces, led California from gridlocked to governable.

In 1980, California was 76 percent white. This state that used to be northern Mexico was home to many citizens of Mexican descent, and things were changing rapidly. The reforms to immigration law made in 1965 were bringing many new, documented immigrants, in particular, Spanish-speaking people, to the state. Hispanics were one-fifth of Californians in 1980. Ten years later, they were one-quarter, and by 2000, one-third. In the mid-1990s, Hispanics and people of color came to outnumber non-Hispanic whites in the state. In the lead-up to this transition, politicians, mostly Republicans, played to voters' racial anxieties to win elections.

Senator Pete Wilson ran successfully against Dianne Feinstein for governor in 1990. He campaigned as a prochoice moderate, projecting compassion, for example, by visiting a hospital ward with babies born addicted to crack. Four years later, with the state in a recession and behind in the polls, Governor Wilson took a different approach to reelection. In addition to opposing affirmative action, he infamously blamed undocumented immigrants for California's troubles.

"They keep coming" a sinister voice warned over grainy black-and-white footage of people running across the border. In Wilson's iconic, effective political ad, the ominous voice says that there are "two million illegal immigrants" in California and that the federal government "won't stop them at the border yet requires us to pay billions to take care of them." After informing viewers that Wilson has sent the National Guard to help protect the border, the ad cuts to Wilson, who exudes a practiced toughness. He declares, "For

Californians who work hard, pay taxes, and obey the laws, I am suing to force the federal government to control the border, and I am working to deny state services to illegal immigrants. Enough is enough."

The innuendo was that Mexican immigrants don't work hard, pay taxes, or obey the laws and that they were usurping tax dollars by relying on state services. In truth, most undocumented immigrants work very hard; pay payroll, sales, and income taxes; and often don't file for income tax refunds they might be entitled to. Studies suggest that they are net contributors to state and national economies and that they contribute more than they take in government services.[12] And immigration tends to lower local crime rates, not raise them.[13] But, as with the failed antilynching efforts of bygone eras, facts don't matter when a racial passion play takes hold. Add economic anxiety to a race script, and the denouement seemed inevitable. Wilson won reelection by a landslide.

He was aided by an initiative, Proposition 187, also known as the "Save Our State" initiative, which was also on the ballot. The preamble to the proposition illuminates how easy this divide-and-conquer politics was for Republicans. "The People of California find and declare . . . [t]hat they have suffered and are suffering economic hardship caused by the presence of illegal immigrants in this state," it began. In the middle of a recession, promising voters a $200 million annual savings by banning "illegal aliens" from public education, health, and other services and requiring that service providers report these immigrants to the state and federal government proved very popular.

The day after Prop 187 was approved, also by a landslide, Wilson, the man who had once publicly empathized with the plight of crack babies, ordered that prenatal health services be stopped for unauthorized aliens.[14] Legal advocates challenged Prop 187 in court as unconstitutional, a court permanently enjoined it, and it never went into effect. However, the proposition was the first time a state had adopted a law concerning immigration. Republicans would mount the same story line, echoing similar words, to enact or attempt to enact similar laws in fourteen states, including nine states of the former Confederacy, in subsequent decades.[15]

Other race-charged policy battles were waged in the Golden State. On the same day that Prop 187 was approved, voters also overwhelmingly approved Proposition 184, better known as the "Three Strikes and You're Out" initiative. The new law required anyone who was convicted of a felony and had two prior felony convictions to receive a prison term of at least twenty-five years to life. Any felony would do, even a nonviolent offense like serving as a lookout in a twenty-dollar sale of cocaine.[16]

Such laws became the rage in the 1990s. About half of all states and the federal government subsequently adopted them as Democrats and Republicans competed with one another to appear tough on crime. The subtext of these and other harsh crime laws of that era was the so-called crack epidemic and the countless media stories that made it all too easy for voters to associate criminality with blackness.[17] California's three-strikes law, however, was one of the strictest in the nation. Because of this and other harsh laws, its prison population surged fivefold between 1980 and 2007.[18]

A state that was once envied for its public schools and universities became an object lesson on how dog-whistling harms not just scapegoated populations but also white taxpayers. Eventually, California was spending more on prisons than on higher education.[19] Once a national leader, the state was also investing below the national average, and $100,000 less than New York did, in a child's thirteen-year life in public school.[20] Yet in 2008, California was spending about $47,102 annually on each prisoner, permanently throwing away human beings, even for nonviolent offenses, and likely making things worse in the communities they came from.[21]

Ward Connerly, a black Republican, championed the "California Civil Rights" initiative in 1996. Also known as Prop 209, it banned consideration of race and gender by California state institutions, which included college admissions and public contracting. Large majorities of African Americans, Latinos/as, and Asian Americans opposed the initiative, as did 37 percent of whites, but it passed by 54 percent in the general election. When Republicans sponsored similar ballot initiatives in other states, the initiatives passed in seven states. This too was easy politics that exploited racial anxieties. Yet again, California and America were divided houses.

But California changed because the people who constituted a politi-cal majority changed. Again, 37 percent of white people supported af-firmative action in 1996. What type of white person does this? A white male, in particular, doesn't benefit from either race or gender-based affirmative action. Dr. King was looking for these other-regarding souls in 1967—people who were "willing to share power and to ac-cept structural alterations." And this cohort of white persons grew. By 2014, some 57 percent of white Californians supported affirma-tive action.[22] Why such an increase? Presumably, a lot more whites in the state acquired cultural dexterity—empathy for a nonwhite person and knowledge and concern about systemic exclusion.

By the late 2000s, nearly 1 in 4 newly married couples in Cali-fornia were interracial, a much higher percentage than the nation as a whole.[23] As a result, a plurality or perhaps even a majority of peo-ple in the state knew someone or were related to someone who was married to a person of a different race. This contact can cause a shift in mind-set, a degree of acceptance, and conversations within a fam-ily or network—conversations that can transfer the tolerance of the ardent integrator to others. Many Californians also engaged in in-terracial cohabitation, adoption, or friendship, and black-white resi-dential integration increased significantly in the state in the 1990s.[24] Increased proximity likely increased white people's knowledge about what nonwhite people face.

And older whites who tended to have less dexterous worldviews went to see their Maker in those two decades. I don't mean to be un-kind in pointing that out. Death is inevitable for all of us. We are all here for a limited time and must decide, individually, what role we will play in the great American experiment.

Another change in California was the increasing size of Hispanic, Asian American, and other nonwhite populations, although the Af-rican American population held steady at roughly 7 percent in these decades. A perfect storm gathered and contributed to a tipping point. As more whites were gaining cultural dexterity, people of color were not only gaining in numbers, but also engaging more in politics.

African Americans had learned organizing during the civil rights movement and applied that experience to politics after passage of the Voting Rights Act. They already had disproportionate influence in the state legislature, especially via then speaker of the California Assembly, Willie Brown. Many Hispanics were radicalized and offended by the tactics of Pete Wilson. Those who were eligible for citizenship began to naturalize in greater numbers. Latino citizens began to register to vote, organize, and run for office in greater numbers. Between 1994 and 2004, Latino voter registration rose by 69 percent in the state.[25] Loretta Sanchez's razor-thin victory over conservative incumbent flamethrower Bob Dornan for a congressional seat in the center of rapidly changing Orange County was indicative of this trend. The beauty of math began to kick in. As the numbers of culturally dexterous whites and political engaged people of color grew, so did possibilities for "a coalition of the ascendant," as one political scientist labeled them.[26]

California entered an era of gridlock, as a left-of-center coalition was ascending and colliding with conservative Republicans in the assembly. Sacramento, the state capital, soon gained a reputation for dysfunction not unlike that earned and deserved by Congress today. For a while, the state seemed ungovernable. The assembly was gridlocked and stymied in part by supermajority requirements that Republicans had put in place for raising taxes.

When the Wilson administration also deregulated energy in the 1990s, rates for electricity skyrocketed. Market manipulators, including Enron, manufactured an energy crisis, another instance of economic elites preying on ordinary people in the vacuum created by politicians who divided and conquered.[27] By the early 2000s, the state was suffering rolling blackouts that reached 1.5 million people. Voters were angry about the energy crisis and the dysfunction in Sacramento. Republican activists who had honed their skills with ballot initiatives successfully tapped that anger to recall Democratic governor Gray Davis a mere eleven months after he had been reelected.

In a crowded field, Republican actor Arnold Schwarzenegger, the person with the most name recognition and the least-known politics, was voted into the governor's suite with 48 percent of the vote. Schwarzenegger soon learned that he did not have a mandate for conservatism. After losing on four ballot initiatives he had championed, he tapped a Democrat as his chief of staff and moderated his politics, although he campaigned against a ballot initiative that would have reduced the harshness of California's three-strikes law.

In 2010, the ascending coalition approved a ballot initiative that placed redistricting in the hands of a bipartisan citizens' commission rather than a legislature intent on protecting incumbents. Voters also approved an innovation whereby the top two vote-getters, of either party, would face each other in the general election. This innovation dramatically changed the incentive structure of California politics; candidates were forced to compete less on ideology and more on ideas. Two years later, voters approved allowing the commission to redraw lines for congressional seats as well. It was the beginning of unshackling democracy from gerrymandered extremism.

In 2010, voters also replaced outgoing Schwarzenegger with seasoned Democrat Jerry Brown, who had once been a young California governor and now was returning to the office as its oldest. The state, like the country, was climbing slowly out of a recession. It was saddled with a $15 billion budget deficit, even as Republicans had sponsored a successful ballot initiative that imposed another supermajority requirement to raising fees in 2010.

By 2012, the state seemed to have moved past gridlock. Only 39 percent of whites were registered Democrats, and this was enough, a critical mass that helped propel the ascendant coalition into dominance. The coalition included people of color, millennials, and socially liberal, college-educated whites. Californians voted yes to Proposition 30, Brown's initiative to raise $8 billion in taxes to fund education and public safety by raising the sales tax to 7.5 percent and taxing California incomes greater than $250,000 on a graduated scale. With smiling, optimistic Obama also on the ballot for reelection, progressives came out to vote. Democrats that year also assumed a two-thirds majority in both the assembly and the senate for the first time since the Great Depression, enough to enact tax increases and put ballot initiatives before voters without Republican support.[28] Whether one is a Republican, a Democrat, or an Independent, one can admire a functioning democracy that promotes the common good.

By June 2014, Latinos alone outnumbered non-Hispanic whites and the numbers of registered Latino voters continued to grow. The ascendant coalition voted to approve an initiative that would release low-level, nonviolent criminals to alleviate prison crowding and channel the savings into public education and safety. The state of California now automatically restores voting rights to former felons when they exit prison. The statement made by the California secretary of state, Alex Padilla, about this change shows how former prisoners were humanized and welcomed to rejoin the polity, in ways that made sense as a matter of public policy: "If we are serious about slowing the revolving door at our jails and prisons, and serious about reducing recidivism, we need to engage—not shun—former offenders."[29]

California is retreating from the War on Drugs, investing in education and offering an example to the rest of the country of what functioning, multiracial politics looks like. It is far from perfect. There is still much damage to undo. Prisons are still unconscionably overcrowded. Most black and brown children attend separate and unequal schools.[30] Among many needed reforms for a more just California are the training of police officers to reject the stereotypes in their heads and to deescalate tense situations, more decarceration, and excellent educational opportunities for all children. The beginning, though, was restoring democracy so that it can no longer be hijacked by racist bids for the dark recesses of people's hearts and minds. In the Golden State, dog-whistling is a political nonstarter for any candidate with grand ambition.

The state also now helps people who were once demonized. Undocumented immigrants can be admitted to the bar to practice law and can get a driver's license.[31] The state is considering allowing undocumented people to participate in the Affordable Care Act, also known as Obamacare.[32] It currently provides state-funded insurance for undocumented children through Medicaid.[33] The University of California system offers loans to undocumented "dreamers," students who cannot participate in the federal student loan program.[34] Most local authorities will not report individuals to federal immigration authorities solely because of their immigration status.[35] Governor Brown struck the word "alien" from the state's labor laws because of its negative implication.[36] In sum, for most Californians, undocumented immigrants have been humanized so that public policies are more apt to reflect pragmatic realities and the net public benefits of allowing people to come out of the shadows.

By 2016, among likely voters in California, 60 percent were white, 18 percent Latino, 12 percent Asian, 6 percent black, and 4 percent multiracial.[37] Among state legislators, 61 percent are white, 18 percent Latino, 9 percent Asian, 9 percent black, and 2 percent multiracial. Conservative Republicans would be in charge if most white Californians accepted the disinformation that the extreme-right echo chamber serves up elsewhere for breakfast. This is impossible in California, where a plurality of whites share the worldview and political commitments of most people of color. Since gerrymandering has been undermined, the new California requires coalition.

Race mixing in California politics, as in its social culture, is likely to be a permanent and growing feature of this state whose early constitution explicitly limited suffrage to "white males." The founding white fathers of California made clear in the state's first constitutional convention that they wanted only whites to govern the state. They took pains to exclude the few Negroes and many indigenous people and nonwhite Mexicans who resided in that rough, beautiful country.[38] Asians, too, were not welcome when they began arriving in significant numbers. A century and a half later, California's ascendant coalition defeated its founders' racist vision and replaced it with something far closer to what we say America stands for. It is Reconstruction once again, and in many ways, the herculean work of building an inclusive California is just beginning.

A similar story could be told about America in a decade or two. In the 2016 presidential election, candidate Donald Trump did for America what Pete Wilson did for California. Trump accelerated political engagement by Latinos, Muslim Americans, and other groups deeply offended by scapegoating, and many whites began to see racism. For seventeen months, the candidate stoked racial resentment and many other forms of bias, and the strategy was shockingly effective. Add to this the unrelenting stream of heartbreaking videos of unarmed black people killed by police and of protests and counterprotests in myriad cities, and the country had a convulsive conversation about race. No matter how appalling, racist, misogynist, anti-Muslim, xenophobic, homophobic Trump's rhetoric, roughly

46 percent of voters supported a man who never held public office, disdained preparation and paying taxes, bragged about his sexual predations, and had a documented history of financial exploitation, including taking advantage of workers. For many of his supporters, these negatives could be overlooked, denied, or even cast as assets because at bottom, he signaled that he was with them.

Many Trump supporters voted their economic frustrations, their weariness at being underemployed or having no job at all. But in addition to economic concerns, Trump tapped into a distinct cultural binary, the chasm, broadly, between nondexterous and dexterous people. Many Trump supporters were sick of what they deem "politically correct" multiculturalism and of coastal elites and a political establishment that seems dismissive of their values and worldview. At rallies, Trump whipped up furor among overwhelmingly white audiences and encouraged them to attack dissenters and shoot his opponent.[39] Here was another American passion play, in which many reveled in hate or appreciated being in a space where it was okay to be nondexterous.

This new low in American presidential politics rendered transparent how embedded supremacy and patriarchy are. Trump rode a torrent of white fragility to victory in the Electoral College among people who just couldn't deal with economic and cultural displacement at the same time. A pus-filled American sore still oozes. Exploiters continue to betray economically vulnerable people while playing on those same people's fears, in an effort to divide and conquer—old story, despicable story. Those with faith in a greater idea can write a new narrative. It requires acceptance, though, of the self-evident truth of our founding. If all are created equal, then America should not have been constructed as a white country. A pluribus that renders white just one among many is a new America that some can't accept. If you are white, you have an obligation to at least understand where the concept of whiteness comes from and to decide how you will proceed with that knowledge. I hope your journey will include an intentional choice to acquire dexterity.

A coalition may yet rise to lance this recurrent boil and wipe away the stench. In 2012, the Pew Research Center projected that the Hispanic electorate would double by 2030. And that was before the frightening election of 2016. Many Hispanics are young citizens who are waking up to their potential at the ballot box. Hispanic millennials constitute 44 percent of eligible Latino voters.[40] From 2012 to 2016, Hispanics increased their share of the electorate from 10 to 11 percent. Asian Americans increased from 3 to 4 percent of the electorate in the same period. Meanwhile, whites declined from 77 percent of the electorate in 2004 to 70 percent in 2016.[41]

Soon, Hispanics and Asian Americans combined will cast as much as a quarter of all votes in presidential elections.[42] Most likely, white supremacy will not be on their agenda, and equality and fairness will. Count black and multiracial people in that column, and other people of color, and large numbers of whites. At the same time, the Silent Generation, those born between 1928 and 1945, is the whitest of extant generations and the least accepting of the cultural and demographic changes in American society.[43] The youngest of the Silents will have reached American life expectancy by 2025. By 2030, in just thirteen years, most Silents will be eternally silent.

It is not hard to imagine an ascendant coalition rewriting the ground rules to unleash American democracy. In individual states, these coalitions might create more citizen commissions that end political gerrymandering. Surely they will support laws that encourage rather than discourage voting. They can also create organizations that help people who want to acquire dexterity to develop these skills and relationships, organizations that are intentional about bridging divides.

Everyone—particularly whites who are used to being central—must work at adjusting to new realities. Passivity is also a choice, and part of the problem. As an African American, I can only write authentically about being black. There are a million ways to be black in America, but for virtually all of us, denying the existence of antiblack racism is not one of them. One scholar has suggested that there are also multiple ways to be white in America. She recommends being *actively* antiracist and this is likely the most joyous path.[44]

Although they are not the answer to all America's ills, ardent integrators are helping to spread dexterity. And in communities that integrators gravitate to, there is the possibility of a refreshing redo on race—not imaginary color blindness, but seeing difference and smiling at it. In small utopias that are very intentional about inclusion and valuing difference, strangers may see a dark-skinned black boy as adorable, beautiful, and full of potential, the same way his parents see him. That view, unfortunately, is a radical concept, but one that prevails today at my kids' thoroughly multiracial public charter school. With ardent integration and activism, such an ethos can spread.

The cultural dominance of integrators will be most palpable in dense metropolitan areas, where intense diversity will be inescapable. Emerging global neighborhoods, places where no particular group or culture dominates, will also contribute to the rise of the culturally dexterous. An influx of global aspirants changes the complexion of a former white-flight suburb, and many whites decide to stay rather than escape to whiter exurbs.

While agitating for a saner future, we can create small utopias now—a school, a nonprofit, a gospel choir, a neighborhood—spaces that are open to all comers, where people can build trust and something new and enduring, something that works for all participants. In the United States, we need to reinvigorate and reimagine public spaces where people practice pluralism. In small utopias, citizens can break things and start anew. They can change the narrative from hatred or denigration of government to putting the people back in the idea of *public* and viewing government as the enabler of good lives. Effective public institutions are critical for middle-class and poor folks who cannot afford to opt out of them. Middle-class utopias where government functions for the common good may rise because old baby boomers with no savings and young people with meager starts in life desperately need excellent, well-funded public institutions, including public transportation, libraries, schools, free or low-cost community colleges, and public universities.

Geography is one key to the successful coalescing of multihued reformers. White supremacy in pre-civil-rights America required exclusion, as did the so-called American Dream, which idealized suburban single-family living for one type of family (traditional, heterosexual, white, middle class) while discouraging entry by others.

In the twenty-first century, the American Dream is broken for all but wealthy people. Exclusion and exclusivity squelch opportunity for the nonaffluent. Technology and its creative destructions leave the masses struggling to create viable lives from what plutocrats will hire and pay them to do. Economic survival requires access, and access requires institutions and communities that include rather than exclude.

Creative innovators tend to live and work in communities of dense diversity and tolerance. Because of this, America is likely to remain a magnet for the most talented people in the world. Our country could be the first universal state in world history—a nation where people of all races, ethnicities, classes, religions, genders, transgenders, and sexual orientations are accepted and where public policies support rather than undermine their aspirations. The United States could show the world what pluralism means, while antipluralistic countries continue to be torn asunder by ancient and modern intergroup conflicts.

Hey, I can dream. This is my hope for our country. I live in a small utopia today. Within walking distance of my front door are locally owned, nonartisanal businesses that cater to real middle-class people and cheap and expensive restaurants. Both upper-class and struggling people walk on the same sidewalks. A stroll to the left leads to increasingly tony homes; a stroll to the right leads to a mixed-income development of garden apartments, some of which rent to low-income people at below-market rates.

My kids do not live in an affluent bubble. They are enriched by encounters with people who have more, and some who have less, than they do. At home and at school, there are poor black people and no one thinks of them as scary aliens to be avoided. Real inclusion that works for everyone is not as improbable as you might think.

My children's public charter school is analogous to a magnet school. It enables my children and other people's children to receive an exceptional Mandarin-immersion, international baccalaureate education for free, decoupled from where they live. There are no high-stakes tests to gain entrance, no interviews or psychological evaluations that screen out those who don't "fit" in-group norms. Only an online application that takes a minute to fill out and the luck of winning a lottery are required. The school draws from all eight wards of

Washington, DC. Parents revel in the genius of children of all colors and economic backgrounds learning a five-thousand-year-old language and culture. Beyond a rigorous, inquiry-based academic curriculum, the school intentionally teaches children to value and talk about racial and ethnic differences.

The principal wears dreadlocks. She is African American and wields power confidently. She speaks Mandarin, as do the black kids that make up the largest demographic group at the school, although no group has majority representation. On the parent Listserv, an unwritten egalitarian rule emerged. Parents identify themselves solely by their names and the classroom and name of their children. No one trades in professional titles or self-importance. Disagreements happen, but they are civil. A dispute about whose children got to perform for Michelle Obama and the First Lady of China was resolved with a new practice of inclusion. The next time the school received such a prestigious invitation, all children were invited to audition. A school choir was born, one that looked like America and the world. We make it up as we go along, and we sometimes stumble. Yet trying and sometimes failing at creating an inclusive small utopia, or a small republic, is so much better than accepting systemic exclusion.

Some communities already approximate the saner, inclusive spaces of the future. More than four hundred counties, cities, or towns require or offer strong incentives to make new housing development mixed-income, and 5 to 10 percent of the US population currently lives in these communities. Integrated places typically result from permissive zoning laws that allow more density in residential development, including apartments and town houses, and these communities exhibit lower levels of racial prejudice. Integrated jurisdictions like Montgomery County, Maryland; West Hartford, Connecticut; and Portland, Oregon, also tend to invest more in education and offer more social mobility for poor children. In contrast, segregated communities usually have highly restrictive zoning that limits density and elevates levels of racial prejudice.[45]

By 2040, much of the country will be intensely colored, although the heartland will remain predominantly white.[46] The majority of Americans will necessarily have adopted the habits of integrators. But will these trends move us from our current gilded, plutocratic age to something more equitable? Rising cultural dexterity may not end the exclusion and marginalization of the black and Latino poor. Accepting a majority-minority nation is one thing, but ending plutocracy and ghettoes is quite another. While half of whites may be culturally dexterous by 2040, some unknowable portion will not. Despite some political liberalization from demographic changes and rising dexterity, we still must mobilize multiracial constituencies to overcome scare tactics and the entrenched political advantages of plutocrats. Freedom is not free. Intentional effort at building coalitions and dismantling the architecture of supremacy is required.

Technology will accelerate a trend of replacing humans for many tasks. Society requires a collective response to a brutal new economy in which there will not be a high-paying job for everyone who wants one. In the upheaval, the temptation to divide will continue. A humane government, supported by a coalition of clear-eyed, empathetic people, is one hope for a country that will enable the economically vulnerable to live decent lives and not simply be thrown away or locked up. This ultimate goal will require innovations that include rather than exclude, and, frankly, it will require higher tax rates for the highly paid.

Most radically, I hope that the dexterous class will lead America to confront what most ails us in race relations: the social and spatial isolation of poor black and brown people. "This innocent country set you down in a ghetto," James Baldwin wrote to his nephew in *The Fire Next Time*, "in which, in fact it intended that you should perish . . . for the heart of the matter is here, and the root of my dispute with my country." Baldwin's dispute should be our dispute. The American ghetto persists, with horrific consequences for those stuck there. The ghetto incubates not just militaristic policing, gang violence, and savage inequality but also nasty othering of the people who live there and false assumptions about blackness that are central to why it has been so difficult to dismantle the structures of supremacy.

This is the unfinished business of the civil rights movement. Martin Luther King Jr. espoused a "Beloved Community" that many Americans embraced in the abstract. The challenge that we did not overcome was how to create enduring integrated communities where people could actually live this ideal. In a small utopia, the willing, privileged integrationist can live in a diverse society without fear, and poor and struggling people can also live and enjoy opportunity rather than be excluded from it. Small utopias enable strangers to practice not only pluralism but also the agape love that King championed. Agape love is not romantic, or the love between friends, but the hardest kind of love to show, a love indifferent to human merit.

This kind of love is as corny and idealistic as utopia itself—a place where empty-nesters willingly pay taxes to educate other people's children. A small, diverse utopia also enables people to escape the oppressions of their in-group's way of thinking, the echo chamber of sameness that can cultivate a righteous sense of entitlement and a dangerous lack of empathy for anyone outside one's tribe. In aspiring utopias, openness to others, progressive taxation, and investment in education and infrastructure make wages rise rather than fall for people who really need their paychecks. This happened in Canada while America endured its Great Recession.

As more of us acquire dexterity and other habits of inclusion, it will become much easier to create winning coalitions and communities of civility, where a debate about school funding is more a spirited exchange about what actually works than a zero-sum fight. Many communities of decency do exist today. They support inclusionary zoning laws that allow struggling people to live near great schools and employers that might hire them. They pass living-wage laws because in 2017, fifteen dollars per hour seems like commonsense fairness rather than a radical left-wing idea.

Imagining the third Reconstruction in dexterous places of the future brings a smile to my face. Such places could embody what radicals envisioned centuries before—what might have been, had integrating, insurgent colonials been politically enfranchised and left to their own devices. Research by Robert Putnam suggests that non-dexterous people burrow in and avoid civic engagement when they enter diverse settings.[47] But this avoidance is less likely in the future, when more people will have acquired comfort with out-groups. Such communities will multiply as the culturally dexterous multiply. There are cities and towns today that welcome immigrants because these places want to bring vitality to their struggling communities. Such welcoming communities work at helping new residents and existing ones get to know and understand one another. They are building new human bridges and, yes, are sometimes whipsawed by the tensions.[48]

America will be radically different from the segregated nation it was when the Lovings married. Oppressions of one kind or another will endure, but oppressed people will have more allies who will fight with them for what is right and fair. I end this book where I began, celebrating those, like Mildred and Richard, who choose to love across boundaries, despite the challenges. As Langston Hughes wrote in his short, sublime poem "Advice," between the miracle of birth and the meanness of dying, the essential point of life is to "get yourself a little loving."

ACKNOWLEDGMENTS

It takes a village to publish a book. Joanna Green, thank you for gently bypassing on a wild idea and suggesting a book about *Loving v. Virginia* instead. It set me on a different path for examining ideas I had been thinking about for decades. Thank you also for editing with grace and guiding me so well. The flowers and the note, "You got this," as I was limping to the finish were inspiring.

Thank you to the three scholars whom Beacon Press tapped to read and critique early drafts of the historical chapters. I don't know your names, as these were blind reviews. But I learned from each of you, and the book was much improved because of your input and wisdom. Thanks also to everyone at Beacon who contributed to the editing, production, and marketing of *Loving*.

Thank you to the scholars, historians, writers, and film documentarians whose work I draw on and cite. You honor a long tradition of truth-telling, and the truth does matter. Thanks especially to Jay Readey, who gave me the idea of a tipping-point theory of race relations.

My dear cousin Dorothy Reed, thank you for reading the entire manuscript. As always, your insights and suggestions were invaluable.

Thanks so much to friends and colleagues who read and commented on manuscript chapters: Jane Kamensky, Ralph Richard Banks, Dan O'Krent, Lolis Elie, Sherally Munshi, Allegra McLeod, Palma Strand, Jenee Desmond-Harris, Karen Hardwick, and Paul Scully, who were especially generous in providing detailed comments on multiple chapters; James Forman Jr.; Darlene Taylor; participants in the Georgetown Law Faculty Workshop, especially Mike Seidman, Paul Butler, Gerry Spann, Larry Solum, Emma Jordan, and Brad Snyder; and participants in law faculty symposia at the University of North Carolina, Chapel Hill, and the University of Texas, Austin. All of you contributed in very important ways that made the book better. Thanks to Julie Cohen for emotional support and counsel as I wrote this book. Thanks to Jill Lepore for answering some of my research questions about Benjamin Franklin and for encouraging me.

Thank you to those who shared their perspectives with me in interviews for this book, including Bill Zavarello, Renee Landers, and her son Nelson. Other interviewees chose anonymity. I am most grateful that you allowed me to share your powerful stories.

Thank you to my students over the years in Race and American Law. Some of your stories and insights found their way into this book. I learned a lot from you about what works and doesn't work in discussing race and how, ultimately, to create a community of trust.

Thank you to my dean, Bill Treanor, and associate dean Josh Teitelbaum for providing me with financial and emotional support and a research leave to write this book.

Stephen Benz, Jasmine Johnson, Emily Wilson, and Dylan Yepez, thank you for working as my research assistants on this project. Time and again, you unearthed sources to support my argument and helped advance my thinking. Heartfelt thanks to Tiffany Jones, Aleshadye Getachew, and Boris Zhao, who provided critical research assistance on projects that preceded but greatly influenced the content of this book. Special thanks to Andrea Muto and the wonderful staff of the Edward Bennett Williams Law Library for critical research support.

My former assistant Johnny Wong was a great aide and ally. Thanks also to Angie Villarreal, Anna Selden, and the entire faculty support staff at Georgetown for your cheerful assistance.

Thanks to Marita Golden, Natalie Hopkinson, Darlene Taylor, and all the women writers of color who lunch quarterly and talk writing. And to the sistah-girl network, thanks as always for sustaining me.

Finally, thank you to my family for enduring another book. Marque, Logan, and Langston, I could not have done this without your love, support, and patience.

NOTES

INTRODUCTION

1. These statements about Richard Loving and his interracial friendships are presented in a documentary film about the couple: Nancy Buirsky, *The Loving Story*, HBO Documentary Films LLC, April 15, 2011.
2. Ibid.
3. Laurence C. Nolan, "The Meaning of *Loving*: Marriage, Due Process and Equal Protection (1967–1990) as Equality and Marriage, from *Loving* to *Zablocki*," *Howard Law Journal* 41 (1998): 248.
4. Peggy Pascoe, *What Comes Naturally: Miscegenation Law and the Making of Race in America* (New York: Oxford University Press, 2009), 6, 8, 10–12.
5. Joseph Carroll, "Most Americans Approve of Interracial Marriages," Gallup News Service, August 16, 2007, http://www.gallup.com/poll/28417/most-americans-approve-interracial-marriages.aspx; Hazel Erskine, "The Polls: Interracial Socializing," *Public Opinion Quarterly* 37 (Summer 1973): 283.
6. Paul Osterman, *Gathering Power: The Future of Progressive Politics in America* (Boston: Beacon Press, 2002), 18–19.
7. Jack Tager, *Boston Riots: Three Centuries of Social Violence* (Boston: Northeastern University Press, 2001), 178–84; John S. Dempsey and Linda S. Forst, *An Introduction to Policing*, 8th ed. (Boston: Delmar Cengage Learning, 2015), 24–25.
8. Martin Luther King Jr., *The Trumpet of Conscience* (Boston: Beacon Press, 2010), 1–18, which includes a transcript of King's Massey lecture, "Impasse in Race Relations."
9. Ibid.
10. See chapter 5 of this book on the *Loving v. Virginia* case.
11. For a comprehensive treatment of antimiscegenation law, interracial intimacy, the construction of color lines, and, hence, whiteness, see, for example, Pascoe, *What Comes Naturally*; Randall Kennedy, *Interracial Intimacies: Sex, Marriage, Identity, and Adoption* (New York: Pantheon Books, 2003); Rachel F. Moran, *Interracial Intimacy: The Regulation of Race and Romance* (Chicago: University of Chicago Press, 2001); Theodore W. Allen,

The Invention of the White Race, vol. 2, *The Origin of Racial Oppression in Anglo-America* (London: Verso, 1997); A. Leon Higginbotham Jr., *In the Matter of Color: Race and the American Legal Process; The Colonial Period* (New York: Oxford University Press, 1978).

12. See chapter 3 of this book for a discussion of Jefferson and Hemings.

13. Gunnar Myrdal, *An American Dilemma: The Negro Problem and American Democracy* (New York: Harper & Bros. 1944), 589–91.

14. Carroll, "Most Americans Approve of Interracial Marriages."

15. See, for example, Susan Svrluga, "Noose Is Found Hanging from Tree on Duke's Campus," *Washington Post,* April 1, 2015, https://www.washington post.com/news/grade-point/wp/2015/04/01/noose-is-found-hanging-from -tree-on-dukes-campus; Manny Fernandez and Richard Pérez-Peña, "As Two Oklahoma Students Are Expelled for Racist Chant, Sigma Alpha Epsi- lon Vows Wider Inquiry," *New York Times,* March 10, 2015, http://www .nytimes.com/2015/03/11/us/university-of-oklahoma-sigma-alpha-epsilon -racist-fraternity-video.html; Justin Ellis, "Blackface Halloween: A Toxic Cultural Tradition," *Atlantic,* October 30, 2015, http://www.theatlantic .com/entertainment/archive/2015/10/blackface-halloween-a-toxic-cultural -tradition/413323; Eliza Gray, "What We Know About South Carolina Shooting Suspect Dylann Roof," *Time,* June 18, 2015, http://time.com /3926263/charleston-church-shooting-dylann-roof.

16. Tom Rosentiel, "Almost All Millennials Accept Interracial Dating and Mar- riage," Pew Research Center, February 1, 2010, http://www.pewresearch .org/2010/02/01/almost-all-millennials-accept-interracial dating-and -marriage; "Millennials' Judgments About Recent Trends Not So Differ- ent," Pew Research Center, last modified January 7, 2010, http://www .pewresearch.org/2010/01/07/millennials-judgments-about-recent-trends -not-so-different/.

17. Malcolm Gladwell, *The Tipping Point: How Little Things Can Make a Big Difference* (Boston: Little, Brown and Company, 2000).

18. See, generally, Thomas F. Pettigrew and Linda R. Tropp, "A Meta-Analytic Test of Intergroup Contact Theory," *Journal of Personality and Social Psy- chology* 90 (2006): 751–83.

19. Wendy Wang, "Interracial Marriage: Who Is 'Marrying Out'?," Pew Re- search Center, June 12, 2015, http://www.pewresearch.org/fact-tank/2015 /06/12/interracial-marriage-who-is-marrying-out; Antoine J. Banks and Nicholas A. Valentino, "Emotional Substrates of White Racial Attitudes," *American Journal of Political Science* 56 (April 2012): 286–97.

20. Overlaying a map of counties that voted for Trump with the counties that are predominantly foreign-born reveals an inverse relationship. Compare the following maps: Pew Research Center, "U.S. Foreign-Born Population Trends," Pew Research Center's Hispanic Trends Project, last modified Sep- tember 28, 2015, http://www.pewhispanic.org/2015/09/28/chapter-5-u-s -foreign-born-population-trends/; "US Election 2016: Trump Victory in Maps," *BBC News,* http://www.bbc.com/news/election-us-2016-37889032.

21. See Drew Westen, *The Political Brain: The Role of Emotion in Deciding the Fate of the Nation* (New York: PublicAffairs, 2007), 223.

22. Juliana Horowitz and Gretchen Livingston, "How Americans View the Black Lives Matter Movement," Pew Research Center, July 8, 2016, http://www.pewresearch.org/fact-tank/2016/07/08/how-americans-view-the-black-lives-matter-movement/.

23. Martin Luther King Jr., "A New Sense of Direction," Carnegie Council for Ethics in International Affairs, http://www.carnegiecouncil.org/publications/articles_papers_reports/4960.html, accessed October 18, 2016; King, *Trumpet of Conscience.*

CHAPTER ONE: GOING NATIVE

1. Arica L. Coleman, *That the Blood Stay Pure: African Americans, Native Americans, and the Predicament of Race and Identity in Virginia* (Bloomington: Indiana University Press, 2013), 70–74, and chap. 5.

2. Edward Maria Wingfield, *A Discourse of Virginia*, appended to Marshall Wingfield, *A History of Caroline County, Virginia: From Its Formation in 1727 to 1924* (Baltimore: Regional Publishing Company, 1969), 497.

3. Edmund S. Morgan, *American Slavery, American Freedom: The Ordeal of Colonial Virginia* (New York: W. W. Norton, 1975), 44.

4. Camilla Townsend, *Pocahontas and the Powhatan Dilemma* (New York: Farrar, Straus and Giroux, 2004), 12, estimates that the entire Powhatan Confederation may have been as large as twenty thousand people. Another scholar estimates that the Powhatan in the immediate area that the English settled numbered eight thousand (Morgan, *American Slavery, American Freedom*, 49).

5. Roxanne Dunbar-Ortiz, *An Indigenous Peoples' History of the United States* (Boston: Beacon Press, 2014), 10, 23, 30.

6. Ibid., 17; Morgan, *American Slavery, American Freedom*, 51–56.

7. Morgan, *American Slavery, American Freedom*, 79–80.

8. Ibid., 72–74; quote at 74. In 1618, in a period of truce between the English and Indians, the "Lawes Divine, Morall and Martiall" would be abrogated so that no one risked a death penalty for "going native" (ibid., 130).

9. Ibid., 100.

10. Frederic W. Gleach, "Controlled Speculation and Constructed Myths: The Saga of Pocahontas and Captain John Smith," in *Reading Beyond Words: Contexts for Native History*, ed. Jennifer S. H. Brown and Elizabeth Vibert (orig. 1996; Peterborough, Ont.: Broadview Press, 2003), 39–74; Morgan, *American Slavery, American Freedom*, 76; Townsend, *Pocahontas and the Powhatan Dilemma*, 52–56, 60, 75. Historians disagree on whether Smith fabricated the story. The legend is eerily similar to another story Smith wrote about being saved by a young woman after being captured by Turks in 1602. For an overview of arguments supporting his veracity, see David A. Price, *Love and Hate in Jamestown: John Smith, Pocahontas and the Heart of a New Nation* (New York: Alfred A. Knopf, 2003), 241–43. Smith had a habit of claiming that a comely young woman saved him in any foreign land he entered, and he made these claims in books that were designed to sell and burnish his legend (Townsend, *Pocahontas and the Powhatan Dilemma*, 52–54, 75). It is also likely that Smith misunderstood an elaborate

ritual of cultural adoption. Powhatan was a brilliant political strategist who had good reasons not to kill Smith, and he did seem to adopt Smith as a son of sorts to engender peace and, for a time, treated him as a friend and an ally (ibid., 14, 56). For a sensitive and convincing account of how the facts presented in Smith's writing could suggest that Powhatan and the people he led had culturally adopted the English and transferred these foreigners from outsiders to insiders, to meet the natives' strategic interests, see Gleach, "Controlled Speculation."

11. Price, *Love and Hate in Jamestown*, 5, 77, 103–4, 173–74, 181. Contrary to entertaining versions of the story by Disney and others, there was never any romantic connection between Smith and Pocahontas (ibid., 5).

12. Ibid., 57, 152; Townsend, *Pocahontas and the Powhatan Dilemma*, 73.

13. Townsend, *Pocahontas and the Powhatan Dilemma*, 69–70; Clara Sue Kidwell, "Indian Women as Cultural Mediators," *Ethnohistory* 39, no. 2 (1992): 97–107.

14. Price, *Love and Hate in Jamestown*, 5, 77, 103–4.

15. Townsend, *Pocahontas and the Powhatan Dilemma*, 81–82.

16. Morgan, *American Slavery, American Freedom*, 77; Price, *Love and Hate in Jamestown*, 225.

17. Price, *Love and Hate in Jamestown*, 84, 98, 106; Morgan, *American Slavery, American Freedom*, 78–79. See also Dunbar-Ortiz, *An Indigenous Peoples' History*, 60 (describing John Smith as a military leader who "threatened to kill all the women and children if the Powhatan leaders would not feed and clothe the settlers as well as provide them with land and labor").

18. Townsend, *Pocahontas and the Powhatan Dilemma*, 12–13, 15–16; Tim Hashaw, *The Birth of Black America: The First African Americans and the Pursuit of Freedom at Jamestown* (New York: Carroll & Graf, 2007), 153 (describing Powhatan's power).

19. Townsend, *Pocahontas and the Powhatan Dilemma*, 56. On the indigenous cultural practices of exogamy and intermingling, see Coleman, *That the Blood Stay Pure*, 87.

20. Townsend, *Pocahontas and the Powhatan Dilemma*, 79, quoting John Smith's account of what Powhatan said.

21. Dunbar-Ortiz, *An Indigenous Peoples' History*, 36–37.

22. Townsend, *Pocahontas and the Powhatan Dilemma*, 103–114.

23. Ibid., 118–19, 123–24, 126. The biblical quotes regarding Rebecca are from the Book of Genesis.

24. Townsend, *Pocahontas and the Powhatan Dilemma*, 12–17, 117–121.

25. Ibid., 114, quoting John Rolfe to Sir Thomas Dale, 1614.

26. Ibid., 98, 108, 112, 115.

27. Ibid., 112.

28. Coleman, *That the Blood Stay Pure*, 46–47.

29. Townsend, *Pocahontas and the Powhatan Dilemma*, 95–96 (noting the death of Rolfe's first in 1610), 115, quoting Rolfe to Sir Thomas Dale, 1614.

30. Price, *Love and Hate in Jamestown*, 156, quoting Rolfe to Dale.

31. Townsend, *Pocahontas and the Powhatan Dilemma*, 119, 132; Price, *Love and Hate in Jamestown*, 159–61.

32. Townsend, *Pocahontas and the Powhatan Dilemma*, 128–30.
33. See Johnson v. McIntosh, 21 US 543 (1823), for Supreme Court Chief Justice John Marshall's recitation of the ancient origins of the law of discovery and his holding that the US government consequently had the right to acquire Native American lands by purchase or conquest.
34. Townsend, *Pocahontas and the Powhatan Dilemma*, 128–30.
35. See Nancy Hendricks, *America's First Ladies: A Historical Encyclopedia and Primary Document Collection of the Remarkable Women of the White House* (Santa Barbara, CA: ABC-CLIO, LLC, 2015), 229. On President Wilson's support for racial segregation, see p. 94.
36. Coleman, *That the Blood Stay Pure*, 99, summarizing the specifics and motives of the Racial Integrity Act and quoting Rosaldo.
37. Hashaw, *The Birth of Black America*, 155–59.
38. Coleman, *That The Blood Stay Pure*, 88, 166.
39. Arica L. Coleman, "'Tell the Court I Love My [Indian] Wife': Interrogating Race and Self-Identity in Loving v. Virginia," *Souls: A Critical Journal of Black Politics, Culture, and Society* 8, no. 1 (2006): 67, 72, 75–76.
40. Coleman, *That the Blood Stay Pure*, 165, quoting an anonymous resident of Central Point in a 2005 interview conducted by Coleman.
41. Ibid., 164, quoting Mildred Loving in an interview and citing birth or census records identifying her ancestors as "colored," "Black," "mulatto," or "Negro."

CHAPTER TWO: SEX, LOVE, AND REBELLION IN EARLY COLONIAL VIRGINIA

1. Morgan, *American Slavery, American Freedom*, 31, 44–45.
2. Allen, *The Invention of the White Race*, 78.
3. Morgan, *American Slavery, American Freedom*, 126n86.
4. Ibid., 325–26.
5. Ibid., 126–30; Allen, *The Invention of the White Race*, 129.
6. Hashaw, *The Birth of Black America*, 87.
7. Ibid., 105–7, 249; James Deetz, *Flowerdew Hundred: The Archaeology of a Virginia Plantation, 1619–1864* (Charlottesville: University of Virginia Press, 1993), 19–20, 23.
8. Ibid., 65, 90–91, 127, 139.
9. Ibid., 67.
10. Linda M. Heywood and John K. Thornton, *Central Africans, Atlantic Creoles, and the Foundation of the Americas, 1585–1660* (New York: Cambridge University Press, 2007), 8.
11. Hashaw, *The Birth of Black America*, 105–7, 249; Deetz, *Flowerdew Hundred*, 19–20. See also Martha W. McCartney, "A Study of the Africans and African Americans on Jamestown Island and at Green Spring, 1619–1803," Colonial Williamsburg Foundation (2003), 32–33, which discusses some of the contributions Africans made to agricultural practices in colonial Virginia.
12. Morgan, *American Slavery, American Freedom*, 133–34; Elmer I. Miller, *The Legislature of the Province of Virginia: Its Internal Development* (New York: Columbia University Press, 1907), 19.

13. For example, Governor Yeardley and his heirs held some of these first Africans beyond a normal period of indenture and thus treated them as chattel slaves, as did Abraham Piersey (Hashaw, *The Birth of Black America*, 104–7).

14. Morgan, *American Slavery, American Freedom*, 154, 156–57; Higginbotham, *In the Matter of Color*, 21–22.

15. Hashaw, *The Birth of Black America*, 170.

16. Higginbotham, *In the Matter of Color*, 23; Morgan, *American Slavery, American Freedom*, 333.

17. Morgan, *American Slavery, American Freedom*, 333; Higginbotham, *In the Matter of Color*, 23.

18. Higginbotham, *In the Matter of Color*, 21–22.

19. Hashaw, *The Birth of Black America*, 170–71. See also Higginbotham, *In the Matter of Color*, 22, 24; Heywood and Thornton, *Central Africans, Atlantic Creoles*, 247.

20. Morgan, *American Slavery, American Freedom*, 155.

21. Hashaw, *The Birth of Black America*, 170–72, 174.

22. Ibid., 180.

23. Ibid., 188, discusses Tony Longo and his exchange with John Neene. See also Morgan, *American Slavery, American Freedom*, 156–67.

24. Hashaw, *The Birth of Black America*, 189. See also Higginbotham, *In the Matter of Color*, 23–26.

25. Hashaw, *The Birth of Black America*, 190–91.

26. Higginbotham, *In the Matter of Color*, 27–28; Hashaw, *The Birth of Black America*, 194.

27. Allen, *The Invention of the White Race*, 154.

28. Ibid., 28. After consulting marriage records, property records, and DNA evidence, some genealogists have indicated that President Barack Obama may be a descendant of John Punch. However, because many records no longer exist, Obama's matrilineal connection to Punch has not been definitively established (G. Reginald Daniel and Hettie V. Williams, *Race and the Obama Phenomenon: The Vision of a More Perfect Multiracial Union* [Jackson: University Press of Mississippi, 2014], 13).

29. Allen, *The Invention of the White Race*, 29. See also Morgan, *American Slavery, American Freedom*, 153–54, which discusses the diversity of the colony population.

30. Heywood and Thornton, *Central Africans, Atlantic Creoles*, 242, quoting John Farrer, *A Perfect Description of Virginia* (London, 1649), 3.

31. Morgan, *American Slavery, American Freedom*, 136, 153–54.

32. Allen, *The Invention of the White Race*, 122–23, 154.

33. Morgan, *American Slavery, American Freedom*, 329–30.

34. Allen, *The Invention of the White Race*, 64–69, 120.

35. Ibid., 129.

36. See ibid., 206–7, 210–11, 213–15; Edmund S. Morgan, "Slavery and Freedom: The American Paradox," *Journal of American History* 59, no. 1 (1972): 25–29.

37. William M. Wiecek, "The Origins of the Law of Slavery in British North America," *Cardozo Law Review* (1996): 1753, 1758.
38. Higginbotham, *In the Matter of Color*, 34; Morgan, *American Slavery, American Freedom*, 299.
39. Higginbotham, *In the Matter of Color*, 34–35.
40. Ibid., 43–44; Allen, *The Invention of the White Race*, 134, 197.
41. For a detailed scholarly treatment of Elizabeth Key's case and support for statements about the case in the text, see Taunya Lovell Banks, "Dangerous Woman: Elizabeth Key's Freedom Suit—Subjecthood and Racialized Identity in Seventeenth Century Colonial Virginia," *Akron Law Review* 41 (2008): 799, 799–801, 809–11, 814, 818–23, 818n109, 830–31, 833–36.
42. Ibid., 835.
43. Allen, *The Invention of the White Race*, 161. The author who researched these fornication cases states only that "the plantation bourgeoisie came to regard the mating of European-Americans with African-Americans as a serious problem for themselves" and cites one letter written by a colony governor in the eighteenth century, after white race pride and black chattel slavery had been established (ibid., 161n87, 242). Virginia governor William Gooch's 1736 letter to "Alured people" is a racist justification for the passage of a 1722 law that curtailed suffrage for free blacks and mulattos. He does state that the mulatto sons of interracial couples are inclined to see themselves as equals, a viewpoint he detests, and he supports the 1722 law in part because it will discourage "that kind of copulation." Even so, Gooch primarily argues that the law was designed "to fix a perpetual Brand upon Free Negroes & Mulattos" (ibid., 242). As explained in the next chapter, those in power constructed the ideology of white supremacy to establish and protect the institution of racialized black chattel slavery.

CHAPTER THREE: SLAVERY BEGETS ANTIMISCEGENATION AND WHITE SUPREMACY

1. Moran, *Interracial Intimacy*, 20.
2. Joel Williamson, *New People: Miscegenation and Mulattoes in the United States* (Baton Rouge: Louisiana State University Press, 1995), 7, 38.
3. Ibid., 13.
4. Peter Wallenstein, *Tell the Court I Love My Wife: Race, Marriage and Law; An American History* (New York: Palgrave Macmillan, 2002), 23.
5. Williamson, *New People*, 39.
6. Martha Hodes, *White Women, Black Men: Illicit Sex in the Nineteenth Century South* (New Haven, CT: Yale University Press, 2014), 20–22; "Irish Nell Butler," Archives of Maryland (Biographical Series), July 27, 2011, retrieved May 24, 2016; Wallenstein, *Tell the Court*, 23; Williamson, *New People*, 10; Stephen T. Whitman, *The Price of Freedom: Slavery and Manumission in Baltimore and Early National Maryland* (Lexington: University Press of Kentucky, 2001), 63–66.
7. Whitman, *The Price of Freedom*, 63–66.
8. Williamson, *New People*, 38.

9. Edward E. Baptist, *The Half Has Never Been Told: Slavery and the Making of American Capitalism* (New York: Basic Books, 2014), xix. A Virginia law prohibiting any additional "American Indian" from being "reduced into a state of slavery" was first introduced in 1691 and reenacted in 1705 (Peter Wallenstein, *Race, Sex and the Freedom to Marry: Loving v. Virginia* [Lawrence: University Press of Kansas, 2014], x).

10. Williamson, *New People*, 39.

11. Ira Berlin, *Many Thousands Gone: The First Two Centuries of Slavery in North America* (Cambridge, MA: Harvard University Press, 1998), 60.

12. Higginbotham, *In the Matter of Color*, 287; Williamson, *New People*, 11.

13. Williamson, *New People*, 98; Paul Heinegg, *Free African Americans of Virginia, North Carolina, and South Carolina* (Baltimore: Clearfield Publishing, 2006), 3.

14. Morgan, *American Slavery, American Freedom*, 331.

15. Higginbotham, *In the Matter of Color*, 45–46, 48.

16. Ibid., 36.

17. Ibid., 41, 44–45. While there may have been exceptions, membership in the Virginia Assembly most likely reflected the restrictions on the franchise and the social dominance of whites. Albert McKinley, *The Suffrage Franchise in the Thirteen English Colonies in America* (Philadelphia: University of Pennsylvania Press, 1905), 34, says, "An assembly of 1684, however, passed a resolution which is the first formal act limiting the suffrage to land-holders. From this year until 1830, no one but freeholders could vote in Virginia."

18. Higginbotham, *In the Matter of Color*, 48; "An Act for the Suppression of Outlying Slaves," 1691, Virginia Center for Digital History, http://www2 .vcdh.virginia.edu/xslt/servlet/XSLTServlet?xsl=/xml_docs/slavery/documents /display_laws2.xsl&xml=/xml_docs/slavery/documents/laws.xml&lawid =1691-04-01.

19. See Virginia Slave Codes of 1705, "An act declaring the Negro, Mulatto, and Indian slaves within this dominion, to be real estate, 1705" and "An act concerning servants and slaves, 1705," chaps. 7, 10, 34, Virginia Center for Digital History, http://www2.vcdh.virginia.edu/gos/laws1700-1750.html.

20. Ibid., chap. 4.

21. Ibid., chap. 36.

22. Ibid., chaps. 23, 34, 37.

23. Higginbotham, *In the Matter of Color*, 45.

24. See Virginia Slave Codes of 1705, chaps. 11, 18, 18.

25. See generally, Baptist, *The Half Has Never Been Told*.

26. Virginia Slave Codes of 1705, chap. 35; Morgan, *American Slavery, American Freedom*, 333.

27. Allen, *The Invention of the White Race*, 240; Morgan, *American Slavery, American Freedom*, 331–33; Higginbotham, *In the Matter of Color*, 54.

28. Georgia, Maryland, Massachusetts, North Carolina, Pennsylvania, Rhode Island, and Virginia prohibited interracial marriages. Maryland, Massachusetts, Pennsylvania, and Virginia prohibited interracial fornication. Maryland, Massachusetts, New York, and Virginia defined the races in statutes. Kevin

Mumford, "After Hugh: Statutory Race Segregation in Colonial America, 1630–1725," *American Journal of Legal History* 43 (1999): 280, 304.

29. Williamson, *New People*, 14.

30. Berlin, *Many Thousands Gone*, 78.

31. Virginia Meacham Gould, ed., *Chained to the Rock of Adversity: To Be Free, Black & Female in the Old South* (Athens: University of Georgia Press, 1998); Moran, *Interracial Intimacy*, 24; Monique Guillory, "Under One Roof: The Sins and Sanctity of the New Orleans Quadroon Balls," in *Race Consciousness*, ed. Judith Jackson Fossett and Jeffrey A. Tucker (New York: New York University Press, 1997).

32. Williamson, *New People*, 69, notes that in the slave market for "fancy girls," young mulatto women would attract a price as high as $1,600 in the 1850s, a time when a "prime" field hand might have sold for a thousand dollars.

33. Williamson, *New People*, 42n75.

34. Allen, *The Invention of the White Race*, 240 (quoting Gary B. Nash).

35. Morgan, *American Slavery, American Freedom*, 328, 386.

36. Thomas Piketty and Gabriel Zucman, "Capital Is Back: Wealth-Income Ratios in Rich Countries 1700–2010," *Quarterly Journal of Economics* (2014): 1255–1310, figs. 10–11.

37. Craig Steven Wilder, *Ebony and Ivy: Race, Slavery, and the Troubled History of America's Universities* (New York: Bloomsbury Publishing USA, 2014), 190, 228, 208; Baptist, *The Half Has Never Been Told*, 322. Several universities have now started retrospective commissions to look at their role in slavery. See, for example, President's Commission on Slavery and the University at the University of Virginia, available at http://slavery.virginia.edu/.

38. Morgan, *American Slavery, American Freedom*, 380.

39. Pascoe, *What Comes Naturally*, 21.

40. Williamson, *New People*, 42.

41. "Thomas Jefferson and Sally Hemings: A Brief Account," https://www.monticello.org/site/plantation-and-slavery/thomas-jefferson-and-sally-hemings-brief-account, accessed June 1, 2016.

42. Annette Gordon-Reed, *The Hemingses of Monticello: An American Family* (New York: W. W. Norton, 2008), 145; Annette Gordon-Reed, *Thomas Jefferson and Sally Hemings: An American Controversy* (Charlottesville: Virginia University Press, 2000).

43. Gordon-Reed, *The Hemingses of Monticello*, 169; "Thomas Jefferson to John Adams, 28 October 1813," *Founders Online*, National Archives, http://founders.archives.gov/documents/Jefferson/03-06-02-0446, last updated March 28, 2016; *The Papers of Thomas Jefferson*, Retirement Series, vol. 6, *11 March to 27 November 1813*, ed. J. Jefferson Looney (Princeton, NJ: Princeton University Press, 2009), 562–68; Andrew Burstein, *Jefferson's Secret: Death and Desire at Monticello* (New York: Basic Books, 2005), 168.

44. "Sally Hemings," https://www.monticello.org/site/plantation-and-slavery/sally-hemings, accessed June 1, 2016.

45. Gordon-Reed, *Hemingses of Monticello*, 326; Annette Gordon-Reed and Peter Onuf, *Most Blessed of Patriarchs: Thomas Jefferson and the Empire of Imagination* (New York: W. W. Norton, 2016), 23.

46. Gordon-Reed, *Hemingses of Monticello*, chap. 8.

47. Deborah Gray White, *Ar'n't I a woman?: Female Slaves in the Plantation South* (New York: W. W. Norton, 1999), 78, says, "Southern laws did not recognize the rape of a black woman as a crime." See also State v. John Mann, 13 N.C. 263 (1829), in which a female slave owner pressed charges for "cruel and unreasonable battery" by Mann against her slave, Lydia, and the North Carolina Supreme Court denied the claim, concluding that slave owners, including Mann, who had only hired out Lydia, had to be given "absolute" control "over the body" of the slave "to render the submission of the slave perfect"; and Higginbotham, *In the Matter of Color*, 47, which notes that statutes "encouraged the extensive exploitation of black women by their masters."

48. Kennedy, *Interracial Intimacies*, 46.

49. Ibid., 46–49.

50. Williamson, *New People*, 42–43; Sheryll Cashin, *The Agitator's Daughter* (New York: PublicAffairs, 2008), 37–41.

51. Kennedy, *Interracial Intimacies*, 47; William Cheek and Aimee Lee Cheek, *John Mercer Langston and the Fight for Freedom, 1829–65* (Chicago: University of Illinois Press, 1989).

52. Gordon-Reed and Onuf, *Most Blessed of Patriarchs*, 23, refer to Jefferson arranging for youngest sons Madison and Eston to be apprenticed to their skilled uncle, John Hemings. Several historians who challenge the existence of the relationship, despite the work of Gordon-Reed and others, cite the absence of evidence of caring or provision as a basis for skepticism about any relationship. See, for example, Robert Turner, ed., *The Jefferson-Hemmings Controversy: Report of the Scholars Commission* (Durham, NC: Carolina Academic Press, 2001, 2011), 10, http://www.tjheritage .org/newscomfiles/front_matter_and_report.pdf.

53. *A Humble Attempt at Scurrility, etc.* (1765), 40, cited in Edward Turner, *The Negro in Pennsylvania* (Washington, DC: American Historical Association, 1911). Turner also cites *What is Sauce for a Goose is also Sauce for a Gander,* etc[.] (1764), 6, for the proposition that "Benjamin Franklin was openly accused of keeping negro paramours." Legal scholar A. Leon Higginbotham cited Turner for this proposition (Higginbotham, *In the Matter of Color*, 286).

54. Benjamin Franklin, *Observations Concerning the Increase of Mankind*, National Archives, 1751, http://founders.archives.gov/documents/Franklin /01-04-02-0080.

55. Benjamin Franklin, "From Benjamin Franklin to John Waring, 17 December 1763," *Founders Online*, National Archives, http://founders.archives.gov /documents/Franklin/01-10-02-0214.

56. Thomas Jefferson, *Notes on the State of Virginia*, in Thomas Jefferson, *Writings* (New York: Library of America, 1984), 209.

57. Ibid., 211.

58. Ibid., 212.

59. Ibid., 214.

60. Jonathan Hart, *Contesting Empires: Opposition, Promotion and Slavery* (New York: Springer, 2005), 122.

61. Brent D. Glass, foreword to *The Jefferson Bible*, by Thomas Jefferson (Washington, DC: Smithsonian Books, 2011), 7.

62. Jefferson, *Notes*, 264.

63. Ibid., 264–65.

64. Nicholas Guyatt, *Bind Us Apart: How Enlightened Americans Invented Racial Segregation* (New York: Basic Books, 2016), 67, 115, 26, cites several of Jefferson's contemporaries who criticized his thoughts.

65. Ibid., 116. See also Thomas Jefferson, "Advertisement," prologue to *Notes*, in *Writings*, 124.

66. Jefferson, *Notes*, 266; Jefferson Letter to Marquis De Chastellux, June 7, 1785. In Query XI, Jefferson suggested that Virginia's "Savages" could not be "great societies," because they existed "without government." He also attributed the reduction in numbers of indigenous nations, including those of the Powhatan Confederation to, among other reasons, "spirituous liquors" and being "a people who lived principally on the spontaneous productions of nature" (Jefferson, *Notes*, 220–21).

67. Ronald Takaki, *Iron Cages: Race and Culture in Nineteenth-Century America* (New York: Oxford University Press, 1979), 62–63.

68. Guyatt, *Bind Us Apart*, 107, 110, 129–30.

69. Ibid., 132.

70. Henry Louis Gates Jr., *The Trials of Phillis Wheatley: America's First Black Poet and Her Encounters with the Founding Fathers* (New York: Basic Books, 2010), 74.

71. Jefferson, *Notes*, 267.

72. Phillis Wheatley, "On Being Brought from Africa to America," in *The Poems of Phillis Wheatley* (Chapel Hill: University of North Carolina Press, 1989).

73. Jefferson, Letter to Benjamin Banneker (1791); Letter to Henri Gregoire (1809), in *Writings*.

74. Jefferson, Letter to James Monroe (1801); Letter to Edward Coles (1814); Letter to Albert Gallatin (1820); Letter to Jared Sparks (1824), in *Writings*.

75. Wallenstein, *Tell the Court*, 20–21.

76. Peter Kolchin, *American Slavery: 1619–1877* (New York: Hill and Wang, 1994), 81.

77. Wallenstein, *Tell the Court*, 21.

78. See Zoe Beiser, "A Solution to Slavery or Racist Expulsion? The American Colonization Society, 1816–1860," http://ushistoryscene.com/article/american-colonization-society, says, "Most Americans feared the sexual mixing of blacks and whites, in part because amalgamation undermined the authority of white men, who could conceivably be replaced by black men in both the private and public spheres. In 1838, outraged that white women were mixing with black men, white anti-abolitionist rioters burned Pennsylvania Hall. Following the violence, the American Colonization Society held

its largest colonization meeting ever in Philadelphia." A strong proponent of the American Colonization Society, Congressmen Henry Clay once proclaimed, "unconquerable prejudice resulting from their color, they never could amalgamate with the free whites of this country. It was desirable, therefore, as it respected them, and the residue of the population of the country, to drain them off." See David Walker, "Appeal to the Coloured Citizens of the World, 1830," http://utc.iath.virginia.edu/abolitn/abesdwa2t .html, accessed November 7, 2016.

79. Gordon-Reed and Onuf, *Most Blessed of Patriarchs*.

80. Douglas Egerton, *Gabriel's Rebellion: The Virginia Slave Conspiracies of 1800 & 1802* (Chapel Hill: University of North Carolina Press, 1993), 48.

81. Arnold Rampersad, introduction to *Black Thunder, Gabriel's Revolt: Virginia, 1800*, by Arna Bontemps (Boston: Beacon Press, 1992), xii–xiii, xvii–xx.

82. Jefferson, Letter to the Governor of Virginia (James Monroe) (1801), in *Writings*.

83. Williamson, *New People*, 13.

84. Wallenstein, *Tell the Court*, 41–42, 49–50, 253.

85. See US Constitution, Art. I, Sect. 2, Sect. 9.

86. Guyatt, *Bind Us Apart*, 55.

87. *A Bill Declaring Who Shall Be Deemed Citizens of This Commonwealth*, in Jefferson, *Writings*, 374. Under the amendments to the bill in 1783, 1786, and 1789, noncitizens could technically become citizens, but the bill cautioned against the admittance of enemies and those not familiar with the Constitution. See "55. A Bill Declaring Who Shall Be Deemed Citizens of This Commonwealth, 18 June 1779," *Founders Online*, National Archives, http://founders.archives.gov/documents/Jefferson/01-02-02-0132-0004-0055, accessed November 11, 2016.

88. "Pennsylvania—An Act for the Gradual Abolition of Slavery, 1780," Avalon Project, Yale Law School, http://avalon.law.yale.edu/18th_century/pennst01 .asp, accessed November 7, 2016. For Pennsylvania being the first state to repeal an antimiscegenation law, see Wallenstein, *Tell the Court*, 254.

89. Paul Finkelman, "The Pennsylvania Delegation and the Peculiar Institution: The Two Faces of the Keystone State," *Pennsylvania Magazine of History and Biography* 112, no. 1 (1988): 53.

90. Guyatt, *Bind Us Apart*, 51.

91. Ibid., 56.

92. See, generally, Ian Haney-Lopez, *White by Law: The Legal Construction of Race* (New York: New York University Press, 1996), chaps. 3, 4, and 5.

93. Joseph Ellis, *Founding Brothers: The Revolutionary Generation* (New York: Vintage, 2002), chap. 3.

94. Jefferson, Letter to James Heaton, May 20, 1826, in *Writings*, 1516.

CHAPTER FOUR: MISCEGENATION, DOG-WHISTLING, AND THE SPREAD OF SUPREMACY

1. Thomas R. Gray and Nat Turner, *The Confessions of Nat Turner* (1831), Zea E-Books in American Studies, book 11, http://digitalcommons.unl.edu /zeaamericanstudies/11.

2. John Hope Franklin and Alfred A. Moss Jr., *From Slavery to Freedom: A History of African Americans* (New York: Alfred A. Knopf, 2004), 164–65; 169–72; Theodore W. Allen, *The Invention of the White Race*, Vol 1, *Racial Oppression and Social Control* (London: Verso, 1994), 84.

3. See, for example, Erik S. Root, ed., *Sons of the Fathers: The Virginia Slavery Debates of 1831–1832* (Lanham, MD: Lexington Books, 2010), 30, which quotes the delegate Samuel McDowell Moore from Rockbridge.

4. Darius Lyman, *The Besotted Alien in Leaven for Doughfaces, or Threescore and Ten Parables Touching Slavery* (1856).

5. James Kirke Paulding, *Slavery in the United States* (New York: Harper & Brother, 1836), 59–73.

6. *Beauty, Virtue & Vice Threats: Images of Women in Nineteenth-Century American Prints*, American Antiquarian Society, online exhibition, http://www.americanantiquarian.org/Exhibitions/Beauty/threats.htm, accessed July 14, 2016.

7. See, generally, Werner Sollors, *Interracialism: Black-White Intermarriage in American History, Literature, and Law* (New York: Oxford University Press, 2000), part 2.

8. Marie-Amélie George, "The Modern Mulatto," *Columbia Journal of Gender and Law* 15 (2006): 665, 672; Pascoe, *What Comes Naturally*, 21.

9. Leon F. Litwack, *North of Slavery: The Negro in the Free States* (Chicago: University of Chicago Press, 2009).

10. Haroon Kharem, "The American Colonization Society," in *Curriculum of Repression: A Pedagogy of Racial History in the United States* (Washington, DC: P. Lang, 2006), 91.

11. Reginald Horsman, *Race and Manifest Destiny: The Origins of American Racial Anglo-Saxonism* (Cambridge, MA: Harvard University Press, 1981), 208–13, quotes Bushnell and explains the construction of Anglo-Saxon as a racial category.

12. Nell Irvin Painter, *The History of White People* (New York: W. W. Norton, 2010).

13. Horsman, *Race and Manifest Destiny*, 201–13; John C. Calhoun, Cong. Globe, 30th Cong., 1st Sess. 96–98 (January 4, 1848).

14. Moran, *Interracial Intimacy*, 17; Juan F. Perea, *Race and Races: Cases and Resources for a Diverse America* (St. Paul, MN: West Group, 2000), 294–96, 304.

15. Pascoe, *What Comes Naturally*, 98–100.

16. Alexis de Tocqueville, *Democracy in America* (1835), trans. George Lawrence (New York: Perennial Classics, 2000), 340.

17. Mark O. Hatfield, with the Senate Historical Office, *Vice Presidents of the United States, 1789–1993* (Washington, DC: US Government Printing Office, 1997), 121–31, http://www.senate.gov/artandhistory/history/resources/pdf/richard_johnson.pdf.

18. Ibid.

19. Henry Robert Burke, "Richard Mentor Johnson: Window to the Past," in *Lest We Forget: African American Military History by Historian, Author,*

and Veteran Bennie McRae, Jr., comp. Bennie McRae Jr., Hampton University, http://lestweforget.hamptonu.edu/page.cfm?uuid=9FEC4E7B-AA9D-C0FB-DE4F0A6430F8F448, accessed July 14, 2016.

20. William D. Zabel, "Interracial Marriage and the Law," 1965, in Sollors, *Interracialism*, 54–61, 57.

21. Guyatt, *Bind Us Apart*, 167.

22. Ibid.

23. Ibid., 161–68.

24. Ibid. 191.

25. Ibid., 172.

26. Ibid., 171.

27. Allen C. Guelzo, *Lincoln and Douglas: The Debates That Defined America* (New York: Simon & Schuster, 2008), xxv.

28. Reprinted in "Amalgamation," editorial, *Liberator*, May 1, 1857.

29. Henry Louis Gates Jr., ed., *Lincoln on Race & Slavery* (Princeton, NJ: Princeton University Press, 2009), 132.

30. Coleman, *That the Blood Stay Pure*, 68.

31. Eric Foner, *The Fiery Trial: Abraham Lincoln and American Slavery* (New York: W. W. Norton, 2010), 257.

32. Ibid., 146.

33. Ibid., 158.

34. Ibid., 150–51.

35. Harriet Ann Jacobs, *Incidents in the Life of a Slave Girl, Written by Herself*, ed. Lydia Maria Francis Child (Boston: 1861), 83, electronic edition by Documenting the American South, University of North Carolina–Chapel Hill digitization project, http://docsouth.unc.edu/fpn/jacobs/jacobs.html, accessed July 14, 2016.

36. Ibid., 85.

37. Ibid., 80. See also Hodes, *White Women, Black Men*, 133n24, which quotes Jacobs.

38. Williamson, *New People*, 2, 5, 33.

39. David G. Croly, *Miscegenation: The Theory of the Blending of the Races, Applied to the American White Man and Negro* (New York: H. Dexter, Hamilton & Co., 1864), available at Internet Archive, https://archive.org/details/miscegenationtheo0crol; Sidney Kaplan, "The Miscegenation Issue in the Election of 1864," *Journal of Negro History* 34, no. 3 (July 1949): 274, 277.

40. Lois Brown, *Pauline Elizabeth Hopkins: Black Daughter of the Revolution* (Chapel Hill: University of North Carolina Press, 2008), 333.

41. Kaplan, "The Miscegenation Issue in the Election of 1864," 277–335. See also Pascoe, *What Comes Naturally*, 28–29.

42. Foner, *The Fiery Trial*, 254–61.

43. Elizabeth Keckley, *Behind the Scenes, Or, Thirty Years a Slave and Four Years in the White House* (New York: Oxford University Press on Demand, 1988).

44. Frederick Douglass, *The Life and Times of Frederick Douglass: From 1817–1882*, ed. John Lobb (London: Christian Age Office, 1882), 321.

45. Moran, *Interracial Intimacy*, 26.
46. Peter Carlson, "Lincoln's Feisty Foil: Thaddeus Stevens Fought Even Harder for Black Equality than the Great Emancipator," *American History* (April 2013): 52.
47. Lydia Smith lived with and kept house for Stevens for twenty years in Lancaster, Pennsylvania. They were domestic partners if not romantic ones. She traveled to and from Washington with Stevens and never refuted the accusation that she was his mistress. He could have married her if he had wanted to, as Pennsylvania had long since abandoned its legal prohibition on cross-racial marriage. In his last will and testament, Stevens identified Smith as his "housekeeper" and provided her with ample funds to purchase the house they had shared. During life, Stevens included Smith in social events with friends and family and offered her seats next to him on public transportation. He hired a prominent artist, Charles Bird King, to paint Smith's portrait, not something prominent men were known to do for "the help." In a letter, Smith once chastised Stevens's nephew, showing that she was comfortable intervening in Stevens's family life (ibid.). "The winter is here and you haven't come to visit your uncle at all," she wrote. "Your uncle is not well" (Jack Brubaker, "When Lydia Smith Chastised Thaddeus Stevens Nephew," *LancasterOnline*, http://lancasteronline.com/opinion/when-lydia-smith-chastised-thaddeus-stevens-nephew/article_ccfd9d23-aeda-5724-9e68-e3d36c735a90.html, accessed July 19, 2016).
48. Peter Carlson, *Lincoln's Feisty Foil*, 52.
49. Ibid., 52–55.
50. Douglass, *The Life and Times of Frederick Douglass*.
51. Frederick Douglass, "The Dred Scott Decision: Speech Delivered Before American Anti-Slavery Society, New York, May 11, 1857," cited in Perea, *Race and Races*.
52. Ibid., 135.
53. Sarah Meer, "Public and Personal Letters: Julia Griffiths and Frederick Douglass' Paper," *Slavery & Abolition* 33, no. 2 (June 2012): 251–64.
54. Frank E. Fee Jr., "To No One More Indebted, Frederick Douglass and Julia Griffiths, 1849–63," *Journalism History* 37 no. 1 (Spring 2011): 17, 18–19.
55. Maria Diedrich, *Love Across Color Lines: Ottilie Assing and Frederick Douglass* (New York: Hill & Wang, 1999).
56. T. H. Pickett, "The Friendship of Frederick Douglass with the German, Ottilie Assing," *Georgia Historical Quarterly* (Spring 1989): 92.
57. Ibid., 100.
58. Diedrich, *Love Across Color Lines*, xvii.
59. Kennedy, *Interracial Intimacies*, 73.
60. James O. Horton, "What Business Has the World with the Color of My Wife? A Letter from Frederick Douglass," *OAH Magazine of History* (January 2005).
61. Pascoe, *What Comes Naturally*, 40–41.
62. Ibid., 32; Moran, *Interracial Intimacy*, 27.
63. William Edward Burghardt Du Bois, *Black Reconstruction in America: Toward a History of the Part Which Black Folk Played in the Attempt to*

Reconstruct Democracy in America, 1860–1880 (orig. publ. 1935; New Brunswick, NJ: Transaction Publishers, 2013); Comer Vann Woodward, *The Strange Career of Jim Crow* (New York: Oxford University Press, 1955), 24; Hodes, *White Women, Black Men,* 197.

64. Hodes, *White Women, Black Men;* Pascoe, *What Comes Naturally,* 40–43, including maps of miscegenation laws in 1865 and 1875.

65. Pascoe, *What Comes Naturally,* 148–49.

66. Ibid., 141.

67. Ibid., 147, 151.

68. Sheryll D. Cashin, "Democracy, Race, and Multiculturalism in the Twenty-First Century: Will the Voting Rights Act Ever Be Obsolete?," *Washington University Journal of Law and Policy* 22 (2006): 71.

69. Hodes, *White Women, Black Men,* 157.

70. Ibid., 154–61.

71. Woodward, *The Strange Career of Jim Crow,* 142.

72. Hodes, *White Women, Black Men,* 176–77.

73. Ibid., 181. On Thurgood Marshall and the NAACP's role in fighting lynching and rape cases, see, for example, Gilbert King, *Devil in the Grove: Thurgood Marshall, the Groveland Boys, and the Dawn of a New America* (New York: HarperCollins, 2012).

74. Ida B. Wells, "A Red Record: Lynching Statistics in the United States" (1895); Hodes, *White Women, Black Men,* 197.

75. Pascoe, *What Comes Naturally,* 52, 79–80, 82–84.

76. Ibid., 84–85.

77. Ibid., 65.

78. Pace v. Alabama, 106 U.S. 583, 1 S. Ct. 637, 27 L. Ed. 207 (1883).

79. Williamjames Hoffer, *Plessy v. Ferguson: Race and Inequality in Jim Crow America* (Lawrence: University Press of Kansas, 2012).

80. Cashin, "Democracy, Race, and Multiculturalism," 71.

81. See, generally, Deborah Davis, *Guest of Honor: Booker T. Washington, Theodore Roosevelt, and the White House Dinner That Shocked a Nation* (New York: Simon and Schuster, 2012).

82. Geoffrey C. Ward, *Unforgivable Blackness: The Rise and Fall of Jack Johnson* (New York: A. A. Knopf, 2004), 216.

83. Ibid., 99; Jack Johnson, *Jack Johnson: In the Ring and Out* (New York: Citadel Press, 1992), 76.

84. Ward, *Unforgiveable Blackness,* 21.

85. Pascoe, *What Comes Naturally,* 164–66 (including wedding photo of Johnson and Cameron).

86. Ward, *Unforgiveable Blackness,* 308.

87. Pascoe, *What Comes Naturally,* 166–80.

88. Melvyn Stokes, *D. W. Griffith's* The Birth of a Nation: *A History of "The Most Controversial Motion Picture of All Time"* (New York: Oxford University Press, 2007), 111; John Hope Franklin, "Birth of a Nation: Propaganda as History," *Massachusetts Review* 20, no. 3 (1979): 417–34; John Milton Cooper, *Woodrow Wilson* (New York: Alfred Knopf, 2011), 204–6; Nicholas Patler, *Jim Crow and the Wilson Administration: Protesting Federal*

Segregation in the Early Twentieth Century (Boulder: University Press of Colorado, 2007).

89. Cameron McWhirter, *Red Summer: The Summer of 1919 and the Awakening of Black America* (New York: Macmillan, 2011).

90. See, generally, Herbert Hill, "The Importance of Race in American Labor History," *International Journal of Politics, Culture and Society* 9, no. 2 (1995); David Roediger, *The Wages of Whiteness: Race and the Making of the American Working Class* (London: Verso, 1991).

91. Pascoe, *What Comes Naturally*, 117–18.

92. Audrey Smedley and Brian D. Smedley, "Race as Biology Is Fiction, Racism as a Social Problem Is Real: Anthropological and Historical Perspectives on the Social Construction of Race," *American Psychologist* 60, no. 1 (2005): 16; Ian F. Haney Lopez, "The Social Construction of Race: Some Observations on Illusion, Fabrication, and Choice," *Harvard Civil Rights-Civil Liberties Law Review* 29 (1994): 1.

93. Pascoe, *What Comes Naturally*, 116–18, 142.

94. Mae M. Ngai, "The Architecture of Race in American Immigration Law: A Reexamination of the Immigration Act of 1924," *Journal of American History* 86, no. 1 (1999): 67–92.

95. Pascoe, *What Comes Naturally*, 140–43.

96. Section 5 of the Virginia "Act to Preserve Racial Integrity" of 1924, reprinted in Sollors, *Interracialism*, 24.

97. Buck v. Bell, 274 U.S. 200, 47 S. Ct. 584, 71 L. Ed. 1000 (1927).

98. Pascoe, *What Comes Naturally*, 146, reproduces Plecker's list, annotated by hand on March 14, 1946.

99. Wallenstein, *Race, Sex and the Freedom to Marry*, 72–73.

100. Coleman, *That the Blood Stay Pure*, 163–64.

101. Pascoe, *What Comes Naturally*, 143–50.

102. Ibid., 118–19.

CHAPTER FIVE: *LOVING V. VIRGINIA*

1. *The Loving Story*, dir. Buirsky; Peter Wallenstein, *Race, Sex, and the Freedom to Marry: Loving v. Virginia* (Lawrence: University of Kansas Press, 2014), 79; Pascoe, *What Comes Naturally*, 271–72.

2. Wallenstein, *Race, Sex, and the Freedom to Marry*, xi, 2, 9, 11, 18–19, 78–79; Wingfield, *A History of Caroline County, Virginia*, 167.

3. Don Baker, "Why They Mattered: Harry F. Byrd Jr.," *Politico*, last modified December 23, 2013, http://www.politico.com/magazine/story/2013/12/harry-f-byrd-jr-obituary-101429.

4. W. James Jr., *The Crisis of Conservative Virginia: The Byrd Organization and the Politics of Massive Resistance* (Knoxville: University of Tennessee Press, 1976); Wallenstein, *Race, Sex, and the Freedom to Marry*, 78, 87.

5. Wallenstein, *Race, Sex, and the Freedom to Marry*, 75–79, 90; Simeon Booker, "The Couple That Rocked Courts," *Ebony*, September 1967, 78, 80.

6. Phyl Newbeck, *Virginia Hasn't Always Been for Lovers: Interracial Marriage Bans and the Case of Richard and Mildred Loving* (Carbondale: Southern Illinois University Press, 2005), 9.

7. Wingfield, *A History of Caroline County, Virginia*, 170, 176.
8. Wallenstein, *Race, Sex, and the Freedom to Marry*, 72–73.
9. Ibid., 2, 21, 60–61; P. E. Boyd Byrd is sometimes described as "black," other times "Indian" (ibid., 21). Booker, "The Couple That Rocked the Courts," 79–80, 82, 84, described him as "Negro." As of July 25, 2016, one could still see the grocery building and the sign on Google Street View.
10. Wil Haygood, "The Man from Jet," *Washington Post*, July 15, 2007, http://www.washingtonpost.com/wp-dyn/content/article/2007/07/10/AR2007071001619.html.
11. Booker, "The Couple That Rocked the Courts," 80.
12. Coleman, *That the Blood Stay Pure*, 161.
13. For a tutorial on the brown paper bag test and the colorism that black people historically engaged in, see Lawrence O. Graham, *Our Kind of People: Inside America's Black Upper Class* (New York: HarperCollins, 1999), 1.
14. *The Loving Story*, dir. Buirsky.
15. Booker, "The Couple That Rocked the Courts," 79; ibid.
16. *The Loving Story*, dir. Buirsky.
17. See, for example, Coleman, *That the Blood Stay Pure*, chaps. 5, 6, 7, which discusses long histories of triracial "African, European and Indian" mixture not only in Caroline County but also in Charles City County, Amherst County, and other areas of Virginia; Wallenstein, *Race, Sex, and the Freedom to Marry*, 249–50, which cites scholarship about a twentieth-century Georgia community and about Prince Edward and Albemarle Counties in Virginia.
18. Newbeck, *Virginia Hasn't Always Been for Lovers*, 11–12.
19. *The Loving Story*, dir. Buirsky.
20. Coleman, *That the Blood Stay Pure*, 175; Arica L. Coleman, "Mildred Loving: The Extraordinary Life of an Ordinary Woman," in *Virginia Women: Their Lives and Times*, ed. Cynthia A. Kierner and Sandra Gioia Treadway (Athens: University of Georgia Press, 2016), 323–25. See also Wallenstein, *Race, Sex, and the Freedom to Marry*, 79–80; Newbeck, *Virginia Hasn't Always Been for Lovers*, 219.
21. "The Crime of Being Married: A Virginia Couple Fights to Overturn an Old Law Against Miscegenation," *Life*, March 18, 1966, 88.
22. Wallenstein, *Race, Sex, and the Freedom to Marry*, 81; Pascoe, *What Comes Naturally*, 272; Newbeck, *Virginia Hasn't Always Been for Lovers*, 11; Coleman, "'Tell the Court I Love My [Indian] Wife.'"
23. David Margolick, "A Mixed Marriage's 25th Anniversary of Legality," *New York Times*, December 12, 1992.
24. Wallenstein, *Race, Sex, and the Freedom to Marry*, 82–83; *The Loving Story*, dir. Buirsky.
25. Brent Staples, "Loving v. Virginia and the Secret History of Race," *New York Times*, May 14, 2008, http://www.nytimes.com/2008/05/14/opinion/14wed4.html.
26. Pascoe, *What Comes Naturally*, 272; Wallenstein, *Race, Sex, and the Freedom to Marry*, 82; Newbeck, *Virginia Hasn't Always Been for Lovers*, 12; Coleman, "Mildred Loving," 317.

27. Wallenstein, *Race, Sex, and the Freedom to Marry*, 83.

28. Pascoe, *What Comes Naturally*, 271; Wallenstein, *Race, Sex, and the Freedom to Marry*, 86–87.

29. Pascoe, *What Comes Naturally*, 272–73.

30. Wallenstein, *Race, Sex, and the Freedom to Marry*, 84–85, 97; Victoria Valentine, "When Love Was a Crime," in *The Best of "Emerge" Magazine* (New York: Ballantine Books, 2003), 19.

31. Wallenstein, *Race, Sex, and the Freedom to Marry*, 97.

32. Mildred Loving's handwritten letter is reprinted in Newbeck, *Virginia Hasn't Always Been for Lovers*, among photos inserted between chapters 10 and 11. For those who wish to quibble with my characterization of her use of a capital *W* for "White," compare that *W* with the distinctly different lowercased *w*'s she uses, for example in the sentence "We were to leave the state to make our home."

33. Newbeck, *Virginia Hasn't Always Been for Lovers*, 139–41.

34. Pascoe, *What Comes Naturally*, 273–75.

35. Robert Walters, "Mixed Couple Tests Virginia Law," *Washington Evening Star*, January 11, 1965.

36. Naim v. Naim, 197 Va. 80, 87 S.E.2d 749 (1955), 90.

37. Pascoe, *What Comes Naturally*, 224–31, 275.

38. Wallenstein, *Race, Sex, and the Freedom to Marry*, 118.

39. *The Loving Story*, dir. Buirsky.

40. Newbeck, *Virginia Hasn't Always Been for Lovers*, 215.

41. Pascoe, *What Comes Naturally*, 246–47, 268–67.

42. Wallenstein, *Race, Sex, and the Freedom to Marry*, 125–26; Pascoe, *What Comes Naturally*, 276–77.

43. Wallenstein, *Race, Sex, and the Freedom to Marry*, 129; Pascoe, *What Comes Naturally*, 280–81.

44. Pascoe, *What Comes Naturally*, 205, 207.

45. Perez v. Sharp, 32 Cal.2d 711, 198 P.2d 17 (1948).

46. See Robin A. Lenhardt, "The Story of *Perez v. Sharp*: Forgotten Lessons on Race, Law, and Marriage," in *Race Law Stories*, ed. Devon W. Carbado and Rachel F. Moran (New York: Foundation Press, 2008).

47. Pascoe, *What Comes Naturally*, 293–94.

48. Hirabayashi v. United States, 320 U.S. 81, 100 (1943).

49. Neil Gotanda, "The Story of Korematsu: The Japanese-American Cases," in *Constitutional Law Stories*, ed. Michael Dorf (New York: West Academic, 2009), 249.

50. Sumi Cho, "Redeeming Whiteness in the Shadow of Internment: Earl Warren, Brown, and a Theory of Racial Redemption," *Boston College Law Review* 40 (1998): 73.

51. Philippa Strum, "How Mexican Immigrants Ended 'Separate but Equal' in California," op-ed, *Los Angeles Times*, March 2, 2016, http://www.latimes.com/opinion/op-ed/la-oe-0302-strum-mendez-case-20160302-story.html.

52. Hernandez v. Texas, 347 U.S. 475, 478 (1954).

53. Loving v. Virginia, 388 U.S. 1, 11–12 (1967). See also Wallenstein, *Tell the Court I Love My Wife*, 283–84.

54. Newbeck, *Virginia Hasn't Always Been for Lovers*, 215.

55. "The Crime of Being Married."

56. Patrick Sullivan, "Quiet Virginia Wife Ended Interracial Ban," *Washington Post*, May 6, 2008 http://www.washingtonpost.com/wp-dyn/content/article /2008/05/05/AR2008050502439.html.

CHAPTER SIX: 2017

1. *Public Papers of the Presidents of the United States: Lyndon B. Johnson, 1965*, 2, entry 546, pp. 1037–40 (Washington, DC: Government Printing Office, 1966); Robert Shenkkhan, "LBJ's Second Great Battle: Enforcing the Civil Rights Act," *Los Angeles Times*, June 28, 2014, http://www.latimes .com/nation/la-oe-schenkkan-civil-rights-lyndon-johnson-20140629 -story.html.

2. See Ian Haney-López, *Dog Whistle Politics: How Coded Racial Appeals Have Reinvented Racism and Wrecked the Middle Class* (New York: Oxford University Press, 2015); Michelle Alexander, *The New Jim Crow: Mass Incarceration in the Age of Colorblindness* (New York: New Press, 2012); Sheryll Cashin, *Place, Not Race: A New Vision of Opportunity in America* (Boston: Beacon Press, 2014), chap. 1; Ian Haney-López and Heather McGhee, "How Populists Like Bernie Sanders Should Talk About Racism," *Nation*, January 28, 2016, https://www.thenation.com/article/how-populists -like-bernie-sanders-should-talk-about-racism/.

3. See, for example, chap. 3 of Sheryll Cashin, *The Failures of Integration: How Race and Class Are Undermining the American Dream* (New York: PublicAffairs, 2004); Douglas S. Massey and Nancy A. Denton, *American Apartheid: Segregation and the Making of the Underclass* (Cambridge, MA: Harvard University Press, 1993); Kenneth T. Jackson, *Crabgrass Frontier: The Suburbanization of the United States* (New York: Oxford University Press, 1985).

4. Robin DiAngelo, "White Fragility," *International Journal of Critical Pedagogy* 3, no. 3 (2011): 54.

5. Margery Austin Turner and Zachary McDade, "Neighborhood Diversity Increases for Whites," MetroTrends, Urban Institute's Report Card on Social and Economic Trends in Urban America, last modified 2011, http://www .metrotrends.org/commentary/neighborhood-diversity.cfm.

6. DiAngelo, "White Fragility," 57–65.

7. Jordan Weissmann, "Sorry, Marriage Is a 'Luxury Good,'" *Atlantic*, October 30, 2013, http://www.theatlantic.com/business/archive/2013/10/sorry -marriage-is-a-luxury-good/281016/.

8. Sabrina Tavernise, "Married Couples Are No Longer a Majority, Census Finds," *New York Times*, May 25, 2011, http://www.nytimes.com/2011/05 /26/us/26marry.html.

9. US Census Bureau, "2010 Census Shows Interracial and Interethnic Married Couples Grew by 28 Percent over Decade," US Census Bureau Public Information Office, April 25, 2012, www.census.gov/newsroom/releases /archives/2010_census/cb12-68.html.

10. Wang, "Interracial Marriage: Who Is 'Marrying Out'?"

11. Andy Kiersz, "These Maps Show the Geography of Interracial Marriage," *Business Insider*, February 7, 2014; Wendy Wang, "Appendix 2: State and Regional Rates," Pew Research Center's Social Demographic Trends Project, February 16, 2012.
12. Wang, "Appendix 2: State and Regional Rates."
13. Reynolds Farley, "Racial Issues: Recent Trends in Residential Patterns and Intermarriage," in *Diversity and Its Discontents: Cultural Conflict and Common Ground in Contemporary American Society*, ed. Neil J. Smelser and Jeffrey C. Alexander (Princeton, NJ: Princeton University Press, 1999), 85–128, cited in Kiersz, "These Maps Show the Geography of Interracial Marriage."
14. Emily Heil, "John McCain's Son to the 'Ignorant Racists' Criticizing an Old Navy Ad with an Interracial Couple: 'Eat It,'" *Washington Post*, May 2, 2016; The Reliable Source, "Jack McCain, Son of John McCain, Weds Renee Swift in San Francisco," *Washington Post*, June 2, 2013.
15. Roland G. Fryer, "Guess Who's Been Coming to Dinner? Trends in Interracial Marriage over the 20th Century," *Journal of Economic Perspectives* 21, no. 2 (2007): 71–90. In 2008, the number of white women who married black men was double the number of white women who married Asian men. But white men married Asian women at nearly double the rate they married black women. In addition, white men married Native American women at roughly the same rate that they married black women, but white women married Native American men at half the rate they married black men. Zhenchao Qian and Daniel T. Lichter, "Changing Patterns of Interracial Marriage in a Multiracial Society," *Journal of Marriage and Family* 73, no. 5 (2011): 1065–84, 1072.
16. Wang, "Interracial Marriage: Who Is 'Marrying Out'?"
17. Ibid.
18. "America's Families and Living Arrangements: 2015: Unmarried Couples (UC Table Series)," US Census Bureau, Demographic Internet Staff, table UC-3, www.census.gov/hhes/families/data/cps2015UC.html, accessed September 18, 2016.
19. Qian and Lichter, "Changing Patterns of Interracial Marriage." In 2008, nearly one-fifth of cohabiting black men had a white female partner, while less than 5 percent of cohabiting black women lived with a white male. About 40 percent of cohabiting Asians and a third of cohabiting Hispanics had white partners, regardless of their sex. Between 40 and 35 percent of Native Americans who were cohabiting did so with non–Native Americans (ibid.).
20. Richard Alba and Nancy Foner, "Mixed Unions and Immigrant-Group Integration in North America and Western Europe," *Annals of the American Academy of Political and Social Science* 662, no. 1 (2015): 38–56.
21. Zheng Hou, Zheng Wu, Christoph Schimmele, and John Myles, "Cross-Country Variation in Interracial Marriage: A USA-Canada Comparison of Metropolitan Areas," *Ethnic and Racial Studies* 38, no. 9 (2015): 1591–609.

22. Gary J. Gates, *LGB Families and Relationships: Analyses of the 2013 National Health Interview Survey* (Los Angeles: UCLA Williams Institute, 2014), http://williamsinstitute.law.ucla.edu/research/census-lgbt-demographics-studies/lgb-families-nhis-sep-2014/.

23. Evan Wolfson, founder and president of Freedom to Marry and widely considered the architect of the marriage equality movement, outlined these key elements to their victory during a lecture and in answer to my question about the influence of *Loving*. Evan Wolfson, "The Freedom to Marry Win: Transformation and Triumph to Celebrate, Lessons to Adapt and Apply," Phillip A. Hart Memorial Lecture, Georgetown Law, Washington, DC, September 28, 2016.

24. Mildred Loving, "Loving for All," National LGBTQ Task Force, June 12, 2007, www.thetaskforce.org/static_html/downloads/release_materials/loving_for_all.pdf.

25. Brian Powell, Lala Carr Steelman, and Oren Pizmony-Levy, "Transformation or Continuity in Americans' Definition of Family: A Research Note," NCFMR working paper 12, Bowling Green State University, Bowling Green, OH, 2012; Alison Keleher and Eric Smith, "Growing Support for Gay and Lesbian Equality Since 1990," *Journal of Homosexuality* 59, no. 9 (2014): 1307–26.

26. Michael J. LaCour and Donald P. Green, "When Contact Changes Minds: An Experiment on Transmission of Support for Gay Equality," *Science* 346, no. 6215 (2014): 1366–69.

27. "22% of Americans Have a Relative in a Mixed-Race Marriage," Pew Research Center's Social Demographic Trends Project, March 14, 2006; Rosentiel, "Almost All Millennials Accept Interracial Dating and Marriage."

28. Rosentiel, "Almost All Millennials Accept Interracial Dating and Marriage."

29. Wendy Wang, "Chapter 4: Public Attitudes on Intermarriage," Pew Research Center's Social Demographic Trends Project, February 16, 2012.

30. One study found evidence of brain activity consistent with disgust even among college students reporting conscious acceptance of such couples. See "Most People Are Accepting of Interracial Marriage, Right? The Brain Shows a Different Story," *Salon*, September 13, 2016, http://www.salon.com/2016/09/13/most-people-accepting-of-interracial-marriage-right-the-brain-shows-a-different-story_partner. This finding is consistent, however, with most research on implicit bias. Many people who are avowedly antiracist will register implicit biases, for example, favoring whites over blacks (see Jerry Kang, "Trojan Horses of Race," *Harvard Law Review* [2005]: 1489–1593).

31. Wang, "Public Attitudes on Intermarriage."

32. Noor WazWaz, "It's Official: The U.S. Is Becoming a Minority-Majority Nation," *US News & World Report*, July 6, 2015, http://www.usnews.com/news/articles/2015/07/06/its-official-the-us-is-becoming-a-minority-majority-nation.

33. Marisol Clark Ibáñez and Diane Felmlee, "Interethnic Relationships: The Role of Social Network Diversity," *Journal of Marriage and Family* 66, no. 2 (2004): 293–305.

34. Melissa R. Herman and Mary E. Campbell, "I Wouldn't, But You Can: Attitudes Toward Interracial Relationships," *Social Science Research* 41 (2012): 343–58.
35. Amanda B. Brodish, Paige C. Brazy, and Patricia G. Devine, "More Eyes on the Prize: Variability in White Americans' Perceptions of Progress Toward Racial Equality," *Personality and Social Psychology Bulletin* 34, no. 4 (2008): 513–27.
36. Samuel L. Perry, "Multiracial Church Attendance and Support for Same-Sex Romantic and Family Relationships," *Sociological Inquiry* 83, no. 2 (2013): 259–85. See also Samuel L. Perry, "Racial Composition of Social Settings, Interracial Friendship, and Whites' Attitudes Toward Interracial Marriage," *Social Science Journal* 50, no. 1 (2013): 13–22, concludes that "greater presence of blacks, Latinos, or Asians in neighborhoods and congregations of whites predicts favorable attitudes among whites toward interracial marriage with each respective racial group."
37. George Yancy, "Experiencing Racism: Differences in the Experiences of Whites Married to Blacks and Non-Black Racial Minorities," *Journal of Comparative Family Studies* 38, no. 2 (2007): 197–213.
38. Frederick Kunkle, "Pew: Multiracial Population Changing the Face of the U.S.," *Washington Post*, June 11, 2015.
39. Pew Research Center, *Multiracial in America: Proud, Diverse and Growing in Numbers* (Washington, DC: June 11, 2015), 5, 11.
40. Ibid., 12, 39–44.
41. Ibid., 12, 41.
42. Ibid., 49, 65.
43. Jenee Desmond-Harris, "6 Things I Wish People Understood About Being Biracial," *Vox*, August 11, 2015, http://www.vox.com/2015/3/11/8182263/biracial-identity.
44. Kenneth Prewitt, "Racial Classification in America: Where Do We Go from Here?," *Daedalus* 134, no. 1 (2005): 5–17.
45. US Census Bureau Public Information Office, "U.S. Census Bureau Projections Show a Slower Growing, Older, More Diverse Nation a Half Century from Now," US Census Bureau Public Information Office, December 12, 2012, www.census.gov/newsroom/releases/archives/population/cb12-243.html.
46. See Prewitt, "Racial Classification in America," 81.
47. D'Vera Cohn, "Census Considers New Approach to Asking About Race—by Not Using the Term at All," Pew Research Center, June 18, 2015, http://www.pewresearch.org/fact-tank/2015/06/18/census-considers-new-approach-to-asking-about-race-by-not-using-the-term-at-all/.
48. Renée M. Landers, "'What's *Loving* Got to Do with It?' Law Shaping Experience and Experience Shaping Law," in *Loving v. Virginia in a Post-Racial World: Rethinking Race, Sex, and Marriage*, ed. Kevin Noble Maillard and Rose Cuison Villazor (New York: Cambridge University Press, 2012), 128–31.
49. Pew Research Center, *Multiracial in America*, 55.
50. Sarah S. M. Townsend, Hazel R. Markus, and Hilary B. Bergsieker, "My Choice, Your Categories: The Denial of Multiracial Identities," *Journal of Social Issues* 65, no. 1 (2009): 185–204, 187.

51. Carol Morello, "Virginia's Caroline County, 'Symbolic of Main Street USA,'" *Washington Post*, February 10, 2012; Coleman, *That the Blood Stay Pure*, 173.

52. Eduardo Bonilla-Silva, *Racism Without Racists: Color-Blind Racism and the Persistence of Racial Inequality in the United States* (Lanham, MD: Rowman & Littlefield, 2003).

53. This is a true, albeit second-hand story told to me by a student. The movie version of this can be seen in *Dear White People*, directed by Justin Simien, Homegrown Pictures, 2014. On the disappearance of black men due to mass incarceration and other structural forces, see Alexander, *The New Jim Crow*; Bruce Western, *Punishment and Inequality in America* (New York: Russell Sage Foundation, 2006).

54. "Sisters," like "brothers," is a colloquial term that many black people, particularly church folk, use to refer to one another. At my church home, the pastor calls me "Sister Cashin," and it makes me smile. Regarding the increased probabilities of affluent black men marrying out, see Ralph Richard Banks, *Is Marriage for White People? How the African American Marriage Decline Affects Everyone* (New York: Penguin, 2011).

55. Ibid., chaps. 4 and 7.

56. See, for example, "Interracial Love," YouTube, https://www.youtube.com /channel/UC9n48bDqGxlWOIsBJyNyJzA, posted November 8, 2014.

57. Hettie Jones, *How I Became Hettie Jones* (New York: Grove Press, 1990).

58. Matthew D. Bramlett and William D. Mosher, "Cohabitation, Marriage, Divorce, and Remarriage in the United States," *Vital Health Statistics* 23, no. 22 (2002): 1–32.

59. Angela Onwuachi-Willig and Jacob Willig-Onwuachi, "Finding a *Loving* Home," in Maillard and Villazor, *Loving v. Virginia in a Post-Racial World*, 181–95.

60. See "Biracial Cheerios Girl and Parents Interview 'Excited' About Negative Comments 6 12 13," YouTube, uploaded February 10, 2014, https://www .youtube.com/watch?v=h4zSkcF4SVc.

61. An analysis of seventeen hundred television commercials aired in April 2012 found that 98 percent of families portrayed were of the same race and that when interracial characters were portrayed, it was usually as platonic friendships or strategically ambiguous situations in which the relationship between characters was not defined (Julie Stewart, "Colorblind Commercials: Depictions of Interracial Relationships in Television Advertising," PhD diss., University of Cincinnati, 2013).

62. Sharon Bramlett-Solomon, "Interracial Love on Television: What's Taboo Still," in *Critical Thinking About Sex, Love, and Romance in the Mass Media: Media Literacy Applications*, ed. Mary-Lou Galician and Debra L. Merskin (Mahwah, NJ: Lawrence Erlbaum Associates, 2007), 85.

63. Stephanie Buck, "Star Trek's Interracial Kiss the Deep South Almost Never Saw," *Tech Insider*, July 22, 2016, http://www.techinsider.io/star-treks -interracial-kiss-deep-south-almost-2016–7.

64. Bramlett-Solomon, "Interracial Love on Television."

65. "Interracial Couples More Common in Media," National Public Radio, December 30, 2005, http://www.npr.org/templates/story/story.php?storyId =5075626; Willa Paskin, "Network TV Is Broken: So How Does Shonda Rhimes Keep Making Hits?," *New York Times*, May 11, 2013, http://www .nytimes.com/2013/05/12/magazine/shonda-rhimes.html.

66. "'Grey's Anatomy' Creator, Actress Discuss Media Diversity," CNN.com, May 22, 2012, http://inamerica.blogs.cnn.com/2012/05/22/greys-anatomy -creator-and-actress-discuss-media-diversity/.

67. Erica Chito Childs, "What's Class Got to Do with It? Images and Discourses on Race and Class in Interracial Relationships," in *Multiracial Americans and Social Class: The Influence of Social Class on Racial Identity*, ed. Kathleen Odell Korgen (New York: Routledge, 2010), 25. See also Myra Washington, "Interracial Intimacy: Hegemonic Construction of Asian American and Black Relationships on TV Medical Dramas," *Howard Journal of Communications* 23, no. 3 (2012): 253–71.

68. Stewart, "Colorblind Commercials"; Wendy Wang and Paul Taylor, "For Millennials, Parenthood Trumps Marriage," Pew Research Center, March 9, 2011, www.pewsocialtrends.org/2011/03/09/for-millennials-parenthood -trumps-marriage.

69. Molly Fitzpatrick, "2015 Was a Huge Year for Interracial Relationships on TV," *Fusion*, December 31, 2015, http://fusion.net/story/249859/interracial -relationships-tv-mixed-race-couples.

70. Brianna A. Lienemann and Heather T. Stopp, "The Association Between Media Exposure and Interracial Relationships and Attitudes Towards Interracial Relationships," *Journal of Applied Social Psychology* 43, no. S2 (2013): E398–E415.

71. Ed Schiappa et al., "The Parasocial Contact Hypothesis," *Communication Monographs* 72, no. 1 (2005): 92–115.

72. Hongyu Wang and Grace Kao, "Does Higher Socioeconomic Status Increase Contact Between Minorities and Whites? An Examination of Interracial Romantic Relationships Among Adolescents," *Social Science Quarterly* 88, no. 1 (2007): 146–64. Socioeconomic status, measured by educational attainment, may affect decisions about interracial marriage, as opposed to dating. See, for example, Zhenchao Qian, "Who Intermarries? Education, Nativity, Region, and Interracial Marriage, 1980 and 1990," *Journal of Comparative Family Studies* (1999): 579–97 (noting, for example, that among white women, increased educational attainment was associated with a declining likelihood of marrying black or Hispanic men but an increased likelihood of marrying Asian men).

73. Herman and Campbell, "I Wouldn't, but You Can," 343–58.

74. Saleem Alhabash et al., "Effects of Race, Visual Anonymity, and Social Category Salience in Online Dating Outcomes," *Computers in Human Behavior* 35 (June 2014).

75. C. Rudder, "Race and Attraction, 2009–2014," *OkTrends*, September 10, 2014, https://blog.okcupid.com/index.php/race-attraction-2009–2014; Christian Rudder, *Dataclysm: Who We Are (When We Think No One Is Looking)* (New York: Crown, 2014), 106–7.

76. Rudder, *Dataclysm*, 112; American Sociological Association, "Study Identifies 'Bonus Effect' for Certain Multiracial Daters," press release, American Sociological Association, August 18, 2014, http://www.asanet.org/press-center /press-releases/study-identifies-bonus-effect-certain-multiracial-daters.

77. Kevin Lewis, "The Limits of Racial Prejudice," *Proceedings of the National Academy of Sciences* 110, no. 47 (2013): 18814–819.

78. Gerald A. Mendelsohn, Lindsay Shaw Taylor, Andrew T. Fiore, and Coye Chesire, "Black/White Dating Online: Interracial Courtship in the 21st Century," *Psychology of Popular Media Culture* 3, no. 1 (January 2014).

79. Tara, "Dating Between Races: The Best Sites for an Interracial Romance," *Dating and Relationship Advice* (blog), August 22, 2012, http://blog.dating wise.com/2141/interracial.

80. David Knox, Marty E. Zusman, Carmen Buffington, and Gloria Hemphill, "Interracial Dating Attitudes Among College Students," *College Student Journal* 34, no. 1 (2000): 69–72.

81. Nian Hu, "Yellow Fever," *Harvard Crimson*, February 4, 2016, http:// www.thecrimson.com/column/femme-fatale/article/2016/2/4/yellow-fever -fetishization.

CHAPTER SEVEN: MORE LOVING

1. Sharon Rush, *Loving Across the Color Line: A White Adoptive Mother Learns About Race* (New York: Rowman & Littlefield, 2000), 6.

2. Ibid., 1–5, 9, 59–69, 71–79, 109, 117, 162–63.

3. Lynette Clemenson and Ron Nixon, "Breaking Through Adoption's Racial Barriers," *New York Times*, August 17, 2006.

4. Leslie Doty Hollingsworth, "Sociodemographic Influences in the Prediction of Attitudes Toward Transracial Adoption," *Families in Society: The Journal of Contemporary Social Services* 81, no. 1 (2000): 90–100.

5. Frances A. DellaCava, Norma Kolko Phillips, and Madeline Engel, "Adoption in the U.S.: The Emergence of a Social Movement," *Journal of Sociology & Social Welfare* 31, no. 4 (December 2004): 145–46.

6. Clemenson and Nixon, "Breaking Through Adoption's Racial Barriers."

7. Leslie Hollingsworth and Verlie Mae Ruffin, "Why Are So Many US Families Adopting Internationally? A Social Exchange Perspective," *Journal of Human Behavior in the Social Environment* 6, no. 1 (2002): 81–97, cited in DellaCava et al., "Adoption in the US," 141, 146; Darryl Fears, "Study of '94 Adoption Law Finds Little Benefit to Blacks," *Washington Post*, May 27, 2008, quoting a 2003 study in which children adopted from Sri Lanka and Colombia expressed the wish to be white, were obsessed with the desirability of white skin, tried to wipe off the brown color, and had behavioral problems.

8. Kathryn A. Sweeney, "Race-Conscious Adoption Choices, Multiraciality, and Color-Blind Racial Ideology," *Family Relations* 62, no. 1 (2013): 42–57; DeLeith Duke Gossett, "If Charity Begins at Home, Why Do We Go Searching Abroad? Why the Federal Adoption Tax Credit Should Not Subsidize International Adoptions," *Lewis & Clark Law Review* 17 (2013): 839, 853–54; R. Richard Banks, "The Color of Desire: Fulfilling Adoptive

Parents' Racial Preferences Through Discriminatory State Action," *Yale Law Journal* 107, no. 4 (1998): 875–964.

9. US Congress, *House Ways and Means Committee Green Book* (Washington, DC: Congressional Research Service, 2014). Ravinder Barn, "'Doing the Right Thing': Transracial Adoption in the USA," *Ethnic and Racial Studies* 36, no. 8 (2013): 1273–91, says that "domestic TRA rates, between 1995 and 2001, appear to have almost doubled for Hispanic children but have only marginally increased, from 14.2 per cent to 16.9 per cent, for African American children." Gossett, "If Charity Begins at Home," 846; Abbie E. Goldberg and JuliAnna Z. Smith, "Predicting Non-African American Lesbian and Heterosexual Preadoptive Couples' Openness to Adopting an African American Child," *Family Relations* 58, no. 3 (2009): 346–60.

10. US Department of State, Bureau of Consular Affairs, *FY 2015 Annual Report on Intercountry Adoption*, (Washington, DC: US Department of State, 2015), https://travel.state.gov/content/dam/aa/pdfs/2015Annual_Intercountry _Adoption_Report.pdf.

11. Nikki Khanna and Caitlin Killian, "'We Didn't Even Think About Adopting Domestically': The Role of Race and Other Factors in Shaping Parents' Decisions to Adopt Abroad," *Sociological Perspectives* 58, no. 4 (2015): 570–94. On adoption of African American children by people from Canada, the United Kingdom, and the Netherlands and the still-extant hierarchy that places black Americans at the bottom in the adoption market, see ibid., 571–73, 590.

12. Kathryn Joyce, *The Child Catchers: Rescue, Trafficking, and the New Gospel of Adoption* (New York: PublicAffairs, 2013), explains how the demand created for "orphans" by American adoptive parents has resulted in child selling and misrepresentations of the circumstances of some children in some countries.

13. Ibid., 73.

14. Numbers based on Immigration Naturalization Service, United States Citizenship and Information Services, *Yearbook of Immigration Statistics* (published yearly by Immigration Naturalization Service, US Citizenship and Information Services); Gossett, "If Charity Begins at Home," 863–65; Southern Baptist Convention Resolution No. 2, On Adoption and Orphan Care, adopted 2009.

15. See, for example, Bonilla-Silva, *Racism Without Racists*, which describes a tripartite system of whites and assimilated white Latinos at the top; an intermediate group of "honorary whites," including light-skinned Asians, below them; and a "collective black" group at the bottom, including blacks and dark-skinned Latinos and Asians.

16. Khanna and Killian, "'We Didn't Even Think about Adopting Domestically,'" 573, notes that some private agencies charged as much as $16,000 more for a white baby and that even agencies specializing in minority infants were known to charge more for black-white biracial babies than black babies. See also Six Words: "Black Babies Cost Less to Adopt," The Race Card Project: Six-Word Essays (series), *Morning Edition*, NPR, June 27,

2013, http://www.npr.org/2013/06/27/195967886/six-words-black-babies
-cost-less-to-adopt.

17. Clemenson and Nixon, "Breaking Through Adoption's Racial Barriers."
18. Rose M. Kreider and Daphne A. Lofquist, *Adopted Children and Stepchildren: 2010* (Washington, DC: US Census Bureau, April 2014), table 10, "Characteristics of Transracially Adopted Children," http://www.census.gov/prod/2014pubs/p20-572.pdf.
19. Goldberg and Smith, "Predicting Non-African American Lesbian and Heterosexual Preadoptive Couples' Openness to Adopting an African American Child," 349; Rachel H. Farr and Charlotte J. Patterson, "Transracial Adoption by Lesbian, Gay and Heterosexual Couples: Who Completes Transracial Adoptions and with What Results?," *Adoption Quarterly* 12 (2009): 187–204.
20. Child Welfare Information Gateway, *Transracial and Transcultural Adoption* (Washington, DC: US Department of Health and Human Services, Child Welfare Information Gateway, 1994), https://childwelfare.gov/pub PDFs/f_trans.pdf, recommends that parents who will transracially adopt examine beliefs about race and ethnicity.
21. Clemenson and Nixon, "Breaking Through Adoption's Racial Barriers."
22. Russell D. Moore, "Jim Crow in the Nursery," in *Adopted for Life: The Priority of Adoption for Christian Families and Churches* (Wheaton, IL: Crossway Books, 2009).
23. Dan Cruver, "The Gospel and Transracial Adoption," Together for Adoption, November 24, 2008, http://www.togetherforadoption.org/?p=383.
24. Michelle Hainer, "Foreign Culture Brought Home; Adoptees Discover Themselves at Camp," *Washington Post*, May 3, 2005.
25. Clemenson and Nixon, "Breaking Through Adoption's Racial Barriers"; Lonnae O'Neal, "Sandra Bullock and How We Talk About Adoption," *Washington Post*, December 7, 2015.
26. Vaunda Micheaux Nelson, *Bad News for Outlaws: The Remarkable Life of Bass Reeves, Deputy US Marshal* (Minneapolis: Carolrhoda Books, 2009).
27. This information is based on my own independent analysis of data from the General Social Survey at the National Opinion Research Center University of Chicago, available at www.gss.norc.org.
28. Sandra Graham, Anke Munniksma, and Jaana Juvonen, "Psychosocial Benefits of Cross-Ethnic Friendships in Urban Middle Schools," *Child Development* 85, no. 2 (2014): 469–83.
29. Thomas F. Pettigrew and Linda R. Tropp, "Allport's Intergroup Contact Hypothesis: Its History and Influence," *On the Nature of Prejudice* 50 (2005): 262–77.
30. Thomas F. Pettigrew et al., "Recent Advances in Intergroup Contact Theory," *International Journal of Intercultural Relations* 35, no. 3 (May 2011): 271–80.
31. Kevin Eagan, *The American Freshman: National Norms Fall 2014* (Los Angeles: Higher Education Research Institute, 2014), http://www.heri.ucla.edu /monographs/TheAmericanFreshman2014.pdf.

32. Linda R. Tropp and Elizabeth Page-Gould, "Contact Between Groups," in *APA Handbook of Personality and Social Psychology*, vol. 2, *Group Processes* (Washington, DC: American Psychological Association, 2015), 535–60.

33. Ibid.

34. See, for example, Fiona K. Barlow et al., "The Contact Caveat: Negative Contact Predicts Increased Prejudice More Than Positive Contact Predicts Reduced Prejudice," *Personality and Social Psychology Bulletin* 38, no. 12 (2012): 1629–43. See also Stefania Paolini, Jake Harwood, and Mark Rubin, "Negative Intergroup Contact Makes Group Memberships Salient: Explaining Why Intergroup Conflict Endures," *Personality and Social Psychology Bulletin* 36, no. 12 (2010): 1723–38, which notes that negative contact can make group identity more salient and discourage future contact with other groups.

35. Cashin, *The Failures of Integration*, chap. 3; Cashin, *Place, Not Race*, chap. 2.

36. David Binder, "Look Different," MTV, last modified 2014, http://www.lookdifferent.org/about-us/research-studies/1-2014-mtv-david-binder-research-study.

37. Ted Gregory, "Most Tolerant but Desensitized? Today's Teens Present a Thorny Contradiction," *Chicago Tribune*, November 13, 2010.

38. Cashin, *Place, Not Race*, chap. 2.

39. Rush, *Loving Across the Color Line*, 160.

40. Natalie J. Shook and Russell H. Fazio, "Interracial Roommate Relationships an Experimental Field Test of the Contact Hypothesis," *Psychological Science* 19, no. 7 (2008): 717–23.

41. Noah P. Mark and Daniel R. Harris, "Roommate's Race and the Racial Composition of White College Students Ego Networks," *Social Science Research* 41 (2012): 331–42.

42. Sarah E. Gaither and Samuel R. Sommers, "Living with an Other-Race Roommate Shapes Whites' Behavior in Subsequent Diverse Settings," *Journal of Experimental Social Psychology* 49, no. 2 (2013): 272–76.

43. See Cashin, *Place, Not Race*.

44. Sylvia Hurtado and Adriana Ruiz Alvarado, "Discrimination and Bias, Underrepresentation, and Sense of Belonging on Campus," Higher Education Research Institute research brief, October 2015, www.heri.ucla.edu/PDFs/Discriminination-and-Bias-Underrepresentation-and-Sense-of-Belonging-on-Campus.pdf.

45. Eagan, *The American Freshman*.

46. Nicole Chiang, "Students Combat Intolerance on Campus," *USA Today College*, May 13, 2013, http://college.usatoday.com/2013/05/13/students-combat-intolerance-on-campus.

47. For example, an analysis of five measures of racial prejudice taken from the General Social Survey conducted by the National Opinion Research Council at the University of Chicago (available at gss.norc.org) in 2010, 2012, and 2014 found that on a given question, only 9 to 38 percent of white millennials gave answers that exhibited prejudice against blacks, percentages that for all but one indication were a few points lower (i.e., showed

less prejudice) than what white Gen Xers, baby boomers, and Silent Generation members gave. In other words, dominant majorities of white millennials did *not* exhibit racial prejudice in answers to questions like "Are Blacks less well-off due to a lack of motivation?" (a majority of Silents said yes). Although the author of the analysis focused on the "substantial minority" of millennials who were racist, the *Washington Post* led with a highly misleading headline. See Scott Clement, "Millennials Are Just About as Racist as Their Parents," *Washington Post*, April 7, 2015, https://www.washingtonpost.com /news/wonk/wp/2015/04/07/white-millennials-are-just-about-as-racist-as -their-parents.

CHAPTER EIGHT: THE FUTURE
1. Myron Orfield and Thomas Luce, *America's Racially Diverse Suburbs: Opportunities and Challenges* (Minneapolis: University of Minnesota Law School, Institute of Metropolitan Opportunity, July 20, 2012), https://www1 .law.umn.edu/uploads/e0/65/e065d82a1c1daobfef7d86172ec5391e/Diverse _Suburbs_FINAL.pdf. See also John R. Logan and Wenquan Zhang, *Global Neighborhoods: New Evidence from Census 2010* (US2010 Project, November 2011), http://www.s4.brown.edu/us2010/Data/Report/globalfinal2 .pdf; William H. Frey, "Melting Pot Cities and Suburbs: Racial and Ethnic Change in Metro America in the 2000s," Metropolitan Policy Program, Brookings Institution, May 4, 2011, http://www.brookings.edu/~/media /research/files/papers/2011/5/04%20census%20ethnicity%20frey/0504 _census_ethnicity_frey.pdf.
2. Other authors have made similar although not precisely the same arguments. See, for example, William H. Frey, *Diversity Explosion: How New Racial Demographics Are Remaking America* (Washington, DC: Brookings Institution Press, 2015); Jennifer Hochschild, Vesla Weaver, and Traci Burch, *Creating a New Racial Order: How Immigration, Multiracialism, Genomics, and the Young Can Remake Race in America* (Princeton, NJ: Princeton University Press, 2012); Jay S. Readey, *The Coming Integration* (Race and Poverty, 2013), http://www.raceandpoverty.org/the-coming -integration; Paul Taylor, *The Next America: Boomers, Millennials, and the Looming Generational Showdown* (New York: PublicAffairs, 2014).
3. Jens Manel Krogstad and Gustavo Lopez, "Roughly Half of Hispanics Have Experienced Discrimination," Pew Research Center, June 29, 2016, http:// www.pewresearch.org/fact-tank/2016/06/29/roughly-half-of-hispanics -have-experienced-discrimination/; "The Rise of Asian Americans," Pew Research Center, Social & Demographic Trends Project, June 19, 2012, http:// www.pewsocialtrends.org/2012/06/19/the-rise-of-asian-americans/; "Many Multiracial Adults Have Experienced Racial Discrimination," Pew Research Center, Social & Demographic Trends Project, June 8, 2015, http://www .pewsocialtrends.org/2015/06/11/multiracial-in-america/st_2015-06-11 _multiracial-americans_00-04/.
4. See, for example, Rebecca Griffin, "For White People Who Believe Black Lives Matter," *Huffington Post*, July 10, 2016, http://www.huffingtonpost .com/rebecca-griffin/for-white-people-who-beli_b_10917900.html; Collier

Meyerson, "Dear White Friends: Here's How to Support BLM Without Making It About You," *Fusion*, July 27, 1016, http://fusion.net/story/329680 /black-lives-matter-white-allies/.

5. Horowitz and Livingston, "How Americans View the Black Lives Matter Movement."

6. Brian Stevenson, "We Need to Talk About an Injustice," TED: Ideas Worth Spreading, March 2012, www.ted.com/talks/bryan_stevenson_we_need_to _talk_about_an_injustice/transcript?language=en; Tim Adams, "Bryan Stevenson: 'America's Mandela,'" *Guardian*, February 1, 2015, https://www .theguardian.com/us-news/2015/feb/01/bryan-stevenson-americas-mandela.

7. Cashin, *Place, Not Race*, chap. 1; Alexander, *The New Jim Crow*; Haney-López, *Dog Whistle Politics*.

8. See, generally, Arlie Hochschild, *Strangers in Their Own Land: Anger and Mourning on the American Right* (New York: New Press, 2016).

9. Bryan Stevenson, *Just Mercy: A Story of Justice and Redemption* (New York: Spiegel & Grau, 2015), 290.

10. For a detailed explanation of how anger and racial resentment by sizable numbers of whites undermines American democracy, see Cashin, *Place, Not Race*, chap. 1.

11. Gladwell, *The Tipping Point*.

12. National Research Council, *The New Americans: Economic, Demographic, and Fiscal Effects of Immigration*, ed. James P. Smith and Barry Edmonston (Washington, DC: National Academy Press, 1997); Council of Economic Advisers, "Immigration's Economic Impact," Washington, DC, June 20, 2007; Rand Corporation, "Rand Study Shows Relatively Little Public Money Spent Providing Health Care to Undocumented Immigrants," November 2006, http://www.rand.org/news/press.06/11.14.html.

13. Peter Beinart, "The Republican Party's White Strategy," *Atlantic*, July–August 2016, http://www.theatlantic.com/magazine/archive/2016 /07/the-white-strategy/485612/.

14. This was part of an executive order that also called for suspension of long-term care to elderly, unauthorized immigrants ("Prop. 187 Approved in California," *Migration News* 1, no. 11 [December 1994], https://migration .ucdavis.edu/mn/more.php?id=492).

15. "Anti–Illegal Immigration Laws in States" (graphic), *New York Times*, April 22, 2012, http://www.nytimes.com/interactive/2012/04/22/us/anti -illegal-immigration-laws-in-states.html?_r=0.

16. See, for example, the story of Shane Reams. His first two strikes were felonious burglary. Both of those crimes were reported by his mother. His third strike was serving as a lookout when a friend sold twenty dollars' worth of cocaine to an undercover cop. His mother was part of the chorus that rose up against the law. See "Two Torn Families Show Flip Side of 3 Strikes Law," National Public Radio, October 28, 2009, http://www.npr.org /templates/story/story.php?storyId=114219922.

17. Alexander, *The New Jim Crow*, 199.

18. "California Profile," Prison Policy Initiative, http://www.prisonpolicy.org /profiles/CA.html, accessed October 17, 2016.

19. Prerna Anand, *Winners and Losers: Corrections and Higher Education in California* (United States Common Sense, September 5, 2012), http://uscommonsense.org/research/winners-and-losers-corrections-and-higher-education-in-california/?cacs_redirect=True.

20. "States in Motion: Visualizing How Education Funding Has Changed over Time," EdSource, November 6, 2015, https://edsource.org/2015/states-in-motion-school-finance-naep-child-poverty/83303.

21. "How Much Does It Cost to Incarcerate an Inmate?," Legislative Analyst's Office, California State Legislature, http://www.lao.ca.gov/PolicyAreas/CJ/6_cj_inmatecost, accessed October 17, 2016; Tracey L. Meares, "Social Organization and Drug Law Enforcement," *American Criminal Law Review* 35 (1998): 191.

22. Julianne Hing, "Poll: Californians' Support for Affirmative Action on the Rise," *Colorlines*, September 26, 2014, https://www.colorlines.com/articles/poll-californians-support-affirmative-action-rise.

23. Rebecca Trounson, "California, West Show Surge in Interracial Marriages, Study Finds," *Los Angeles Times*, February 16, 2012, http://articles.latimes.com/2012/feb/16/local/la-me-interracial-marriage-20120216.

24. William A. V. Clark and Julian Ware, "Trends in Residential Integration by Socioeconomic Status in Southern California," *Urban Affairs Review* 32, no. 6 (1997): 825–43, 831; "California Adoption Facts," North American Council on Adoptable Children, https://www.nacac.org/policy/statefactsheets/California%20ADOPTION%20FACTS.pdf, accessed October 21, 2016. Lindsay Dunsmuir, "Many Americans Have No Friends of Another Race: Poll," Reuters, August 8, 2013, http://www.reuters.com/article/us-usa-poll-race-idUSBRE97704320130808, says, "As a group, Pacific states—including California, the most populous in the nation—are the most diverse when it comes to love and friendship."

25. Beinart, "The Republican Party's White Strategy."

26. Ronald Brownstein, "How the Democrats Are Taking Over California," *Atlantic*, January 18, 2013, http://www.theatlantic.com/politics/archive/2013/01/how-the-democrats-are-taking-over-california/429849/.

27. Bethany McLean and Peter Elkind, "Gaming California," chap. 17 in *The Smartest Guys in the Room: The Amazing Rise and Scandalous Fall of Enron* (New York: Penguin, 2013).

28. Brownstein, "How the Democrats Are Taking Over California."

29. Edwin Rios, "California Just Restored Voting Rights to 60,000 Ex-Felons," *Mother Jones*, August 7, 2015, http://www.motherjones.com/politics/2015/08/california-voting-rights-felons.

30. UCLA Civil Rights Project, "California, the Most Segregated State for Latinos," press release, May 14, 2014, https://civilrightsproject.ucla.edu/news/press-releases/2014-press-releases/ucla-report-finds-california-the-most-segregated-state-for-latino-students.

31. Tatiana Sanchez, "There's Been a Boom in Driver's Licenses Issued to Immigrants Here Illegally," *Los Angeles Times*, February 8, 2016, http://www.latimes.com/local/california/la-me-0208-immigrant-drivers-licenses-20160208-story.html; Teresa Ruano, "California Supreme Court Admits Undocumented

Immigrant to State Bar," *California Courts*, July 2, 2014, http://www.courts
.ca.gov/24673.htm.

32. Kimberly Leonard, "California Moves Toward Extending Obamacare to Illegal Immigrants," *US News & World Report*, June 3, 2016, http://www
.usnews.com/news/articles/2016-06-03/california-moves-toward-extending
-obamacare-to-illegal-immigrants.

33. Souya Karlamangla, "Medi-Cal Will Soon Cover Children in the U.S. Illegally. The Real Battle? Getting Adults Insured," *Los Angeles Times*, April
27, 2016, http://www.latimes.com/local/politics/la-me-immigrants-medi
-cal-20160427-story.html.

34. "California Dream Act," University of California, Office of Admissions,
http://admission.universityofcalifornia.edu/paying-for-uc/whats-available
/ca-dream-act, accessed October 17, 2016.

35. Julia Preston, "In Debate over Sanctuary Cities, a Divide on the Role of the
Local Police," *New York Times*, September 1, 2016, http://www.nytimes
.com/2016/09/02/us/in-debate-over-sanctuary-cities-a-divide-on-the-role-of
-the-local-police.html.

36. Melanie Mason, "California Gives Immigrants Here Illegally Unprecedented
Rights, Benefits, Protections," *Los Angeles Times*, August 11, 2015, http://
www.latimes.com/local/california/la-me-california-immigrant-rights
-20150811-story.html.

37. Public Policy Institute of California, "California's Likely Voters," http://
www.ppic.org/main/publication_show.asp?i=255, accessed October 17, 2016.

38. Robert F. Heizer and Alan F. Almquist, *The Other Californians: Prejudice
and Discrimination Under Spain, Mexico, and the United States to 1920*
(Berkeley: University of California Press, 1971), 96.

39. Nick Corasaniti and Maggie Haberman, "Donald Trump Suggests 'Second
Amendment People' Could Act Against Hillary Clinton," *New York Times*,
August 9, 2016, http://www.nytimes.com/2016/08/10/us/politics/donald
-trump-hillary-clinton.html.

40. Jens Manuel Krogstad et al., "Millennials Make Up Almost Half of Latino
Eligible Voters in 2016," Pew Research Center, Hispanic Trends Project, January 19, 2016, http://www.pewhispanic.org/2016/01/19/millennials-make
-up-almost-half-of-latino-eligible-voters-in-2016/.

41. John Huang et al., "Election 2016 Exit Polls," *New York Times*, November
8, 2016, http://www.nytimes.com/interactive/2016/11/08/us/politics/election
-exit-polls.html?_r=0. CNN's exit polls estimate that the white electorate de-
creased from 72 percent to 71 percent of the population from 2012. Compare "Exit Polls," *CNN Politics*, November 23, 2016, http://edition.cnn
.com/election/results/exit-polls/national/president, with "President Race,
Exit Polls, 2012," *CNN Politics*, December 10, 2012, http://www.cnn.com
/election/2012/results/race/president/. Jens Manuel Krogstad, "2016 Electorate Will Be the Most Diverse in U.S. History," Pew Research Center, February 3, 2016, http://www.pewresearch.org/fact-tank/2016/02/03/2016
-electorate-will-be-the-most-diverse-in-u-s-history/.

42. Paul Taylor, "An Awakened Giant: The Hispanic Electorate Is Likely to
Double by 2030," Pew Research Center, Hispanic Trends Project, Novem-

ber 14, 2012, http://www.pewhispanic.org/2012/11/14/an-awakened-giant
-the-hispanic-electorate-is-likely-to-double-by-2030/; Taylor, *The Next
America*, 84, which suggests that Asians and Hispanics will be 25 percent
of the presidential electorate in "a few decades," but again, this process
could accelerate.

43. Taylor, *The Next America*, 35–36.
44. Beverly Tatum, "*Why Are All the Black Kids Sitting Together in the Cafeteria?*": *And Other Questions About Race*, rev. ed. (New York: Basic Books,
2003), 12.
45. Orfield and Luce, *America's Racially Diverse Suburbs*; Raj Chetty et al.,
"Where Is the Land of Opportunity? The Geography of Intergenerational
Mobility in the United States," working paper 19843, National Bureau of
Economic Research, Cambridge, MA, 2014; Jacob S. Rugh and Douglas S.
Massey, "Segregation in Post-Civil Rights America," *Du Bois Review: Social Science Research on Race* 11, no. 2 (2014): 205–32.
46. PolicyLink, "Map of America's Tomorrow," *Vimeo*, May 18, 2011, https://
vimeo.com/23913159.
47. Robert D. Putnam, "E Pluribus Unum: Diversity and Community in the
Twenty-First Century the 2006 Johan Skytte Prize Lecture," *Scandinavian
Political Studies* 30, no. 2 (2007): 137–74.
48. See generally "Welcoming Cities and Counties," at Welcoming America,
https://www.welcomingamerica.org/programs/member-municipalities, accessed January 11, 2017.

INDEX

abolition
  Bacon's rebellion and, 37
  Douglass's stance on, 82–85
  Franklin's views on, 54, 63, 64–65
  ideology of, 70
  Jefferson's views of, 58, 59
  in Northern states, 63–64
  in Pennsylvania, 63
  and race-mixing fears, 67–68,
    73, 74
"An act concerning Servants and
  Slaves" (1705), 6, 46–48
"An act for suppressing outlying
  slaves" (1691), 45–46
Adams, John, 84, 92
Adams, John Quincy, 84
adoption, 20, 150–162
advertising, and multiracial people,
  141–142
"Advice" (Hughes), 189
affirmative action, 176–177
Affordable Care Act, 180
African Americans. *See also* Africans;
  slavery
  acquisition of cultural dexterity,
    136, 166
  Black Lives Matter movement,
    13, 172
  black male sexuality, 7, 8, 60, 67,
    86, 87, 88, 120–121

  black studies departments, 123
  citizenship of, 7, 8, 57, 64, 74–75,
    81, 86
  colonization movement, 60–61
  contemporary treatment of, 12
  free blacks, 60–61, 63, 75, 79–80
  free blacks after Revolutionary
    War, 60–61
  interracial marriage and cohabita-
    tion of, 129–130
  interracial marriage statistics, 129
  Native Americans disavowed mix-
    ing with, 25
  rape accusations against black
    males, 88–89
  suffrage, 63
Africans. *See also* African Americans;
  slavery
  adoption of children from, 156
  arrival of, in Virginia, 29–30
  differential treatment of, 36
  early expectations in colonies,
    31–33
  emancipations of, 33–35
  and European women as partners
    or wives, 40
AfroRomance.com, 148
Alabama, 85, 90
Ali, Muhammad, 161
Allport, Gordon, 163